Digital Media, Culture and Education

John Potter • Julian McDougall

Digital Media, Culture and Education

Theorising Third Space Literacies

palgrave
macmillan

John Potter
UCL Knowledge Lab
University College London Institute of Education
London, UK

Julian McDougall
Bournemouth Media School
Bournemouth University
Bournemouth, UK

ISBN 978-1-137-55314-0 ISBN 978-1-137-55315-7 (eBook)
DOI 10.1057/978-1-137-55315-7

Library of Congress Control Number: 2017933329

Printed on acid-free paper

This Palgrave Macmillan imprint is published by Springer Nature
The registered company is Macmillan Publishers Ltd.
The registered company address is: The Campus, 4 Crinan Street, London, N1 9XW, United Kingdom

For my sister Frances, an inspiration to all of us
and remembering Tony (1927–2015) and Bernie (1928–1990)
(John)

For Barrie Kendall – Happy 80th
(Julian)

This book makes a valuable contribution to the fields it inhabits, not least by refusing reductive and easy polarities such as culture and technology, school and not-school, digital literacy and media literacy. Instead, Potter and McDougall set up a dialogue between fields of research, concepts of literacy, and domains of practice, a cooperative rather than adversarial model. They elaborate their central ideas of third-space learning, dynamic literacies, porous expertise, and digital curation with a rich array of researched examples, showing the importance of collaborative learning in practice. This will be an essential read for lecturers, students, and practitioners hoping to understand the landscape of literacy and learning in the twenty-first century.

—Andrew Burn, *Professor of English, Media, and Drama, University College London, UK.*

Here is a hopeful book about dynamic literacies in education that brings to life the lived experience and creativity of young people and makes visible their meaning-making practices. It surfaces ideas in ways that are theoretically and methodologically groundbreaking. This is a refreshing, hopeful, and above all, challenging book that enables, develops, and supports new thinking in media education together with literacy studies. By situating itself within cultural studies the work is re-vitalized. The book gathers together scholarship in the fields of cultural studies, digital literacies, multimodality, and new media but locates this within practice, so that the ideas come alive for educators. Acceptably written, this is a welcome addition to the field, which speaks to the cultural context of civic engagement for young people in and out of school, or 'not-school'. Now, more than ever these voices are needed as resistance is a key part of survival for young people whose modes of participation need to be strengthened and supported in a challenging world. Dynamic literacies are the way forward – and this book articulates and maps out a pathway through to action.

—Kate Pahl, *Professor of Literacies in Education, University of Sheffield, UK.*

This book is for all those who realize we face new and complex problems in education today; that staying in our academic silos and engaging in business as usual will no longer do; and that digital technology can free teachers to be designers, curators, and aggregators, bringing astonishing resources to learners of all ages and in all places. It is a magnificent piece of work and a breath of fresh air.

—James Paul Gee, *Mary Lou Fulton Presidential Professor of Literacy Studies, Regents' Professor, Arizona State University, USA.*

Acknowledgements

Joint Acknowledgements

We wrote this book together after a series of conversations about our research and teaching over a number of years. It is a joint effort, with the bulk of the first half belonging mainly to John, and the second half mainly to Julian. For the final chapter, however, we wanted jointly to reflect on the key themes running through the whole text. We decided to do this as part of a reflective conversation between us and colleagues in the field. This began as an email exchange with Neil Selwyn and Cathy Burnett and we would both like to acknowledge the great contributions they made to our 'Afterword'. They engaged fully and generously with our questions and took on the key themes of the book. We would like to thank Michelle Cannon and Fiona Scott for their support as our co-presenters in the conversation strand at the Media Education Summit in Rome in 2016. We would also like to thank participants in that session for permission to share their contributions: Kathleen Tyner, Ashley Woodfall, Christa Van Raalte, Anne Dawson, James Cohen, Steve Connolly and Spencer Brayton.

John's Acknowledgements

John would like to thank Monash University in Melbourne for the award of a Visiting Fellowship last Autumn, without which his contributions on *Dynamic literacies*, *Third Spaces* and *Curation* would never have been written. In particular, he would like to acknowledge the support, good conversations and good company of members of the Learning and New Media group: Neil Selwyn, Luci Pangrazio, Michael Henderson, Scott

Bulfin and Selena Nemorin. Also in Australia, the encouragement of Catherine Beavis and Michael Dezuanni, talks and seminars with Graham Parr, Nicola Johnson and Julie Faulkner, and participants in the 'Young People and the Digital' event at the Australian Centre for the Moving Image. In London, although study leave didn't quite go to plan for various reasons, John would like to acknowledge the support of Lesley Gourlay and Myrrh Domingo in trying to provide some space in the summer of 2016. Andrew Burn gave constant encouragement as always, as did Michelle Cannon. Alison Gazzard and the whole MA Digital Media team were highly supportive. The UCL Knowledge Lab, directed by Carey Jewitt, and previously by Richard Noss, is an inspiring place to work and I would like to acknowledge the great conversations down the years with colleagues there which have helped to shape my thinking. In Sheffield, in spite of serious illness, my sister was an inspiration, as was her partner, Jimmy. On the home front, in London, John would like to thank Janet, Alice and Jack for everything.

Julian's Acknowledgements

Julian would like to thank everyone involved in the work which led to his chapters, amongst whom were: the PE department at Chew Valley School – Jo Hibbert, Phil Edwards, Dave Hill, Mandy Clarke, Gareth Jones, Jack Hinckley, Celia Butcher and Suzanne Daly. Julian would also like to acknowledge Pete Fraser, for time served in the cause of media education and for putting up with much nonsense from him over the years. Julian also sends thanks to Alex, Lydia, Ned and Stan for all the more important stuff.

Contents

List of Figures

List of Tables

CHAPTER 1

Foreword – Terms and Conditions

In the novel *The City and the City* by China Miéville (2011), two cities on the edge of Europe co-exist in the same space, sharing streets and even buildings in areas which are 'cross hatched' between the two. It is illegal for citizens of these cities to acknowledge that they have seen one another and they go about their lives policed by a shadowy organisation which enforces this law. As children, the citizens of these fictional places walk the same streets as those of the people in the other city but gradually, over time, they learn to 'un-see' them, so that it becomes natural by the time they are grown up to live in a place that is occupied by another city. In the book, an intricately constructed detective story plays out which gradually and inevitably involves crossing over between the two places, as well as a close encounter with the enforcers. But not before the reader wonders at the parallels the author is drawing with the world we live in, our own ways of thinking, in which we choose habitually to see or 'un-see' people, places, even ideas, which co-exist in the same space.

In recent years in the course of our own work, in *media in education*, our perception has been that a number of parallel theories and writers, disciplines and perspectives occupy the very same spaces, just as in Miéville's novel, without ever really acknowledging their co-presence. They work in separate but intersecting fields, as in Bourdieu's concept of 'field' (1977), essentially as social actors autonomously occupying discrete domains within the same social space of their research. It seems to us that the same kinds of phenomena around media, education, learning, technology and the like are

J. Potter, J. McDougall, *Digital Media, Culture and Education*,
DOI 10.1057/978-1-137-55315-7_1

routinely written about, contested and debated by people who inevitably 'un-see' each other in separate conferences, special interest groups and the like. Very occasionally the act of 'un-seeing' becomes obvious. In a recent email exchange with an organisation running international conferences in the field of literacy, one of us discovered that a Special Interest Group called 'Digital Literacy' had formed in parallel with one he'd already started called 'Media Literacy'. Happily, the members of both were willing to acknowledge that they could see each other and find ways in which to pool knowledge and build new projects together in years to come.

It is not even an issue of disagreement (because at least some of these groups are potential allies) so much as it is a way of working in which theories and knowing about the world are in parallel but apparently invisible to each other. The worlds of educational technology, digital media and learner culture co-exist and it appears that the theoretical constructs do too, but they do not always intersect usefully. The contention of this book is that in attempting to understand and communicate the lived experience of learners in and around media and technology, we may well find useful models in common which could usefully be exchanged and shared. Indeed, some writers have noticed that when studying a cultural phenomenon with connections to learning, that it would be essential to work in the interstices between text and culture in order to describe the authorial practices better, more fully, more usefully. Andrew Burn (2009), for example, points out that the fields of both cultural studies and semiotics need each other more than they sometimes appear to acknowledge; the one to study the textual practices, the other to understand better the educational-cultural act of production.

In the two examples quoted above, the fields concerned do at least catch occasional glimpses of one another and do acknowledge their presence, even as they do not share perspective and sometimes fail to respect the different intellectual positions at work. In more extreme cases, there is an absence of any kind of theoretical work in the field, as if theory itself had no place; in this world the phenomena stand apart from any critical positioning. This happens where problematising the role of technology as a part of lived experience and wider culture and its relationship to learning is a non-starter. In this non-contested world, technology simply enhances learning, provides solutions for those with 'problems' and generally acts as a neutral force for good. This approach is useful if you have something to sell because in this world-picture, research is actually just 'market research'. The writing which results in this case masquerades as a quasi-scientific process and produces tables and statistics to prove the effectiveness or otherwise of a technological intervention. It all points to some scientific process which barely exists and which demonstrably fails to show any lasting benefit to learners. It could all be done better if there were some attention paid to the worlds in which the learners and their teachers actually live, the economic and social circumstances of those people and the nature of the interaction with and through the many technologies they use. Indeed, some of the best writing about educational technology usefully incorporates learning theory and psychology and here there is at least a sense in which a level of criticality has been developed which is aware of a wider cultural experience, churn and change. Nevertheless, in too many 'ed-tech' studies, rich descriptions of actual leaners and learner lives remain just out of reach.

In this book, we want to put learners and their cultural experiences back at the heart of what we consider learning to be. We would like to discuss projects and places in which we have worked in the past few years, beyond the life of the research done there, in order to reflect on the ways in which lived experience with media and technology was revealed. We may have been going into those areas with our own perspectives and with our own agendas, often as dictated by our various funders, because our own agency is not limitless, but nevertheless on returning and comparing across fields we have found useful things to say. We want to contribute to the 'maturation' phase of enquiry into technology, learning and literacy. In this phase we move beyond reductive opposition between emancipatory '2.0' ideas and rejectionist discourse to observe the complex interplay between democratising, neoliberal and regulatory agencies around literacies in multimodal fields, the intersection of technologies, literacies, education and self.

In order to position the book further for our readers we will address how we will go about this in answer to the most common questions we've been asked whilst working on it:

In Which Field Is This Book Actually Located?

This book is located at the intersection of a number of fields and we hope it reaches an audience who are not satisfied with simple answers to complex issues around education, learning and the digital. In some ways it would be easier for us to address one of the different constituencies with which we are familiar and in which we spend some of our time: *Cultural studies, media literacy, digital literacy, media studies, film studies, multimodality, digital making*, *educational technology* and so on. But what we wanted to do instead was to give voice to some thinking about how some of these worlds might be *usefully* drawn together. Here, and in each chapter, we state an important disclaimer. For many people, a technology-enhanced, fluid digital *third space* context in which their voice can be heard and knowledge can be co-constructed is not their experience of education. Their being outside of these developments are, in some cases by virtue of being offline, for reasons of geography or economics. For others, the opportunities for blended learning are restricted by a conservative epistemology, transmitted in traditional classroom settings in schools with a strong resistance to integrating digitally enabled learning from the 'first space'. That said, in short, whether we say that this book is about 'digital literacy', or 'media literacy', we are concerned to bridge some of the gaps that currently exist between people and institutions studying essentially the same phenomena. We would like some of the people concerned to stop 'un-seeing' each other and join in a more purposeful debate, formulating a new criticality around learning, media and technology.

Are There Other People Working in This Intersection Between Fields?

We recognise that there are other people who have reached similar conclusions and who want to invent new ways of thinking and exploring some of these phenomena. We want to align ourselves with some of the studies and ways of thinking which have begun to emerge which are similarly concerned with acts of boundary crossing but who want to develop criticality in their work, to address a paucity of theory in the field. We are thinking here about writers and colleagues from the worlds of critical education technology studies, from digital and new literacies, from play and learning, from digital humanities and anthropology and from multimodality, media and cultural studies. One such boundary-crossing recent work is *The Class: Living and Learning in Digital Culture*, a richly detailed ethnographic study of a cohort of young people across a year in a school, considering their use of technology and social media in the context of their learner lives (Livingstone and Sefton-Green 2016), and we recognise in this work a wish to look closely at what happens when social and other practices with digital media meet educational practices. Another would be the recent study of children's playground games in the new media age (Burn and Richards 2014) which drew on a wide range of cultural and media theory to describe the remixing of the lived cultural experience in children's play. Our own approach is to look across a variety of projects we've been engaged with in recent years, at a variety of theoretical/critical positions and to build some new and deeper understanding of these phenomena.

Who Should Read the Book?

We would like to address this book to anyone working in the context of lifelong learning, formally or informally, and digital media/technology. This of course includes learners themselves, teachers, parents, carers, researchers, students and more. We would like these people to read the book and find chapters which speak to them about the situation they are currently in, which describe recent research projects in the fields of learning, media and technology and which try to explore and explain these in terms of new and useful hybrid concepts. We hope that these concepts can be developed in future research projects and collaborations. We hope that if you are a student of any kind, not only of media or technology education, you will find a description of a project or a concept which calls to you as something you would like to try to research, to make your own. If you are an academic colleague, we hope you would consider boundary crossing and collaborating. We want to foster an active debate and a curiosity about how the world of learning is changing in response to the pervasive use of media technologies in wider culture. We want to attract readers who are willing and able to develop critical thinking about what they see in front of them, the media in which they swim every day, and how this affects what they do when they are learning.

How Do You Conceptualise This Intersection in Terms of 'Education'?

We want to think about the ways in which education is experienced as a cultural phenomenon which hails and interpellates people as learners of a particular kind. At the present time, in many performative systems, learners are positioned as databots who must be ranked and scored in order for the neoliberal hegemony to play out its acts of privatisation and commercialisation and so that people may, quite literally, know their place. Formal settings which have given themselves over entirely to the production line of testing are at risk of producing learners who misrecognise themselves as failures. However, rather than becoming locked in those debates around performativity for too long, we want to identify better ways of thinking about teaching and learning now, celebrate schools, colleges and places of learning which are striving to enlarge their ambition, their vision. We want to look at examples of places and spaces in which digital media are purposefully integrated into pedagogy in ways in which the intersection between culture and media, learning and technology becomes a rich potential source of motivation, of agency on the part of learners.

In Addition to Boundary Crossing, Do You Have Any New Concepts to Offer or Develop?

We would like to have a go at defining further some terms which might be useful in thinking about the way learners experience the world in the second decade of the twenty-first century. In saying this we are not allowing ourselves to be seduced by the endlessly deferred future which bedevils a lot of the writing about technology in which tomorrow is optimistically described but never actually arrives. Rather we are interested in looking more critically at one or two concepts which may be useful in formulating the whole project in terms of media, practices and social and cultural worlds.

Firstly, we have written elsewhere about 'curation' and something we call 'porous expertise' (McDougall and Potter 2015). These need some further elaboration and the development of criticality around them. We will address this for c*uration* by further defining it as a new literacy practice in digital media which sets it apart from a celebration of preference or choice, exhibition or collection. We will show how this is not a simple celebratory construct, how it can be better problematised and we will try to reclaim it from ubiquity in social media; we aim to show how it is more than simply *editing* or *life-building* for those with existing high social and cultural capital and access to online spaces. In particular, we want to emphasise its nature as an overarching new literacy practice which subsumes others, with particular consequences for teaching and learning.

Porous expertise will likewise be developed further as a concept which addresses a key issue of in the digital age, namely that of 'powerful knowledge' and how this may be encountered and negotiated. We want to ensure that our understanding of this concept is clarified in terms of roles, rights and responsibilities in pedagogy on the part of all the social actors in the field of education, formal and informal.

Gee (2015a) suggests that when we research literacy in digital media contexts we are looking at: 'Person(s) with tools in specific practice(s) sponsored by specific sorts of social or cultural group(s) or institutions' (2015a, p. 103).

Gee sets this up as an alternative to generalising ideas about whether technology is simply good or bad in relation to learning. We want to extend Gee's helpful statement to include a new dimension, as follows: People who are living and working with digital media, engaged in specific educational practices and power relations, involving co-creation and curation, sponsored by specific sorts of cultural groups or institutions in particular spaces and networks. We want to examine critically the extent to which technology enables transformations in practices, spaces and power relations.

Why Do You Have a Subtitle Which Invokes the 'Third Space'? What Do You Mean by This?

We have chosen to position the book as being at least partly about better theorising notions of literacy, in particular, the concept of the '*third space*'. When we talk about this we will go back to the source of the term (Bhabha 1994) and we will navigate a path through its incorporation into a sociocultural vision of literacy (Gutierrez 2008), derived from new literacy studies. We want to suggest that this *third space* has a literal and metaphorical meaning. We understand it as a space which is a negotiated and contested area in which meanings are made and shared, some of which may relate to encountering new knowledge, learning or developing new skills and dispositions. Its literal, physical location could also be an after-school club, a museum, a lunchtime activity. It could be a metaphorical location in which the learning is negotiated through agentive activity on the part of both learner and teacher, even in a formal setting. Either way, we will be precise about what we mean and about how it can be explored and in each chapter we will pose, and return to, two key framing questions:

- What happens to people doing education in a (digital) *third space*?
- How do engagements in the (digital) *third space* influence practices back in the second space?

How Will You Organise the Book, Its Chapters and Topics?

Each chapter takes a particular position in terms of relevant theory and offers some example research projects which enable an elaboration of key concepts. Following this introductory chapter, we will approach the world of *digital media, cultural theory and education in third spaces* as follows:

Chapter 2 Dynamic Literacies

Because this book is concerned with the issues around digital media and education, as seen through a sociocultural and political lens, we have chosen to begin by looking at the ways in which these issues are represented in recent definitions of 'literacy' which have been mobilised by a range of different theorists and interest groups. We will suggest that the term 'dynamic literacies' could extend concepts in the 'new literacy studies' to generate an inclusive, umbrella term which is inclusive enough to encompass the changing nature of meaning-making in the context of digital media and culture. This chapter, then, will outline key debates in the field of literacy/new literacies, describe the changing landscape of education in the wider context of the digital and propose a theoretical approach to understanding such developments. As media educators, we understand that the ways in which an education system engages positively, negatively, or not at all with media texts and practices is framed by what is admissible in its formal structures and educational settings as 'literacy'; any definition of literacy frames and defines pedagogy. We want to suggest that a working definition of literacy in the digital age should be inclusive, not exclusive, and should be one which gathers together a series of sub-categories, as suggested above, of *dynamic literacies*, all of which are founded on the idea that literacy is ideological, contingent and bound by context, which is currently dominated by digital media and digital culture.

Chapter 3 Third Spaces and Digital Making

We use this chapter to articulate our understanding of the term '*third space*' and position our use of it as part of an evolving semantic which takes in metaphorical, virtual and physical spaces which are all interstitially located between larger institutional organisations: home, school, work and so on. These spaces are locations for thinking, working, negotiating, playing and more, in the context of digital media, education and culture. They are all places in which 'literacy events' (Street 2003) take place, in which meanings are shared and in which pedagogical framing of those meanings is a key determinant of action in education. In other words, we see '*third spaces*' as connected to the notion of 'dynamic literacies' introduced in Chapter 1. We see such spaces existing as potential locations for learning in which hierarchies are also fluid; there is the potential to be more open to learners' skills and dispositions arising out of practices which are representative of wider culture and lived experience. We wish to further understand such spaces by thinking about 'sociomateriality', a concept which implies that we should try to understand more about how meaning is made in respect to the interactions between learners and artefacts, bodies and spaces, just as much as it is from their lived experience in wider culture.

This chapter also addresses 'maker theory', which seeks to encourage the craft skills of making as learning and to develop reflexivity through the curation of a person's digital presence as an 'open portfolio' (see Peppler 2013; Sefton Green 2013; both of whom have conducted recent literature reviews in the field). We will connect this movement with the established practice of making media in learning including looking for synergies between those who wish to emphasise texts and practices (semioticians, multimodal theorists), those who invoke media and cultural studies as a touchstone (as in the joining of the two fields proposed in Burn 2009) and those who wish to reposition Media Studies as a 'maker discipline' (Gauntlett 2015).

Frau Meigs (2014) brings to our attention the hitherto under-theorised emergence of coding education as a seemingly neutral pedagogic space, with attendant discourses of '21st century literacy' and a 'common sense' economic modality. We will explore the social and cultural implications of this approach and connect coding much more closely to the idea of a wider, reimagined version of literacy. We are interested in exploring the ways in which coding and collaboration can be reframed as a particular instance of (im)materiality in spaces of learning in which the relations between the various social actors are mediated (after the recent work of Burnett and Merchant). This chapter will consider how and why in this way computational thinking can be characterised as part of material culture and how this presages a new cultural alignment within the curriculum. We will also explore in this chapter a set of socio-pedagogical strategies which might apply to this area of learning. In the developmental view of writing, children come to know that the marks which they make stand for them when they are not there. They learn this not only because of direct technical instruction but also through seeing the impact of writing in the lives of the those around them: in shopping lists, text messages, web pages, letters, forms, notes from school and so on. For coding, we will consider how powerful it would be if beyond thinking of it only as a set of technical operations children came to know, at a very young age, that coding not only stands for them when they are not there but produces action on the world and the things in it? It works like language but also like language with another dimension to it. The marks, if written in the right way, in the right order make devices and objects on screens do things that cause other things to happen in the world. They make things happen in a range of devices but they also make things happen in a range of media. Children need only see that things do not work in the way they wanted to know that their instructions need looking at again. They can debug incorrect code from seeing that a floor robot does not travel or behave in an expected way. Just as they learn to edit writing to make it clearer, to stand for them when they are not there they can see that they can adjust, draft and check through immediate feedback where they are going wrong and where they are going right. We will connect this to the growing interest in game design and game making.

Chapter 4 Digital Curation/Digital Production: Storying the Digital Learner

What does curation as a new literacy practice imply for learning across the lifecourse? How can new literacy studies help us take theoretical stock of the situation? In this chapter we will invoke and develop critically new theories of self-curation in digital media as well as exploring the limitations and presumptions of previous versions of multiliteracies (as in the critiques offered by Leander and Boldt 2012). We will describe instead how a theory of curation is operationalised and turns into social action inside and outside places of learning whilst acknowledging that this clearly is the subject of much debate, in which very similar questions are being asked using different analytical frames drawn from sociocultural theory, psychology, literacy studies and more. In sociocultural theory the curatorial impulse towards artefacts is explored as a specific analogue for relations to people (see the work of Daniel Miller 2008). From cultural psychology the relation to self-storying is seen as a way of building the self (Bruner 1987). In new literacy studies we see that this is a practice in which it is possible to work intertextually with different representational artefacts to represent aspects of the self for exhibition and distribution (Merchant; Potter et al.). We believe that we can bring aspects of these perspectives together and use them in shaping future research agendas for further exploration of home-school transition in the context of learning. We will attempt to pin down to a set of (tentative) strategies.

Chapter 5 Porous Expertise and Powerful Knowledge

Chapter 4 asks – in the twenty-first century, it is argued that education operates in a 'mixed economy' of schooled and informal learning (including digital), but in that environment, whose knowledge counts? We are told that traditional modes of delivery and standardised units of learning are threatened by MOOCS, peer networks and digital divides.

For those who are experiencing a fusion of learning contexts, in this state of ongoing transition, how are boundaries of expertise negotiated formally and informally across and between various knowledge domains? In this chapter we think through what (discursively) frames these epistemological sites of struggle. We will argue that the potential for digitally mediated cultural practices to enable a more 'porous' exchange of expertise between teacher and student is 'kept in check' by the ongoing operation of power in the form of education's role in sustaining inequality. We return to Stuart Hall and the legacy of cultural studies to provide a conceptual framework for an investigation of how digital media learning is situated as a site of struggle – a 'new popular culture'. This framework will then be applied to a contemporary 'case' where we can assess how expertise is negotiated in digital *third spaces.*

Chapter 6 The Networked Educator and Open Learning

This chapter will employ actor network theory (ANT) to assess the research evidence (not the conjecture) that supports the view that the social network is an emerging human/non-human agent in contemporary education and learning. Examples under scrutiny here will include

Teachmeets, learner networks, MOOCS (both established and emergent) and 'we media' peer pedagogy. In each case, ANT will be deployed to evaluate the place of the 'affordance' in the educational landscape and the degree to which validation is present, and on what terms. A major case study will be the Open Education movement (Hall et al. 2014), and their project to disturb 'either or' models of networked learning from within the educational mainstream, in favour of 'either and' disruptions which problematise conditions of possibility for expertise, discipline boundaries and the commodification of learning, whilst existing in the same space as profoundly neoliberal 'providers'. Crucially, the extent to which each network operates within a pedagogic rationale will be explored, from the perspectives of providers and users.

Chapter 7 Cultural Studies Goes to (Not) School: Digital Struggles

What frameworks of education anywhere in the world are negotiating with the different ways to make meaning? How can multimodality and sociocultural theory work together in the context of learning? This chapter will provide a framework for aligning these hitherto distinct – and sometimes conflicting – theoretical 'lenses' to assess digital education as the social practice of 'horizontal' meaning making rather than a 'vertical' regime of value/legitimation. This chapter will be 'bookended' by a consideration of the implications of digital networks and *third spaces* for the explicitly pedagogic legacy of the Birmingham Contemporary Centre for Cultural Studies (including the works by Stuart Hall, Richard Hoggart, Dick Hebdige, Richard Johnson, Angela McRobbie and Tessa Perkins), its development in the 'seminal' *Cultural Studies Goes to School* (Buckingham and Sefton-Green (eds)) and the recent revisiting of these approaches in a literacy studies context in *Learning and Literacy Over Time* (Sefton-Green and Rowsell 2014).

Chapter 8 Afterword – An Exchange with Cathy Burnett, Neil Selwyn and Others

In this closing chapter we restate the theoretical position taken throughout the book, drawn from cultural studies, new literacy studies and educational research, to discuss the implications of the themes and findings from each chapter for learners, teachers, educational developers, policymakers and researchers. This will take the form of a summary overview, bringing together the key strands into a set of 'conditions of possibility' rather than recommendations. This concluding chapter will be presented as a transcribed 'reflexive' conversation between the two authors and two critical friends from the field of literacy and technology in education, Cathy Burnett and Neil Selwyn, reflecting on some of the key issues in the preceding text. Finally, we discuss the book and its key issues with attendees of the Media Education Summit, an annual, international conference which runs a conversation strand and, with the delegates' permission, we present a range of views on issues we have raised.

Overarching Aim

As we stated at the beginning of this chapter, our perception has been that a number of parallel theories and writers, disciplines and perspectives, drawn from media education, media literacy, cultural studies, semiotics, digital cultures, actor-network theory, educational technology and more have occupied similar spaces in recent years without being brought together into the same space. In the chapters which follow we attempt to do just that and to present some of our own research and thinking through the resulting frameworks. We begin, in the chapter which follows, by exploring contemporary versions of 'literacy' in the context of digital media, culture and education.

CHAPTER 2

Dynamic Literacies

This book is about the impact of digital media on education, as seen through a sociocultural and political lens; it examines critically some of the key themes and issues relating to media, technology and learning. We have chosen to begin by looking at the ways in which these issues are represented in recent definitions of 'literacy' which have been mobilised by a range of different theorists and interest groups. Each of these theories and definitions seeks in some way to respond to the changes brought about by the increasingly all-pervasive nature of digital media texts and artefacts in lived experience in the past few decades, in the developed world and, in different ways, in the majority world. We would like to suggest that the term 'dynamic literacies' is one way to think about an inclusive, umbrella term which is responsive and inclusive enough to describe the changing nature of meaning-making in the context of digital media and culture. 'Dynamic literacies' is, for us, a term which brings together the shifting and contested versions of literacies which have emerged out of semiotics and multimodality (Kress 2003), media education (Buckingham 2003), the new literacy studies (NLS) (Gee 2004, 2015a; Street 2003; Heath 1983) and many more, all of which in differing ways stand in contrast to the view of literacy as a static, narrow and autonomous set of codes and conventions, a view which is widely applied in educational institutions and contexts and which forms the basis of many neoliberal 'reforms' in systems all over the world.

J. Potter, J. McDougall, *Digital Media, Culture and Education*,
DOI 10.1057/978-1-137-55315-7_2

Later in the book we will also make use at various points of the term '*third space*' and position our use of it as part of an evolving semantic which takes in metaphorical, virtual and physical spaces which are all interstitially located between larger institutional organisations: home, school, work and so on. These spaces are locations for thinking, working, negotiating, playing and more, in the context of digital media, education and culture. They are all places in which 'literacy events' (Street 2003) take place, in which meanings are shared and in which pedagogical framing of those meanings is a key determinant of action in education. In other words, we see '*third spaces*' as connected to 'dynamic literacies' and existing as potential locations for learning in which hierarchies are themselves fluid; there is the potential to be more open to learners' skills and dispositions arising out of practices which are representative of wider culture and lived experience. We will illustrate these concepts by reference to key writers in the field who have influenced us, but, importantly, also by reflecting on work in a range of research projects we have engaged with in recent years. We will suggest that employing both 'dynamic literacies' and '*third spaces*' as terms offers useful frames of reference which can bring together a wide range of parallel but hitherto previously discrete contemporary discourses on digital media, education and culture.

Beginning, then with 'dynamic literacies', a key concern of this book is the changing nature of teaching and learning in response to the widespread consumption and production of digital media texts and artefacts in wider culture. We recognise, in turn, that this has a great deal to do with how we define 'literacy' because literacy is in some senses in a symbiotic relationship with 'pedagogy'; our shared understanding of what it means to be literate determines not only *what* we learn but *how* we learn and even *what* it means to be a learner. In other words, a working definition of 'literacy' shapes the whole political and pedagogical discourse around formal education and establishes much of its content and many of its performative structures.

For some, including many people who work in education, literacy is an inarguable, uncontested, neutral set of skills and competencies around communicating and making meaning. For others, at the same time as recognising those skills and competencies should be developed and practised, literacy is nevertheless inherently contentious and contested, changing in response to wider social and economic conditions represented in new communicative modes and practices; for some, the codes and conventions of meaning-making themselves change in response to what Lievrouw and Livingstone describe as 'the changed artefacts, social arrangements and practices' (LievrouwI and Livingstone 2006) in and around new media.

As media educators, we understand that whether or not an education system engages positively, negatively, or not at all with media texts and practices is framed by what is admissible in its formal structures and educational settings as 'literacy'. We also know that the situation is varied across the developed world and the majority world. The case studies and vignettes we present from our research projects will help us to discuss recent and relevant developments in educational systems close to home, in England, whilst we will also include commentary and perspectives from other parts of the world. In any case, we will consider throughout what literacy actually *is* for those social actors involved in education, for teachers, parents, carers and students alike, who move daily across the boundary between institutional space and wider lived experience. One of our approaches in the book will be to look at projects in which participants exhibit apparent awareness of their own dynamic, their own movement between those spaces and the possibility for social action in each one. This will necessarily result in us suggesting that spaces between home and school are places in which conditions can be said to constitute a '*third space*' for literacy and meaning-making (Gutierrez 2008; Bhabha 1994), as noted above, and that such spaces can be literally and physically located (e.g. in the after-school club) or metaphorically present (e.g. even accessible under certain conditions in formal settings for learning). There will be further discussion of this concept in Chapter 3.

Finally, a key interest for us at the outset is finding ways to incorporate into our understanding of literacy some of the emergent ways of thinking about the materiality of literacy and classrooms, *third spaces* of learning and media (Dezuanni 2015; Burnett and Merchant 2014). We want to suggest that a working definition of literacy should be inclusive, not exclusive, and be one which gathers together a series of sub-categories, as suggested above, of *dynamic literacies*, all of which are components of the systems and elements in the spaces of learning. We will begin by outlining some of the ways in which definitions of literacy shape pedagogy and the thousands of interpersonal interactions in a school day. The sections which follow will each address some of the key ways of thinking about literacy with particular relevance for us, working in the enlarged definition which includes all forms of media in its scope and range.

Defining Literacy, Shaping Pedagogy

For many organisations, institutions and countries around the world, *literacy*, by definition and by action, is an undeniable and constant force for good. The web pages for the United Nations Educational, Scientific and Cultural Organisation (UNESCO) state that:

> Literacy is a fundamental human right and the foundation for lifelong learning. It is fully essential to social and human development in its ability to transform lives. For individuals, families, and societies alike, it is an instrument of empowerment to improve one's health, one's income, and one's relationship with the world. (UNESCO 2016)

There is very little to disagree with here, particularly when that statement is elided with such obvious social good. In both the majority world and the developed world alike, concerns over literacy remain high on the agenda, routinely invoked by politicians as the basis for urgent, performative actions designed to act as simple and effective solutions to mutually agreed problems. However, the definition of 'literacy' itself remains both complex and highly contentious, not least because accepting it as an immutable and uncontested force for good disconnects it from cultural, political and social contexts and risks reducing it to a set of technical codes and conventions. By themselves, knowledge of these codes does not *guarantee* access to wealth and success in life, though, of course, they hardly impede it. However, factors such as higher economic, social and cultural capital, the background of parents and carers and the location and type of schooling, *alongside* a working knowledge of the technical codes *are* all, accounted for together, much more likely to have an impact on life chances.

For the majority of children and young people, from all classes and backgrounds, the definition of literacy and the operation of that definition remain of crucial importance because of the way it *includes* or *excludes* aspects of their wider social and cultural life. If a curriculum is narrow and exclusive of children and young people's experience beyond school, they are likely to be interpellated into a system in which they misrecognise themselves as learners in the prevailing pedagogy. They are likely to find themselves positioned in the narrowest terms of success and failure, judged against normative standards in a performative culture which runs the risk of introducing negative effects by focusing on a reductive set of measures which are portrayed as the only ones worth knowing about. Our argument is that, in addition, to being narrowly focused and quick to label the social actors in educational systems as failures (be they schools, children, students, parents and teacher) that this is simply not ambitious enough a design for learning for the challenging and changing times in which we live.

There is another way to view the impact of wider culture on pedagogy. The literature on 'funds of knowledge', for example, suggests, there are significant gains for learners where teaching and learning settings admit outside cultural life into classroom discourse and where the pedagogy is inclusive; in other words, where literacy is seen as contingent, culturally situated and bound in context (Moll et al. 1992). The codes and conventions of grammar, syntax, semantics and more can *still* be central in the curriculum experience, but this view of pedagogy suggests that they should be located in learning which is inclusive of the outside culture, which values the knowledge and lifeworlds of children, parents and carers in the community and which takes note of differently held 'ethnotheories' about learning (Brooker 2003). From the school side, a working knowledge of the cultural and literacy practices of those being taught is likely to benefit all social actors in the process. It remains a question of cultural capital and the ascribing of values to the detail and lived experience of the wider mass of children and young people in the care of the various systems (Alanen et al. 2015). For media itself, of course, where questions of value arise out of its exclusion in the formal life of the curriculum in our own country, there is an additional problem. The moving image, the precise location of much of children's cultural knowledge and social capital is not necessarily present in a school, formally in a curriculum subject, or even informally, as we will discuss at a later stage. And yet, as has been argued in recent years, it is a fundamental source of rich literacy practices which enables a more equitable and vital curriculum experience (Parry 2013).

Turning to the curriculum itself, as even the most cursory study of semantic and grammatical shift in England reveals, the codes and conventions of literacy are in a constant state of evolutionary change; we should expect nothing less from a living language, responsive to wider cultural influence, though such happenings are routinely lamented by conservative commentators, even as they are celebrated by others. Attempting to preserve and fossilise literacy in a narrow and prescriptive way robs it of it, if it is potential for dramatic and playful use which, in turn, denies its expressive potential for human communication across a variety of modes and means. We might also argue that it *potentially* inhibits the development of future digital makers and artists, although, as we shall note in later chapters, there may yet be potential for this activity in other spheres. Certainly, to try and pretend that the world is otherwise and that literacy is unchanging is to deny the obvious, profound and accelerated experience of change in the context of the new century, however complex and often inequitable those changes may be.

It is important to be clear that we are not arguing for a literacy curriculum which fails to attend to 'the basics'. After all, children and young people are arguably more than ever in need of many of those skills, not least because they are reading more than ever. If we factor in the way that text is shared in ever multiplying ways, on screens on myriad devices, as well as continuing to have a life on the printed page, then children and young people are daily attending to myriads of words, maybe even more than at any time in history. Accessing the codes, making sense of them and learning how to use them are all tasks which are inseparable from the world in which they are actively and routinely used to make and share meaning. Unfortunately, in England, as research has shown, our curriculum currently pays more attention to technical decoding skills than to the exchange of meaning even at the level of print literacy (Davis 2014) and even as such politically instigated pedagogy has long been shown to represent only one, albeit important, component of the way in which people learn to read fluidly, strategically and critically (Scarborough 2001).

Our main argument, then, is that we should be more ambitious for our children and young people in the way we design their schooled literacy experiences and in the ways in which we ascribe value to them. If we had a curriculum for literacy which, alongside the basic precepts, made time for the dominant modes of contemporary popular communication, the still and moving image, the music file and more, we would arguably have a living, responsive educational experience. Many children and young people are using a plethora of conventions and protocols outside of the conventions of the school, none of which is static or immutable, all of which are changing and dynamic and all of which have huge potential for learning and life. We should really expect our education systems to shift and widen their range to accommodate some of these changes to the ways in which we make meaning to take account of media, as many have argued over a long time (e.g. Buckingham 2003; Hobbs 2014; Burn 2009; Cannon 2016). However, in too many recent examples in the developed world (for reasons which we will explore later), including the current National Curriculum for Primary Schools, ages 5–11, in England (DFE 2013b), the direction of travel is back to narrower definitions and, we would suggest, back to concomitant narrower visions for pedagogy. In summary, our argument around the curriculum is not actually about excluding or diminishing the place of print; the argument is essentially about being more inclusive and widening the definition of literacy, so that we can be more ambitious with our pedagogy, more ambitious for learning in digital media culture.

Case Study: Persistence of Vision

How might a pedagogy for literacy be made to be inclusive of learning about and making media as well as retaining relevance to text, enabling children to achieve in both? This is the challenge outlined in the preceding section and a small number of studies have begun to suggest ways forward. In the United Kingdom, from the ways in which Cary Bazalgette first envisaged a curriculum which explored learning about the unique properties of media and time-based texts (Bazalgette 1989, 2000), there has been a tradition in media education of connecting literacy and media learning (Parry 2013). But this is not to suggest that one is to be learned *through* the other, that media is a useful prop for *real* learning in the traditional subjects. It is simply to suggest that, as in lived experience, print and media are bound up together. We stated that literacy and pedagogy were in a symbiotic relationship. So too are print literacy and media literacy, with neither acting as the sole driver of communicative experience or of expressive potential for meaning-making.

As one case in point, a few years ago, there was a project which brought together poetry, animation and social media as part of wider initiative to demonstrate the value of a wider definition of literacy in learning. 'Persistence of Vision' took the premise that non-narrative poetry could be taught alongside animation production and, potentially, benefit younger learners in primary schools (Bazalgette et al. 2011; Bazalgette 2010). Animation, as a form, shares many of the characteristics of non-narrative poetry: an emphasis on time, image, rhythm, repetition and more. In three rural, local authorities children made simple animations from poetic starting points and, subsequently, made poems from animated starting points, reverse engineering images back into playful experiences with words. In one of the locations, the work was enhanced and supported by a social media space on a video sharing platform. It became a network for exchanging ideas and opinions about starting points for both poetry and animation. As reported soon afterwards,

> In terms of observable existing theoretical frameworks, some of the characteristics of Etienne Wenger's (1998) "communities of practice" were in evidence, most notably the ways in which the tripartite notions of "mutual engagement, joint enterprise and shared repertoire" were represented in the exchanges in the comment spaces. (Bazalgette et al. 2011, p. 5)

Many short animated films were made over the course of the year in the project, and teachers reported enhancements to children's understanding of both animation and poetry, as well as to their writing. Projects like this are always open to challenge. How generalisable are these findings after all? What numbers of children were involved? Firstly, we can make a claim that the project went further than a simple celebratory experience of a one-off project in a single school, massively staffed by specialists who came in, conducted a creative classroom experiment in widening the definition of literacy and subsequently left. The reason for this being that the work was designed, alongside the principles of the 3D Creative, Cultural and Critical model of literacy (derived from Bill Green's Operational, Cultural and Critical model, see Green 2002) to be iterative and recursive. It took place over the period of a year, with multiple visits to classrooms on the part of the researchers. Were specialist animators involved? Yes, but not to work directly in the classroom. Instead they were to provide the teachers with initial methods at in-service training sessions throughout the year. The idea was to create a replicable model that a busy primary school class teacher could implement. Was there a vast amount of technical knowledge and support required? Not really, though it would be wrong, and in keeping with some of the enthusiastic commentaries on educational technology to pretend it was implemented without any difficulty. However, simple, inexpensive software, a webcam and a laptop were all that was required in terms of equipment, layered in alongside the supportive training model described above. If the project were to be repeated now, with the advent in many classrooms of tablet devices, it could conceivably be easier still; though to begin to argue in this way is to drift towards determinism and start to think about technology. The biggest shift was not engineered by technology alone, indeed recent history is littered with examples of 'technology enhanced learning' as, at best, a questionable idea (Selwyn 2013), which we will discuss again in later chapters. The really successful outcomes in this project were in the changing perceptions of the teachers over the pedagogy which was implemented, which saw a productive engagement with media as a vehicle for widening both the definition and enactment of literacy in the classroom. As we wrote at the time:

> Teachers on the whole reported that POV was successful in driving up writing standards. We came to see that this was because of the creative connections which could be made between curriculum areas and knowledge domains. Writing had a purpose and was holistically connected to a curriculum experience. It makes sense to children to work in this way as many have pointed out: firstly, for reasons of fashioning and maintaining creative flow (Csikszentmihalyi 1996) and secondly because situated learning and the development of literacy skills go hand in hand (Gee 2004). In textual terms, at both functional and formal level, the poetry supported the animation and vice versa. In one of the project schools, a teacher reflected on the ways in which working in a complementary way in the different modes of text and visual production supported the children' s overall literacy development in ways envisaged by writers and academics in the field. (see, for example, Bearne 2009, pp. 156–187), (Bazalgette et al. 2011, p. 6)

The New Literacy Studies

Clearly, then, our version of literacy, one which seeks to connect classrooms to lived, cultural experience, especially of media, is an *ideological* one with connections that go back to the NLS and the work of Brian Street and others (see, for example, Gee 2015b for one account of the development of NLS). Street introduced the 'ideological' version of literacy (Street 2003) as a binary to the 'autonomous' version, in which, as we've discussed above, becoming literate *by itself* confers success and status upon an individual. He also argued for a fundamental break with the autonomous version in social terms:

> What has come to be termed the "New Literacy Studies" (NLS)... represents a new tradition in considering the nature of literacy, focusing not so much on acquisition of skills, as in dominant approaches, but rather on what it means to think of literacy as a social practice. (Street 2003)

Certainly the autonomous version dominates the agenda for education and testing in those countries which work with the narrowest of definitions of literacy. In those systems it is both context and abstraction; its meaning is apparently fixed but its nature actually makes it contingent and bound to context in use. Whilst the curriculum for English in schools (DFE 2013a) contains many fine statements about its aims and promising an enriching experience for all, in recent years it has become operationalised as a reductive activity for the times in which we live with a focus on arcane technical competence. So-called traditional literacy of the kind described above exerts a powerful influence over school pedagogy. In its purest form it corresponds with constructivist notions of child development, of ages and stages, of the step-by-step acquisition of knowledge, even as it over-privileges phonological awareness as the only predictor of successful reading development (Scarborough 2001). As Gee has pointed out, it is a version of literacy which is backed by a particular kind of thinking about child development, informed by the view that literacy develops individually, internally and *solely* by mental processes in the brain (Gee 2015a, Ch.2). Over time we have come to an understanding of how these processes are augmented by *social* factors which actually influence literacy development. Literacy is in the mind, yes, but also involves learning how to take part in communicative acts which are shaped in the particular social and economic circumstances around and between people. In the early years of the twenty-first century and beyond, this means finding ways for literacy learning to account for materiality and pedagogy in the context of digital media, the dominant modes of communication.

In recent years scholarly engagements with *literacy* and, in particular, the NLS with its connection to pedagogy have sought to reconfigure its relationship with wider media and visual culture, to move its definition and scope away from a technical and reductivist focus on the codes and conventions of print and to include the many modes in which meaning is made in the digital age. Some of the key figures in this approach are identified with the NLS which James Gee has pointed out arises out of work from a range of disciplines. He lists the following key domains contributing to the NLS way of thinking about literacy, as follows: '... linguistics, history, anthropology, rhetoric and composition studies, cultural psychology, education and other areas ...' (Gee 2015b). Brian Street, for example, a key figure in the NLS, cited in the section above with the terms 'autonomous and ideological literacy', is an anthropologist. He has argued that the study of literacy is concerned with all the practices and arrangements around making meaning; that it is therefore inherently 'ideological' and contested

(Street 2003). Within this key founding principle, the NLS has made room for a broad range of approaches which, in addition to arising from the fields which Gee lists, concern themselves with a range of practices, texts and artefacts. Consider the ways in which the editors of *The Routledge Handbook of Literacy Studies* (Rowsell and Pahl 2015) have recently organised their contributors into specific gatherings of topics and approaches: *foundational, space-focused, time-focused, multimodal, digital, hermeneutic, every day* and *community based*. All of these are in some way concerned with being inclusive of wider definitions of literacy and none of them is solely print-focused. Some are inherently focused on everyday practices in wider digital culture whilst others, *multimodality* for example, focus on different kinds of texts and take semiotics as their starting point, examining the many ways in which meaning is made from an orchestration of different modes, from still and moving images, through gesture, speech and the design of texts in the dominant meaning making space of the screen (Kress 2003; Burn and Parker 2003; Jewitt 2011). In recent years this has been extended into thinking about what this may mean for learning of many different kinds in many different settings and set out as a set of unifying principles for materials gathered in many different projects. Bezemer and Kress identify three connected matters when reflecting on this work, all of which are important for any account of what it is to be literate and act in the world to make meaning:

> First was the core, the 'substance': the connection between *communication* and *learning* as the constant, recurring issue throughout the different projects we (had) worked on. The second was our use of a *social semiotic theory*, which meant we were bound to look at all of the means for making meaning. It provided us with the overarching frame of *multimodality*. The third, equally crucial, matter – the other large constant – as and is our settled understanding of the significance of the social as the *frame*, as the shaping force for all actors and all action. (Bezemer and Kress 2016, p. ix)

Scholars who have identified themselves with the NLS have all in some way moved the debate on literacy into a closer alignment with more contemporary forms of meaning making (Cope and Kalantzis 2000; Lankshear and Knobel 2006; Gee 2004). Along with the NLS has come a raft of attempts to renegotiate literacy's engagement with the changing social arrangements and practices in wider digital culture. In 'Literacy and Education', a recent re-appraisal of these approaches, Gee (2015a) describes distinct phases of thinking about literacy and traces their antecedents through the constructivist, the 'social mind' and up to 'digital media'. In the final section of the book he argues that our understanding of literacy must be inflected by our knowledge that different kinds of textual production have different affordances, some of which we barely understand. Certainly this is the case with 'Digital media' as he notes:

> All of this raises questions about digital media: What are their connections to oral language? To print? How are they transforming oral and written language and changing their ecologies? What effects in digital contexts are digital media having and likely to have? What institutions or groups sponsor or serve as catalysts for digital media to have certain sorts of effects in certain sorts of practices and contexts? How are digital media transforming human talk, text, action, interaction, mind, and memory, and how can they do this?
>
> We do not yet know the answers to these questions. Things are too new and changing too fast to have answers yet. (Gee 2015a, p. 103)

This allusion to a *dynamic* conception of literacy and literacy research is important and we will return to this towards the end of the chapter.

Case Study: Image Making and Voice

At this point, here is a recent example of an observation from a research project. How might some of this 'orchestration of modes' take place and in what sense can they be part of a school's offer and a pupil's experience? In the vignette which follows we see one small example of connecting to the 'funds of knowledge' of a group of children.

On a Monday morning in a secondary school classroom in the north of England, a group of eight young people, aged about 12–13 years, is taking part in a project which is aiming to enable them to operate as researchers of their own lives. There are two parts to this activity which is being facilitated by youth workers and a teacher/academic. Firstly, they must record words and emotions which describe aspects of their own lived experience under difficult socio-economic circumstances, made up of collaged images and words cut from magazines on a tablecloth-sized sheet of paper. Secondly, they are tasked with recording this activity in still and moving images made on tablet devices. The group divides into two and undertakes these activities in parallel, taking a turn at making the collage and filming their friends doing the making. Each member of the group has something to say about the filmmaking part; one in particular wants to demonstrate the best way to connect to the network and show how he edits and uploads videos to his own online channel. Another, in contrast, wants to know which way up to hold the device and how best to open the applications needed. The rest are confident exploring the devices, based on their past experience with touchscreens, their own or other people's. For all of them, however, it is the first time they have had the opportunity to make any still or moving image representation of their lives on a Monday morning in a classroom. All are enthusiastic and motivated. However, the session is not without its difficulties and issues, and once the technology has receded into its place as the tool rather than the locus of the activity, the focus shifts to the means by which shots and edits can be used to convey emotions, make a documentary record or tell some kind of story.

Looking back at the clips and simple edits now, performed over a period of an hour, with the integrated still shots and music added from the software's demo sound files, there is a genuine if nascent facility with the modes and means of contemporary media, which is familiar from similar projects in previous years (Potter 2012; Burn and Durran 2007). Along with the collage activity the work reveals a knowledge of process and product which is more usually employed in social media (for those with the equipment and online accounts to facilitate it). Close-ups and two shots are skilfully taken; in moving image pieces the camera moves slowly round the table varying in height. The tablet screen enables constant review within something that looks like a viewing screen, so that the finished product and the process elide in the same space, as has been noted in studies of mobile filmmaking (Potter and Bryer 2014).

Up to this point in their school lives, in the country in which this scene takes place, these young people have had no *formal*, sustained engagement with the means and modes of contemporary communication. Informally, of course, and to varying degrees, many of them are likely to have encountered 'making' with digital media. They will have experienced at first hand the issues of power and control which accompany any digital representation of identity and experience. At times, in the space beyond this room, the young people, as well as the adults who are facilitating the work, will have counted both positive and negative effects amongst those issues. In the room itself, they are acutely aware of this, even in the safe environment in which they are operating, sometimes laughing *at* each other, sometimes *with* each other, sometimes switching to the front camera to create 'selfies' and to parody selfie culture. At all times, they realise that without control over the deletion and retention of these digital images, they become something that can be used to tell stories with them, about them, around them. They know and the adults working with them know how these images find an audience, how they are placed together, and in what spaces and for how long is integral to the practice of making images in digital media. They will know this practice but perhaps will not have the word 'curation' as their first choice of name for it. We have written elsewhere about curation as a new practice arising out of the pervasive use in wider culture of the tools of new media representation (Potter 2012; McDougall and Potter 2015), and there is more on this subject in a subsequent chapter. Certainly the connections between making, editing and exhibiting inhere in their conversations and are part of a whole nexus of practices and arrangements in lived culture.

For now, there are some questions worth asking about the activity as a whole. What was creating the sense of agency and urgency in the room? Was it the act of representation itself, familiar from outside culture, less familiar, in this format in school time? Was it the permission inherent in the activity to be off-topic, to be off-timetable, to work in a different space within the school? This group had, after all, previously jumped at the chance to be part of the research project and to spend some of their time disentangled from their usual routine. If a curriculum subject name had been used to label these hours on the timetable, what name would it have taken?

Answers to these and related questions lie in the domains of literacy, of agency and of location. Overarching all of these is the sense of the *dynamic* which we experience whenever we pick up a device with the intention of making a record of something happening to us or our family or friends. And these images which we make, moving and still, are always in motion from somewhere to somewhere. When they are first taken they are called back to life in a thumbnail gallery, arranged chronologically moment to moment for deletion, selection, editing, curation in what some have described as the 'multimodal mixing desk' (Burn and Parker 2003). In the background they may already be duplicated and placed in a file server in the 'cloud'. They are sometimes under our control or, in the best of cases, of those we trust. In the worst cases, control of these images is ceded to those institutions or individuals who would curate them in different ways or mine them for usable, useful and, sometimes, sellable, data (of which more in later chapters).

It is certainly the case that representational and communicative practices have changed rapidly since the times in which the earliest digital images were made. The young people making the stories of the self which are described above were unused to making such representations in the context of a safe and distancing critical space. They were cared *for* and cared *about* by their school, but their experience of these newer and nascent forms of literacy were strictly external and subject to personal social and political capital, to control or lack of it outside. Unless any of them were to go on in the following years to take a media-related subject, should it be on offer to them, they were unlikely to encounter this kind of literacy practice again in this kind of setting.

In England with the focus on literacy as a 'basic' subject and with the huge swathes of time devoted to its study and practice in both primary and secondary schools, it could be said to be in a unique position to allow for exploration of critical, creative and cultural contexts of people's lives. However, since it is defined narrowly here and in many other countries of the developed world and majority world, we find that the general experience of the curriculum, both in its content and how it is enacted in pedagogy, is similarly narrowed. In other words, arguably, the definition of literacy in a society determines the limits of its pedagogy, its range and scope of ambition as a site for explorations of the social world. We might ask ourselves: How has this limiting of pedagogy been allowed to happen? But perhaps with more immediate impact on life and learning in mind, we should also ask: What would an alternative view of literacy look like, one which admitted *dynamic* processes into its construction? And, furthermore, what kinds of spaces would support work which enabled this to happen?

Categorising Multiple Literacies

How many literacies can we name now? Adding the qualifier 'education' and searching on the terms in this sub-heading will result in many thousands of returns. From *Digital literacy* to *Media literacy, Multimodal literacy* and more, the field is crowded with terms and definitions which are interrelated and overlapping, though sometimes contradictory and even oppositional to one another. The major difference between the possible positioning of pedagogy resulting from each version of literacy is revealed by looking more closely at its origin. In all cases, appending literacy has conferred some kind of status and a demand to pay attention to it as a serious phenomenon. Some members of the 'New London Group' anticipated the plethora of forms which new definitions of literacy would take when they called their key text 'Multiliteracies', further anticipating its connection to economic and cultural life when they subtitled it: 'Literacy, learning and the design of social futures' (Cope and Kalantzis 2000).

To take one or two of the major, extant forms of literacy and examine them, beginning with *Media literacy*... in the United Kingdom, as has been noted, 'Media literacy... has never been an accepted and cohesively defined idea' (McDougall et al. 2013, p. 7) whilst *Media education* as a concept has a much longer tradition and an, arguably, much better defined historical and political identity (Buckingham 2003). Meanwhile OFCOM, a government agency in the United Kingdom, issues continual reports and advice under the term 'Media literacy' although it is mainly focused on accounting for trends and patterns of use of media artefacts and texts in the wider population (see Ofcom 2015, for a rationale for its work). Educationalists are invited to the launches of reports, and the data are useful for academics and educators to build on. But the agencies themselves do not argue for intellectual and educational curriculum change in the same way as the main lobbying groups (such as the Media Education Association) do and have done for a number of years.

In these debates 'Media literacy' is sometimes seen as a politically pragmatic term, accruing respectability for the study of media in schools whilst flawed in itself as a description and lacking a focused and coherent vision for its future. Media studies in England, on the other hand, are the main curriculum presence there for media education, a subject which is only available on an optional basis for children at secondary school age. Here too there is an issue which is particular to the United Kingdom of the habitual, political mainstream belittling of 'media' as a serious subject of study, particularly, but not exclusively, where children of primary school age are concerned. Many have written in its defence (Buckingham 2009; McDougall 2012) and invoked similar arguments made in this account for enlarging literacy itself; it remains a subject which faces continual threats to its existence in England. Even as an exam subject Media Studies is far from safe in the United Kingdom, with attempts by government to curtail its practical work, even as it attempts to cram in a range of disparate theorists, perhaps in an attempt to make it appear more rigorous and intellectual, more fit for academic purpose in the way a 'traditional' subject is (for an account of recent struggles to save Media Studies in England).

In Europe, the terms 'Media education' and 'Media literacy' are also existentially split but they depend on one another in a number of country contexts, including, for example, for the partners in the ongoing E Media Education Lab project where a series of training scenarios are being built for use across the EU which stress the interconnectedness of media education and media literacy, two dimensions of essentially the same phenomenon (EMEL 2014).

In North America, 'Media literacy' has a longer tradition from the early twentieth century and the dawn of popular radio onwards (Rowe 2014). In the USA the terms 'Media education' and 'Media literacy' cross over one another and are used interchangeably by leading figures in the field (see, for example, Hobbs 2014) but all point to an enlarged and media-centric curriculum for all citizens, even as it is harder to envisage it happening consistently across such large areas in a distributed and regionally regulated system. However, one thing which these definitions and others around the world have in common (e.g. Wilson et al. 2011) is that their agenda extends from understanding media texts to a protectionist rhetoric around wider e-safety and stretches to encompass claims for e-citizenship as an enhanced, positive, media-led and supported version of participation in democracy. The UNESCO curriculum is a key example of this, whilst studies have shown that by itself, new media, including social media, affords little in the way of actual civic participation except under very specific circumstances (Banaji et al. 2009).

In the case of the term 'Digital literacy' there are very many recent instances and multiple points of origin, from the education technology agenda through the e-safety agenda. It has generally been taken up in connection with 'new technologies', 'educational technology', 'technology enhanced learning' and other related branches of study and play. In most cases, this seems to refer to the skills connected with using technology is used to gain access to information as well as to assess its usefulness and provenance. In its Wikipedia definition, the range and scope of the term is expanded exponentially to the point of including almost everything else within the umbrella term. There is a little of the 'cultural' represented here though, nor even the various words listed previously, and most of it seems to refer only to its instrumentalist properties, and its relationship to the software and hardware of new technologies. We will see in Chapter 3 how this is accounted for in a slightly different way in emergent work on literacies and sociomateriality. For now, though it appears that 'Digital literacy' shares some common ground with some definitions of 'Media literacy', in most versions of this term the social and cultural life of digital texts and practices is downplayed at the expense of emphasising the technological. Because of this it has become, to an extent, a politically expedient way of attempting to generate interest in an intellectual and educational programme which incorporates new technologies and new media. The reason for this, perhaps, is the fact that it does not have the negative connotations of the word 'media' which appear to be politically difficult for some to use; 'media' is after all, a school and academic subject which is frequently mocked and discredited in some public commentary in England (for a useful, short article exploring the arguments see Buckingham 2009). We shall see in a later chapter how the relatively new computing curriculum in England avoids the word media by referring to 'digital texts', and, useful though this is for teachers who would like to access the modes and means of contemporary communication with their students, it is, of course, no substitute for a complete media education programme for children and young people.

Can there even be such a thing as a vision of a critical digital literacy, one which does not simply allow the word 'digital' to provide a techno-centric gloss on a range of sweeping and fundamental shifts in our understanding of what it is to be literate? In one possible set of responses to this question Luci Pangrazio provides a detailed review of the terrain, exploring a number of complementary and occasionally contradictory positions. She notes that 'Defining what is meant by digital literacy…has proven complicated, as the spaces, texts and tools which contextualise such practices are constantly changing' (Pangrazio 2014, p. 2). She argues that this is why the brush strokes of some commentators are broad and sweeping and often without much nuance or criticality, focused on instrumental rather than ideological skill sets.

Where can we turn to find new critical theory in literacy which is located in fields that are not purely text-based, nor debating the cultural and political at a surface level? Emergent and interesting ways to account for literacy practices in the digital age which are cognisant of bodies, space, artefacts, systems and the *performance* of literacy in the context of digital media are starting to be made in the fields of sociomateriality, (im)materiality and fractionality (Dezuanni 2015; Burnett and Merchant 2014). The rich descriptions of classrooms and after-school clubs, employing the language of fractionality and materiality, arguably point to a significant new turn in literacy studies which is focused on practices and performance. In these circumstances literacy studies returns to an almost anthropological view, telling stories of artefactual versions of sociomateriality, layered with aspects of actor-network theory (Latour

2005; Law 2004), and these are themes to which we will return in future chapters devoted to unpacking them in the context of digital making and digital curation.

'Dynamic Literacies'

The literacies we have considered – *Digital literacy, Multimodal literacy, Sociomaterial literacy, Media literacy* and more – are they not all in some way *dynamic*? And could we see them as subsets of an overarching ideological set of 'dynamic literacies' with distinct traditions which, nevertheless, frame a genuine attempt to account for the changes to the ways in which meaning is made in the digital age? Some are undeniably social, technological and cultural frames (media literacy, digital literacy, sociomateriality), whilst others are concerned with the design of texts made up of different semiotic resources in a range of modes (multimodal literacy). All share the basic tenet of responding to changes to the way we think about making and sharing meanings in the course of living, and ultimately learning, with digital media. All therefore share the quality of being *dynamic* resisting static, fixed positions on what literacy can and cannot be in the twenty-first century. This is not to say that they are essentially the same, because they most certainly are not, and many do not share cultural or even critical perspectives in common. Their starting points are different, but the historical circumstances under which they have arisen are the same: the screen has emerged from its place as a medium of distribution in the corner of a room and has entered social and material life in ways which were inconceivable in times gone by. This rapid dynamic in material culture and lived experience has spawned a parallel dynamic set of literacies which are all in some way ideological, recognising that literacy is bound to context and to the means of production and reading of texts. These new media texts are different, the artefacts are different and the social arrangements which pertain to them both are utterly changed (Lievrouw and Livingstone 2006) and we must add to this the fact that *literacy* as a means for describing these changes has also changed.

Why might this be important as a unifying concept? Because conceptions of literacies with a sociocultural emphasis can fail to focus on important aspects of text and design, on the ways in which meanings are shared and read. On the other hand, literacies which focus solely on text and design run the risk of failing to pay attention to important aspects of lived, aesthetic and embodied experience (Leander and Frank 2006;

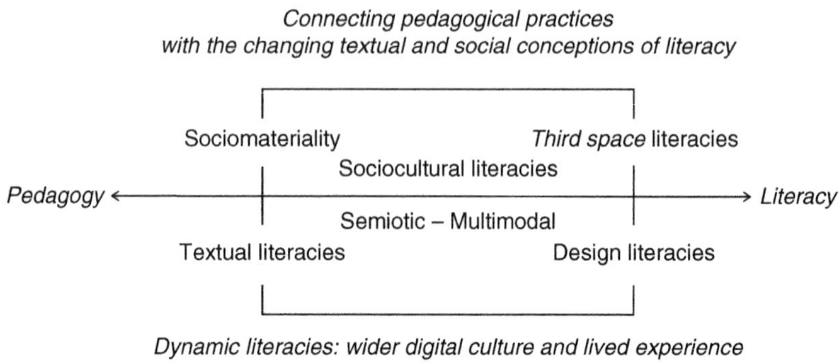

Fig. 2.1 Dynamic literacies and pedagogical practices

Burn 2009; Dezuanni 2015). Bringing them together in this way may be a useful and productive way to explore literacies and learning.

In the diagram in Fig. 2.1 we have brought sociocultural and semiotic literacies together in the same frame. Those above the line are emergent literacies which are sociocultural in nature, located in the spaces, actions and practices of digital media. Those below the line are semiotic, focused on text and design, the changing nature of both in the context of the screen and digital media. Both sets belong in the same space and on a continuum between a vision for literacy and a set of pedagogical responses and actions. These are our overarching groupings for 'dynamic literacies' and our frame of reference for including wider digital culture and lived experience in pedagogical practices which will be elaborated in different contexts of digital media, culture and education in the chapters which follow.

Of course, it could be argued that *literacy* has *always* been dynamic and responsive to changes in technologies and practices (Ong 1982). However, the accelerated nature of these changes in the late twentieth and early twenty-first century and the cultural dissonance which arises from the static nature of systems around them, such as those in neoliberal educational assessment-driven models, make for challenging and unresolved tensions. Because of their response to societal change, their inherently ideological approach and their design for inclusivity for all forms of communication, it seems to us that the word *dynamic* is a useful way to bracket together the conceptions of literacy we have discussed, from the sociomaterial and (im)material to the multimodal and semiotic. If we do this of course, having argued above that there is a symbiotic connection between literacy and pedagogy, we need to think about a response to conceptions of *dynamic literacies* which connects back to pedagogy and to systems for learning, formally and informally. Both the textual and socio-cultural sets of definitions contribute to the push and pull on teaching and learning in a system, especially one which operates at a time of such rapid change in the artefacts, texts and arrangements around digital media. We therefore need to account for those practices and arrangements which inhere in literacy events in the widest sense, whilst at the same time acknowledging the actual physicality of the screen, its place in embodied arrangements, in other words, we should be concerned with the *socio-materiality* of the digital. How might these events which take place on screen, between social actors and artefacts in a range of locations become part of the pedagogical frame? What kinds of things might people do? What kinds of interactions are possible formally organised spaces? Do we need to start thinking about other kinds of (third) spaces? And where does the term 'dynamic literacies' fit into the argument?

Beginning with the final question above, 'dynamic literacies' first came to our attention as a term when it arose out of a seminar series run by Prof Pål Aarsand at Trondheim University. At that point Aarsand was attempting to develop work in the field which explores this possibility using the term 'dynamic literacies' to group together the approaches as they embark on studies in pedagogical practice, making the connection between a conception of literacy and pedagogy stronger. Indeed, this is now the subject of some curriculum development at Trondheim. A recent course there in 'dynamic literacies' is described as follows:

> We will pay attention to dilemmas, tensions, challenges and changes that can be identified in studies of literacies. To illustrate what could be seen as multimodal and dynamic aspects of literacies, the focus will be directed to media literacy practices and related to phenomena such as learning, identity, and agency. Anchored in a sociocultural perspective, it has been claimed that literacy is situated. This raises questions: What is literacy? Can literacy be any kind of competence with regard to reading, understanding and writing texts in its broad sense? Different prefixes put to 'literacy' indicate that this is the case. These, for instance are: digital literacy, media literacy, visual literacy, information literacy, and multi-literacy. Viewing literacy as situated has actualised, among others, the notions of time, place and mobility. How do we capture literacy practices that seem to appear across different activities? How can this be studied? (Aarsand 2015)

We would argue further that *dynamic literacies* is a term which is both *synchronic*, inclusive of current situated practices, and *diachronic*, a term which opens the possibility of movement through time as an incorporated principle. It holds within it several of the terms mentioned above, but has its own momentum as a sharp contrast with the static nature of the literacy of 'the basics', of performative systems. In other words, it is aligned more closely with the ideological version of literacy because it suggests that literacy is always context-bound and contingent. For the moment, it is a necessary additional term which stands for a version of literacy which is usefully inclusive of various other liminal, spatial and technological literacies gathered together in the NLS. More than this, it provides an immediate contrast with the static nature of curriculum and assessment design for literacy in many performative systems. Elsewhere we will argue that reform of the curriculum to take account of dynamic literacies in an agentive and inclusive way is a prerequisite to addressing inequality and disconnections in educational settings. We will also see how, in the chapters which follow, these concepts are related to a number of current positions around 'networked learning' and 'porous expertise' in digital media and education.

CHAPTER 3

Third Spaces and Digital Making

In the previous chapter we grouped certain practices and ways of framing meaning-making in the digital age under the umbrella term, 'dynamic literacies'. The idea was to try to bring together definitions and constructions of literacy/literacies which enabled potential enactments of pedagogy which were fluid and suited to the hybrid and fast-changing ways in which meanings circulate in digital culture and within the lived experience of learners. But we are aware, also, of the fact that such suggestions are at risk of being located alongside optimistic and techno-evangelistic discourses for education. We are not interested in advocating for technology use per se; it is happening anyway, though not in ways which are always appropriate or beneficial for the complex ecosystem of the school (for a further discussion of which, see Selwyn 2013). Our main interest is in securing definitions of digital practices in wider culture which take into account the particular circumstances under which they are socially produced and we proceed from a cultural perspective, not simply a technological one. In fact, we are only too aware of how technological 'solutions' for education are designed to serve many purposes other than enabling learners to connect to lived culture. They can be used to reinforce and even develop arid and mechanistic practices under the weight of performative pressure in neoliberal education systems which demand rapid and widespread 'results' as measures of improvement and in which children are not only measured but become the measure itself (Yandell 2014). Indeed, the widespread and increasing

J. Potter, J. McDougall, *Digital Media, Culture and Education*,
DOI 10.1057/978-1-137-55315-7_3

use of big data in education is the subject of increasing critical attention and analysis which is rapidly becoming a field of study in its own right (Williamson 2015). Questions are being asked about the ways in which data is gathered, stored, manipulated and used to construct the wider educational agenda in tables of attainment and elsewhere. And we will address 'school' and 'not-school' later in the book.

So, whilst positive about the potential for change and cognisant of the necessity for static systems to shift in the light of the 'dynamic' we tried to outline previously, we would like to distance ourselves from the idea that introducing digital technology into educational settings is straightforward and always carried out with the best of intentions. We would like, always, to temper our definitions of what is possible with our understanding of what actually happens within performative education systems when technology arrives, particularly when it is framed outside of its cultural position and presented as a neutral force for good. Just as there is an autonomous version of literacy by which being literate is said to confer status on all who gain a mastery of it, there is an autonomous version of technology, a clarion call, a set of apparently inarguable factual assertions about its usefulness, all of which are easily manipulated by larger power brokers in the global educational marketplace. These are resisted and challenged in many studies now, of course, and good, critical questions are raised about high- and low-level educational interventions around technology. We resist this idea and suggest, as of course many others have done, that technology is not neutral but, rather, is part of both material culture and lived experience, impossible to divorce from its historical specificity and its political moment.

Our interest is in what gets made by the technology, by whom and how. It lies with media in education: with video, music, audio, animation, coding, remixing, social media, gaming, locative, augmented, virtual activity and more. We are not focused primarily on the devices and technologies which are used to make and share these practices which, we would argue, are all media texts. We are centred on how meanings circulate in digital culture, how they are produced and what this means for pedagogy and for the future of learning. The technology takes its place in our thinking as an artefactual entity, bound up in the texts and practices but not privileged in and of itself. For this reason, we are drawn to writers who are critically engaged, culturally sensitive and interested in looking more closely at what could be constituted as creative and developing pedagogical practice. Hence the opening chapter in which we mentioned those literacies which seem to us to open the frame of the picture wider than the merely technological, even as it includes that lens. We are drawn to writers who employ theories and methods which bring together technology, culture and creativity, as well as to those who operationalise those theories in the actual contexts of learners, their playful, cultural practices and their habitus, their ways of being in the world. And we would like to develop further some of this thinking in the light of our research over a number of years, some of which has taken place in what has come to be known as the *third space*, described variously as a 'not school/not home', as the halfway house of museum education or an after-school club or similar, and even sometimes as a metaphorical space which can be created out of sensitive pedagogy, of which more later.

In this chapter, then, we will look into the definitions and operationalising of the *third space* as a fruitful location for 'dynamic literacies' and for the sorts of practices around media which are harder to develop in some formal settings of education. However, although our aim in this part of the book is to do this in a way which looks beyond the classroom, our overarching aim is to think more deeply about how the loop of practice can be arced back to the classroom, given the right conditions, if we can find a way to describe them. We are further interested in exploring some of the activities which go on in the *third space* from a critical point of view and compare our experiences and our frameworks with those who are researching in the field. Our aim is to work with '*third space* literacies', 'sociomateriality' and with lenses from 'fractionality' and more, which have been used by others in the field in recent years to explore the digital and media literacy practices of children and young people who are making digital artefacts and texts (Cannon 2016; Dezuanni 2015; Burnett et al. 2014).

In any case, like most terms which come into the zeitgeist, the *third space* has moved far from its original definition; we begin the next section by looking at this line of development. We go on to explore what we see as a 'sociomaterial turn' in the ways in which media, technology and literacy are being written about in recent studies before exploring, as in previous chapters, some examples from some of our own research projects. This will lead us to a consideration of the phenomenon of the 'digital maker movement' as an instantiation of making in *third spaces* which seems to offer the potential for a connection between the sociocultural and the digital which is, in turn, realised in both onscreen and physical spaces for learning. We will make the case for the cultural and artistic lives of the learners around these spaces to be reflected in curricular designs which may run the risk of narrow definitions of computational thinking and coding. Finally, we will draw the strands of the chapter together and link the work back to our previously defined 'dynamic literacies'.

The Third Space and Digital Media in Education

In arguing for the expansion of schooled literacy into an inclusive incorporation of digital media in education, we want to mobilise the concept of a *third space* in specific ways by reference both to its origins in the work of Homi Bhabha (1994) and as an important component in designing pedagogy for equity and social justice, as in the work of Kris Gutierrez (2008) and others. Its origins lie outside of education, in different intellectual and academic discourses, pitched between humanities, cultural and literacy studies. For Bhabha (Bhabha 1994), the term *third space* was developed and enlisted as a way of defining communication both as the production of meaning and, more importantly perhaps, as a complex act of 'cultural performance'. In this short passage he outlined this by reference to the 'pact of interpretation' in the communicative act between the designated cultural locations of 'I' and 'You'. In this situation,

> the production of meaning requires that these two places be mobilized in the passage through a *third space*, which represents both the general conditions of language and the specific implication of the utterance in a performative and institutional strategy of which it cannot 'in itself' be conscious. What this unconscious relation introduces is an ambivalence in the act of interpretation. (Bhabha 1994)

For Bhabha the space is metaphorical, built into the cultural performance of communication, bounded by institutions and social strategies, always contingent and in an ideologically bound context; this, of course, calls to mind the positioning of the NLS and suggests ways in which this might be socially organised. It also brings to mind orientations towards the design of social futures envisaged by the members of the New London Group as a set of 'multiliteracies' (Cope and Kalantzis 2000); by suggesting that the implications of communicative acts exist in an unconscious relation to their institutional contexts, it implies a crucial role for a strategic and political pedagogy in the digital age. The use of the word 'ambivalence' is key to the understanding for education of the concept; for pedagogical purposes it sets up a series of essential considerations: of the relative power, positionality and subjectivity of all the actors involved in educational acts; it requires that we consider the messy realities of everyday life, the spaces, bodies, texts and artefacts. It suggests at least that the certainties of 'direct instruction' are hopelessly adrift from the reality of communicative actions in spaces of learning. If none of the parties in communicative acts admits negotiation or complexity as preconditions of the production of meaning, then there is no room for manoeuvre which produces agency, action, or even, change in an educational setting. It may even potentially inhibit pedagogical action and ambition, restricting teaching to a narrow instrumentality.

Some questions to ask about this, therefore, include: How do teachers and teacher educators account for the ambivalence and provisionality in their designs for teaching and learning and how much more complexity is therefore suggested in the era of digital media? How does this concept sit with our discussions and definition of literacy/literacies, dynamic or otherwise? Finally, how does either media in education or the complexity of the *third space* begin to establish itself in the era of performativity, of officially constituted and enforced autonomous definitions of literacy and the ways in which these are bent out of shape by political expediency.

One scholar who has mobilised the concept of the *third space* in pursuit of a culturally sensitive literacy pedagogy is Kris Gutierrez (2008). She reimagined the *third space* as a way to think about the social actors in a given setting, their autobiographical and temporal specificities and how these could be accounted for in the design of an emancipatory form of educational experience. She wrote about how the design for learning in the *third space* could resist the standard binaries of home and school, taking into account the lived experience of movement and changes to context. She did this by locating the work in a study of the University of California, Los Angeles (UCLA) Migrant Student Leadership Institute (MSLI) which provided actual and metaphorical potential in incorporating movement, contexts, 'shifting practices and communities' into pedagogical design. Traditional, earlier operating frameworks of home and school were described as 'deficit portraits' which merely compelled 'educators to fix communities and their members so that they match normative views and practices' (Gutierrez 2008). This was not an option for those working on this programme, where cultural affiliations and dispositions of the learners were at the heart of the day to day experience, and, importantly, up for challenge as well as celebration. However, in accounting for the practices in the institute, she was careful to distance the learning experience from the notional 'challenge' of neoliberal, performative schooling and assessment programmes. She discussed ways in which the resources of the participants' own lives could take on the creation of a new knowledge as, ultimately, a new social history in the setting. All of this, we are informed in the notes accompanying the article, arose from the design and reflection on the work itself and not, at that time, from any reading of the work of Bhabha, though she subsequently incorporated this into the framework: a way to think about pedagogy and culture and a way to structure opportunities for many learners.

For those of us concerned with media education practice as a site for negotiated pedagogy, the central challenge is, and always has been, in defining and operationalising its relationship to this *third space*. Media's location as a subject in the formal literacy curriculum in England for primary school children and lower secondary (5–14 years.) has been marginalised in recent years and its future as a formal school qualification, even for older students, is not assured. It has, in many cases, been quite literally forced into the non-metaphorical, literal *third space* of the after-school club, not that this has been a wholly negative way forward, allowing as it does, for some interstitial activity, of the kind described above, to take place. Back inside the machinery of the formal curriculum in England, a quick scan of the documentation (for enactment outside of the independent or quasi state sector of 'academies' and 'free schools') shows that even the word 'media' has been removed; there are no references to moving image texts or wider culture anywhere. Aside from an oblique reference in the maths curriculum to using media to describe properties of shapes, where media is present at all in the mainstream curriculum orders, post 2013, is, vestigially, in the term 'digital texts' in the computing programmes of study (DFE 2013a). Again, this is something we will return to in a later chapter: the problem of the digital as a descriptor for media, both socially and politically.

For now, though, we must consider under what conditions such *third spaces* may ever really challenge accepted orthodoxies and pedagogies. It is possible to glimpse this in the few studies of such spaces in formal settings which have been undertaken. Some of these have been during actual school time under conditions in which power relations are subverted by the presence of artists in the classroom in projects which seek to partner schools with creative professionals (see, e.g. the work of

Thompson et al. 2012). In their use of particular strategies which go towards risk-taking, inclusion and challenging dialogic interaction, the artists in the classroom depart from some of the conventional and habitual practices of teaching and introduce new 'signature pedagogies' into the settings which are themselves derived from creative arts practice. Such *third spaces* as are created in these acts may only be temporary in nature, existing only whilst the creative professionals are present in the school, under very specific conditions, and existing only because of the way their 'signature pedagogies' create the conditions for purposeful, agentive experiences (Thompson et al. 2012). They are almost always negotiated into existence by the role of the teacher, stepping aside whilst the practice takes place but operating as a controlling and managerially enforcing presence. In this sense the offer to teachers inherent in this concept is frustrating because it suggests it is not possible for them to recreate such practices in the day-to-day life of the formal space of the classroom without some challenging of the inherent power structures and assumptions, the habitus of the social actors in the space. This, of course, is not always possible to enact in systems which de-professionalise teaching professionals and expect them to narrow their own visions of pedagogy. The potential overlay and challenge to practices which usually inhere in these systems is likely to produce a great deal more work for all concerned.

In many studies, then, the *third space* is located outside of the strict temporal structures of the working day of the classroom, in a lunchtime or after school club which may still be located in the formal setting but which exists under very specific conditions. Different theoretical frameworks apply here which invoke not simply pedagogy but also the socio-material relations of bodies, technology and space, along with conditions which are generative of dialogue, construction and creativity (Burnett and Merchant 2014; Cannon 2016; Dezuanni 2015; Hawley 2016). Indeed, there is what could be described as a 'sociomaterial turn' in these recent studies of classrooms, technology and media, which is seeking to complement more textual and screen based literacies with hybrid forms of theory which are better able to account for young people's productive engagement with media in the material world. There are also correspondences with emergent thinking on locative versions of literacy and learning which, in the words of Mills and Comber, attempts to foreground

> place and space as constitutive, rather than a backdrop for real action. Space and place are seen as relational and dynamic, not as fixed and unchanging. Space and place are socially produced, and hence, can be contested, reimagined, and remade. In bringing space and place into the frame of literacy studies we see a subtle shift – a rebalancing of the semiotic with the materiality of lived, embodied and situated experience. (Mills and Comber 2013, p. 412)

Clearly this links back to the concerns of the previous chapter in seeking a dynamic and responsive version of literacy which contrasts sharply with the 'imaginary' of the static educational system (imaginary in the sense that the static system resists anything other than the autonomous version of literacy, which produces mainly imaginary change in the lives of students and teachers). But whilst these disciplinary debates around the spatial turn are increasingly common in the research literature of 'literacy studies', they have not, until recently figured hugely in the research on technology or media in the classroom, where sociological and cultural studies hold more sway. One of the key concerns of this book, stated at the outset, was to find a way to bring some of these complementary approaches into the same academic space and, in common with the writers and studies mentioned above (Burnett and Merchant 2014; Cannon 2016; Dezuanni 2015; Hawley 2016), this is what we hope to achieve.

Screens as Virtual Places of Real Work, Materially Located

Claims are sometimes made for virtual, screen spaces as *third spaces* in and of themselves where newer forms of pedagogy might be possible. It seems to us that whilst this is an attractive claim, it runs the risk of privileging onscreen/online experiences as inherently dynamic, authentic and easily negotiated. Some writers have pointed to the risks of this producing a new autonomy of the screen, when what is really required is a new vision of multiply placed literacies (Bulfin and Koutsogiannis 2012), and, we would argue, associated pedagogies.

Until we are all able to live entirely as holograms in a virtual world, devices and screens are part of the material world, alongside their owners and users. This applies whether they are in the hands of users on the move, whether they are in a classroom, a home, an internet café or an after-school club. For us, the *third space* is where some of them may be located and, in that space, they are subject to certain conditions and social relations. Seeing the virtual itself as an uncontested source of free-thinking, learner-centred experience in education is not a tenable position, ignoring, as it does the material circumstances inherent in producing the interaction, the economic imperatives of screen ownership or the political engagements in the (re)production and (re)-imagining of the world onscreen.

Writers who have addressed the issue of home-school learning from the perspective of the NLS and its antecedents have, of course, looked at more than the screen. They have attempted to describe the virtual in terms of new but everyday practices which have the potential to be integrated into an existing set of relations (Lankshear and Knobel 2006). Others have described the conditions under which learning may occur in functioning online spaces as situated generators of optimal conditions for positive pedagogy (thinking here of the 'affinity spaces' and 'participatory cultures' of Gee 2004; Jenkins et al. 2006). Others have tried to move beyond technology in the debate altogether into a wider engagement with the social, political and personal of education in the new media age (Buckingham 2007).

In their study of children writing in a virtual *third space*, in a series of blogs created at school and maintained at home, Barrs and Horrocks (2014) point to the ways in which traditional literacy was, at that time, operating as a constraining and distorting force on children's writing, focused on the technicalities of grammar and terminology of analysis over production. In their account, the influence of the dominant narrow pedagogy spills over into the ways in which atomised teaching of various learning objectives is skewing writing away from actual communicative acts altogether and replacing them with writing which demonstrates technical ability at the expense of meaning and affect. These values are restored by judicious use of blogging in very particular kinds of pedagogical practices that employ a more nuanced account of technology, media and learners, generating a kind of *third space* which allows for movement of value across the semi-permeable membrane between home and school (Potter 2011). It is important to remember that the success of this activity arose out of the skilled pedagogical practices of the teachers and co-researchers who were looking critically at power relations in the classroom and at wider issues of literacy implied by the use of blogs. There was much more to the whole way in which the blogs were set up than simply seeking an audience, and much more to say about what happened than describing the activity as 'motivating'.

Third Spaces and Sociomateriality

As we noted in the beginning sections of this chapter, more recent research represented in the work of academics in the United Kingdom and Australia is turning from a focus on the virtual to pay attention to the arrangements of bodies, devices and locations with respect to discussing literacy events and pedagogy as an orchestration of all of these factors, describing them as sets of real events, producing real work.

Some of this work in sociomateriality implies that we should think more clearly about how meaning is made in respect to the interactions between learners and artefacts, bodies and spaces, as much as from their lived experience in wider culture. In doing this we should resist a purely romantic or celebratory account of the possibilities of technology and work from a perspective which draws the virtual and the material together in the same space. Whether this theory is pure actor – network theory, describing the relations between artefacts and bodies as assemblages of the social (Latour 2005) or whether new combinations of theory need to be developed is a moot point. At the time of writing, the studies are seeking to create accounts of 'real' classrooms, in all their messy realities, and the ways in which these are integrated into meaning-making onscreen and in the material spaces of learning. These studies engage with more evidence than is usually derived from the recorded performance of onscreen behaviours or the ways in which the virtual represent meaning. They are accompanied by detailed observations and transcripts which build a thick description of the setting and the events taking place (Geertz 1973) including in some cases close attention to video evidence analysed with attention paid to the ways in which many of the modes of meaning making are orchestrated (Jewitt et al. 2016).

In one of these recent studies, the possible use of a sociomaterial frame in thinking about literacy becomes an important component of the account of young children playing Minecraft. The authors talk of the ways in which the girls 'bring themselves into being through talk and digital production in the social spaces of the classroom and within the game's multi-player online world' (Dezuanni et al. 2015, p. 147). In other words, the screen and the design of the virtual world do not have a privileged place in the account of the ecosystem of the classroom. The social life of the classroom is captured as an important element of the play, which the authors characterise as performative representations. An important aspect of the project is the description of the onscreen work of construction in the world of Minecraft as 'real' building. The communicative and representational practices are bound up in the whole experience of being in the world of the classroom which they report as messy and provisional, with expertise valued amongst the girls at many different levels. The authors go on to write that:

> We have identified that these practices include not just digital production and assemblage, but also talk that accompanies gameplay that is an integral aspect of digital participation. We agree that it is vital to understand the practices that occur in the social spaces between making and sharing because these are key sites of identity construction and learning, and therefore central aspects of the girls' learning lives. (Dezuanni et al. 2015, p. 160)

Observing similar activities in the *third space* of a computer club running software which allowed the creation and building of a virtual town, Burnett and Merchant (2014) drew on the work of different authors who have written about the relationships between online and offline meaning making in this *third space*, some of whom are from the tradition of NLS outlined in the previous chapter. Others included scholars of actor-network theory, specifically Latour (2005), in the authors' attempts to account for the 'materiality' of the hardware and the virtual as the children struggle to position artefacts on desks, maintain a focus on the screen, talk to each other and so on. Drawing on Law and Mol (2002) and the notion of objects which are 'fractal', they develop the idea that objects in the zone of action of the children are neither wholly real nor virtual. Writing about one of the children and their movement in both spaces, they note that

> his laptop is both a physical object in the classroom and the portal to the virtual world; he interacts with others both in and out of world. At the same time, the classroom frames not only what he does in physical space but also what he does online. The 'world of his own' (*in which he appears to be*) is perhaps the one he helps construct as he operates across both environments and helps sustain a space that allows both movement and stillness, both autonomy and compliance, both material and virtual actions. (Burnett and Merchant 2014, p. 43, my italics and additions in brackets)

If these accounts problematise physical and virtual space, even as they seek to provide richer accounts of children, computers, real and virtual worlds, how can they be reconciled with the sociocultural notion of a *third space* outlined above, or, more usefully, with a set of practices within them which could be constituted as '*third space* literacies'? The question is perhaps partly answered by thinking about ways in which such projects are pedagogically designed and established. They exist outside the usual time constraints of the classroom (in an after-school club, as in Burnett and Merchant 2014) or are specifically negotiated into a space which is not like the classroom's usual arrangement (as in Dezuanni et al. 2015). In other words, the social and pedagogical arrangements of these spaces taken together constitute a social design which has parallels with the classes described by Gutierrez (2008). The difference in these situations is that the *third space* each case is where the real and virtual come together and where the potential for social action in the world is dictated by more complex and pedagogically ambitious designs than may be possible in performative and static systems which, as we have already noted in chapter one, do not admit the notion that literacy is 'dynamic'.

Some Projects in Third Spaces

In our own work, two projects in *third spaces* are worth considering in the light of these approaches, each offering a different perspective in their own framing but each with potential for reevaluation as instances of sociomateriality, which could suggest ways forward in further explorations of *third spaces*. The first, directed by Prof Andrew Burn and Prof Jackie Marsh and reported in detail in two recent books (Willett et al. 2013; Burn and Richards 2014), was concerned with investigating the primary school playground in the new media age. In part this involved taking on some of the hype around the disappearance of children's games which, it was feared, was driving them away from outdoor play in morning break at school and into an engagement with screens. The project found that, to the contrary, children's playground games were indeed alive and well in the digital age, with changed contexts and different rules of engagement. Involving children as simultaneous subjects and co-researchers in the project, and working with expert playground-embedded ethnographers, Dr Rebekah Willet, Dr Chris Richards and Dr Julia Bishop enabled an understanding of how the social actors brought popular media culture into their performed and embodied play in what was essentially a *third space*. As part of the project, the children became involved in helping to design a website for the British Library (2016) which held a newly digitised selection of playground game histories and resources gathered over a number of years in the twentieth century in the United Kingdom by Peter and Iona Opie (1954). Children contributed their understanding and interpretations of the earlier games, alongside representations of their own contemporary play in the form of text, image, designs for animation and, crucially, a way of navigating the content which was child and non-expert friendly, all of which was designed to engage the children's agency (however difficult a word that is to define and operationalise) in creating the resources. What became evident in viewing their work for the outward facing website was that, in presenting design material about a *third space* for the *third space* of the screen, they largely reincorporated their play in the spaces intertextually. In one video clip when pitching ideas for the site, a girl recreates in her gestures the embodied way of being in the space, amongst the other children, in the actual physical location. The action in the world of the playground became performed again by them for the intended audience to navigate:

> What is new and revealed by taking a closer look at both the drawn and performed elements which are essential to the site for her, in both the still image and in the video, is the embodied and aesthetic response to the activity. She wishes to perform the site as it would be encountered by a visitor and, at the same time, she wishes to meet the demands of the brief and to make the collection accessible to a viewer. This level of construction of the site from the raw material of the collection shows a concern for content as well as process, for production as well as consumption. (Potter 2014, p. 199)

This is a literacy event in the *third space*, then, which is operating within the spatial and the material, the virtual and the lived experience of the child. As the child designs the site, she performs it. The objects surrounding her in the room, adults, pens, paper, children, cameras, books and tables are all co-present with screens and representations of designs. They are all orchestrated in the performance and each aspect is important. Whilst so much of the commentary could be located in the familiar discourse of design, the transduction into the digital involves work in the real world to move the play into a faithful but transmissible form. We would argue that sociomateriality provides additional lenses through which to view human action around media and technological artefacts and that much of the most interesting practice is emerging in *third spaces*.

The work as described in the texts around it could not have been so fully accounted for if it were not for the very careful ethnographic accounts which were built from the observations, though it is fair to say that these were not directed ultimately towards the kinds of theoretical domains under discussion. The playground games project, however, does suggest ways forward for future research which widens the account to incorporate a theorised *third space*, in which sociomateriality and the spatial turn could play a part.

In a subsequent project in a *third space*, children were engaged in making simple computer games from stories which they had previously created. The project was in a summer school club, voluntary to attend, run by two community groups in London, over the course of five full day sessions, running consecutively through a week. One venue was a famous community arts centre which, by association with the project, was aligning itself to the 'digital maker' movement (of which more later). The other was an after school club established with the aim of extending and improving children's literacy experiences (in the sense of print literacy). This latter organisation was part of a three-year evaluation conducted by the University of London, and this was its first attempt to introduce any activity which had substantial levels of digital culture and making in its practices. There were, therefore, a number of interesting pedagogical cross-currents in the setup of the work. For a start, the fifteen children aged between about 10 and 14, mixed in gender, were from two different backgrounds, with half coming from the area around the arts centre and with the others visiting from a relatively poorer part of the city. The spaces provided were in both venues, with the first two days taking place at the literacy club in which the originating stories were created. In the arts centre, where all the children relocated from the middle of the week, the participants worked on coding and programming activities with tutors from an after school children's coding project and a literacy tutor. These sessions were designed to culminate in the children producing, exhibiting and trialling a small computer game designed to run in Scratch, the educational programming software (MIT 2016).

Sessions were very different in each place, with those in the literacy club organised around traditional literacy activities, such as character and setting creation, using print literacy and written language. Children responded in a mode which suggested they were in school, with hands going up for responses and recording made by the tutor on a chalk board. The pedagogical design for these sessions then moved into the territory of computer games even as a discussion opened up about wider digital culture, framed by a series of questions about gaming's harmful effects. At this point, by opening up a dialogue on an aspect of children's cultural experience outside of formal, print literacy, there was great deal of interest from the group. The tutor expressed concern about the likely impact of violent games on the wider community, with people watching and then trying to act out these experiences, a notion which was quickly refuted by a 13-year-old female student and gamer who had a string of anti-effects arguments to make.

When the sessions moved in to the arts centre, the dynamic radically changed. Away from the more formal classroom style setting where some elements of the pedagogy had borrowed heavily from literacy lessons, the activities moved in to the making and programming of the games. There was an immediate change in the nature of the communication between the actors in the setting. It was no less complex nor easily resolved, but there was a qualitative difference which was associated perhaps more with the actual making and doing than any overt 'learning' intention. In this way, the kinds of observations from the studies mentioned earlier in the chapter could be at least partially applied. The setting became one where play with a range of game authoring artefacts was encouraged, as the students moved between devices and interfaces in search of ways of turning their paper plans into something that could be played. At this point, the disjuncture and disconnect between the plans and the outcomes was apparent really early on as the students struggled to turn their characters and settings into a playable experience in the 2-D world of Scratch. The limitations produced some interesting solutions as characters became designed into maze games and race games which were simpler to programme and contained none of the narrative nor any of the 3-D rendering demanded by the students' original stories and designs.

Observing the session, it was possible to be struck by the way in which the hardware devices were part of the world of the project in the ways described in the earlier studies, but overlaid with a layer of traditional print literacy even as sight of this was lost by pragmatism in the decision making by both children and adults. Indeed, interviewed in the chaotic last day with the arts centre being taken over by other, music summer schools and noise from all sides, children in turn expressed nuanced and carefully expressed sentiments about the success or failure of their game. Even when pushed by over-persuasive interviewing techniques the students engaged in the project recognised the tensions between the competing demands of the literacy aims of the project and the programming side of things. These tensions were evident in the exchange below with one of the students in a difficult and noisy *third space* for interviewing:

Student:	On Tuesday and Wednesday I still think it's too long and making stories for like six hours is not like fun ... but making a game for like six hours because a game like technically takes six hours it makes it a little bit more fun
Interviewer:	Would you say that there should be less of the story time and more of the making time?
Student:	Yes
Interviewer:	OK
Student:	That's what I'm saying
Interviewer:	OK
Student:	But that's just my opinion ... I'm always (inaudible) by technology more than stories
Interviewer:	But the two together is pretty interesting?
Student:	Well, it's alright (conciliatory tone) because you kind of need a story to make a game
Interviewer:	Because without a story even with all the technology a game is not that good?
Student:	Yeah but also sometimes if you don't play games you are not good at making the story – you are not good at making games
Interviewer:	So you need to know a bit of both?
Student:	Yep – they go hand in hand

The exchange, in which the interviewer asks some leading questions, is full of thoughtful agency on the part of the interviewee, a student aged 10. The most salient point is the statement about game culture and its overriding influence on the quality of the experience of game making, more significant in this interview, than any negotiated compromise between social actors in the exchange. If you don't play, then you don't know how to design the game well. In itself the interview constitutes an attempt to build a negotiated meaning, a kind of *third space* through which a communicative pact of interpretation is made.

Viewed in isolation as a screen-based piece of work, with no context for the game, it would be difficult to draw conclusions from the project which were anything other than restricted to design elements, or at best some of the simpler ludic elements. On the other hand, if the students were interviewed about only about their experiences of the literacy elements, the story composition and so on, as separate items, then only a commentary about the sociocultural would be possible. What would be lost would be the dynamic of movement in the room, the peer support, the lowered laptop lids and shouted statements, the careful manoeuvring round a darkened room in an unfamiliar space, some kind of way of accounting for the play. The materiality of the room, the artefacts and bodies, the way in which the pedagogy was successfully orchestrated in the space was as much a factor in the (at least partially) successful outcome of the project as the other elements. What was lacking, because at the time the research was not designed in this way, was a way of bringing the material and the virtual together in a commentary which attempted to fully account for digital making in a *third space* from a sociomaterial and sociocultural perspective. Only with these elements in place could conclusions be drawn which would allow us to explore more fully the notion of the *third space* in this context. Creating a frame which approached this would also allow us to more fully and accurately think about the wider digital making movement.

Digital Making and Learning Lives in School and in the Third Space

There is beginning to be interest in the USA and United Kingdom in exploring 'digital making' as a site for more interest and learner-driven work with technology (Sefton-Green 2013; Peppler 2013). Such activity has been characterised by a freedom to explore a more interest and learner-driven agenda than is perhaps possible in the formal arrangements of the school and is frequently written about in the context of *third spaces* (after-school clubs, museums and galleries, hacking events, etc.). In the case of Sefton-Green, the opportunity to explore this world in the form of a commissioned review (by Nominet, the internet charity) sits alongside the work which he and Erstad and others have been doing over a number of years to describe the various trajectories of learning lives, including and incorporating the skills of making with digital media (Sefton-Green and Erstad 2012). The concept of learning lives moved the way of thinking about media, technology and learning practices with the digital into both the actual and metaphorical *third spaces* which we have been discussing. For the Nominet review, Sefton-Green established three areas for exploration: Learning and the Economy; The Individual and Learning; Learning, Community and Society. In each case the need for further research was outlined, with the final space requiring significant work

> investing in and sharing systematic accounts of learning digital creativity in a range of educational locations (at home, in the community, at school, college, university and at work), including case studies and quantitative measures in order develop a more consistent evidence base to support ongoing initiatives. (Sefton-Green 2013, p. 61)

We would argue that the theoretical underpinning of this activity is important and should draw on the domains explored in this chapter, engaging with the problematic but often cited rhetorics of creativity (Burn et al. 2006) but also taking on some of the under-theorised claims made for 'making' as a site for designs for positive user engagements with technology (Quinlan 2015). The *third space* potentially offers a theoretical base which suggests negotiations of contested meanings and criticality and potentially enables researchers to look beyond the hype and context-free assertions made by the proponents of making. It chimes with the findings of the (so far) very few studies there have been which have taken a critical look at the phenomenon of the 'makerspace' inside or outside school (Nemorin and Selwyn 2016; Halvorsen and Sheridan 2014) in which the messy realities of day-to-day life in schools, and 'makerspaces' is delineated in ways which recall the socio-materiality and (im)materiality arguments discussed earlier (Burnett and Merchant 2014; Dezuanni 2015).

In the USA the review conducted by Peppler (2013) is located firmly within the arts and builds on traditions of work which do not begin from the digital. This is a fundamentally different approach which sees the act of making as central and which connects to the digital as part of a continuum of development of tools and practices which have long antecedents in arts practice. Indeed, the 'digital' is only one aspect of the scope of her review as she states at the outset:

> Our framework has four main parts – each a distinct "practice" that can be cultivated by interest-driven arts learning in a digital age:
>
> - technical practices, such as computer coding for artistic projects;
> - critical practices, such as carefully observing and studying an artwork to understand it;

- creative practices, such as making choices how to handle a project by applying artistic principles; and
- ethical practices, such as giving credit to the original creators of a work. (Peppler 2013, p. 7)

Just as Sefton-Green (2013) concluded with recommendations for future research in a field which is not yet explored in depth, so too does Peppler, citing the need to find ways to be inclusive of the range of activities which students in *third spaces* seem to 'move' between. Out of school hours' activity inevitably produces the kind of 'mobility' and spatial activity which others also suggest should be a fruitful location for study in the digital age (Leander et al. 2010). Beyond this Peppler suggests that the subject areas in which work is located themselves are sites of transition and movement. In their lived experience of digital culture, the production which students undertake is hybrid and simultaneous in nature and not divided or parcelled up. We see this as being part of a wider phenomenon of curation through the personally and socially acquired skills of 'curatorship' as a new literacy practice (of which, more in later chapters). But in the meantime, for Peppler, the key action is in ascribing recognition and value to the informal arts learning practices of students and young people on the part of organisations engaged in after school work. And on the part of the young people themselves, the imperative is to build on the digital-curatorial activity they undertake and to 'document their practices and support institutions that use portfolios in their admissions and hiring practices' (Peppler 2013, p. 67).

Peppler seeks, in other words, to move more in the direction of the negotiated space, the one which is cognisant of the world-picture of the young people, which does not confer status on the digital itself but on the whole 'ecology' of the settings of learning through which young people move. Future research effort should be directed to

> investigate the design of interest-driven arts learning social networks, including progression pathways and whether these tools need to operate within a larger ecology of learning environments to best support teens. (Peppler 2013, p. 70)

Peppler's work chimes with research in the United Kingdom which looks specifically at how making or crafting as a resource for pedagogy may bring more culturally relevant and more challenging pedagogy with media, in particular, within reach of learners and classrooms. In her detailed descriptions of such making, Cannon (2016) resists simple definitions in a nuanced argument which calls for digital making, media production in this instance, at the heart of a praxis-orientated creation of a *third space*. Such a study, combined with the work outlined above raises the prospect of a new way of studying this kind of space which moves beyond celebration and builds sophisticated arguments about the connections between learner lives and the curriculum. In many countries this connection can be made formally, of course, but, in England, the digital is restricted in official orders to the subject of computing which we now go on to address.

Curriculum as 'Third Space' for the Digital: Gains and Losses in the English Computing Subject

In 2013 the UK government introduced computing as a subject, a move that looked like opening up a potentially innovative space in the curriculum for all schools. Certainly the consensus amongst some powerful lobby groups was that the previous location for the digital in schools, the information and communication technology (ICT) curriculum was not fit for purpose. Under pressure from the British Computer Society and facing criticism from the likes of Google for its alleged focus on basic office software skills at the expense of computational thinking, the ICT curriculum was replaced by computing (DFE 2013a) and the focus in schools shifted towards coding and programming skills for all children from the ages of 5 to 16. The story of how this curriculum change was navigated through a series of consultations, name changes, shifts in focus and emphasis is told in Peter Twining's blog/wiki hybrid (Twining 2013). For readers in other countries following this link or researching this issue further, and in whose systems there is a tradition of these kinds of skills being taught alongside 'media', there will be some curious omissions. Whilst broadly welcomed as a way to introduce children and young people to more creative encounters with technology, to understand better how the programmed world works and to develop more employable profiles, the computing curriculum nevertheless faced criticism for the way in which it appeared to dispense with some of the cultural references of its predecessor and replace it with an arid and mechanistic experience (Buckingham 2015b). As each iteration was produced and the actual lived experience of code in media receded from view, 'digital texts' made an appearance in the final version and, with it, some kind of watered down reference to wider, popular culture was retained. And yet, the overriding influence on the design of the computing curriculum came from areas outside of the lived experience of coding or media. The curricular influence on this process came from the STEM (Science, Technology, Engineering and Maths) lobby.

In order to see a negotiation with the cultural experiences of young people and the presence of code and programming in the world beyond school, including the world of wider employment, we would propose STEAM(M) as a better way to create subject-related *third spaces* for school, formally and informally. We are inserting the additional letter in there, A for Arts – as recognised in the USA, for example, by campaigners and lobbyists for creative curriculum experiences (White 2015) together with a less usual, silent second M (for Media) at the end. The reason for the silence is that it is almost totally absent from the formal school curriculum for younger learners and only just present in the form of the exam subject, Media Studies, for older students. The reason for its presence in our acronym STEAM(M) is that it is always present anyway, as we have seen in the previous chapter's account of dynamic literacies. Children know this, adults know this, teachers, parents and carers too – their attention to safety as the key issue of the day is symptomatic of this and shouted loudly every time the area is debated. But the M, for Media, is silent and absent in the formal, curriculum organisation for schools in England.

Clearly, as we have seen in some of the examples above, a groundswell of *third space* activity is happening all round this subject area with coding clubs, learning in maker spaces and some very helpful work for teachers who may be struggling with it. We would argue that the next step is to connect this to other curriculum areas, particularly in the arts and media. Because at the same time as there has been a triumph for the STEM lobby, and many positive gains, there have been huge losses to the arts in education in the curriculum. In recent years, they have been downgraded in formal schooling in spite of the obvious connections with the economic arguments (e.g. in-game authoring and special effects have artists, storytellers, composers, designers and filmmakers working alongside programmers; they depend on one another). So, putting the A back into the acronym and building a new campaign have never been more important. There is an interest in enriching the computing curriculum by giving it some wider cultural and pedagogical context. But beyond all this is the well-established need for arts education and its connection with positive outcomes for collaboration, critical engagement, cultural understanding and problem solving.

But what about media as an official subject for study, in or out of a negotiated *third space*? It would potentially be useful for teachers to have some kind of formal permission to access the codes and conventions of the world around them and to have some guidance about what is available to them in, for example, making the connection between animation and poetry (Bazalgette 2010) or filmmaking and using tablet devices (Potter and Bryer 2014). It would be wonderful if pupils could have their efforts in media production recorded somewhere in a portfolio as suggested by Peppler (2013) for interest-driven arts work, preferably alongside their successes in programming so we do not have to endlessly pretend that there is no connection between coding and the wider experience of the world.

As noted above, the silent M of Media in STEAM(M) is all around us. The ways in which art, music, film, animation, sciences and social sciences circulate in wider culture are all in media, sometimes social media, and sometimes broadcast media. And there are ways of becoming productive with both which do not necessarily require permission from curriculum documents. And we are not talking about learning media through other subjects, which always reduces media education to a technical support or simple AVA role. We are talking about systematic ways of connecting the arts and STEM by means of Media Education which develops the skills of making and the language of the moving image, its grammar and lexis (cf. Burn 2009).

For some time, it seemed possible that 'Media Literacy' might be a way of suggesting rigour and a conjunction of the M word with the L word (a word with undoubted resonance) looked like a good way to represent the inherent subject discipline. It is just possible that the various other distributed versions of literacy may be able to carry some of this weight, and some of this rigour into classroom more easily. Certainly 'digital literacy', however ill-defined and lacking in shared understanding of meaning, does seem to be one way to enable productive discussion of engagements with media and essential lessons in safety.

The STEM and computing lobby made their argument very well in England at about the time the new curriculum orders were drafted and we are simply arguing here that we would do well to think about ways to enable children and teachers to go beyond STEM, to embrace the arts and learn about and with media. We suggest in this chapter that the *third space* itself may be the best space for this to happen, in the absence of formal curriculum activity.

'Third Spaces' as Locations for Negotiated Pedagogical Practices

To sum up we are arguing here that school systems which do not work in some way with the lives of their learners in the context of their lived experience cannot, arguably, be said to be fully agentive in their approach, rather they are curriculum-centred and institution-facing. As a result, they cannot build on and develop skills and dispositions which are evident in the earliest social and cultural experiences of learners outside school, which is a prerequisite of the negotiation which enables a *third space*. We should not, of course, expect school and home to operate in the same way in this regard and, certainly, earlier research shows that very young learners themselves know this, expect this and how to negotiate the differences quite successfully (Selwyn et al. 2010). However, recent research from Australia with older students (Bulfin et al. 2016) seems to suggest that schools could be more nuanced in their understanding of, and in their working with, the practices of children and young people across the boundary between home and school. There is no call in this research for urgent action to remedy the apparent disconnect, but rather, the research suggests that 'schools should be looking to complement and extend students' digital practices, rather than simply replicating and reinforcing how technologies are being used elsewhere in their lives' (Bulfin et al. 2016, p. 249). We would suggest that such a complementary and extending approach involves engaging with students in the negotiated *third space*, and recognising that pedagogical practices need not be fixed or fossilised but should somehow be brought into play by developing a new critical digital media literacy (Pangrazio 2014) and acknowledging its dynamic nature.

CHAPTER 4

Digital Curation/Digital Production: Storying the Digital Learner

In the opening chapter we addressed the issue of 'dynamic literacies'. We wrote about it as a potentially useful term to allude to the ways in which literacy in the digital age is both *synchronic*, inclusive of current situated practices, and *diachronic*, a term which opens the possibility of movement through time as an incorporated principle, taking in new texts, artefacts and practices. We suggested that dynamic literacies combined the earlier forms of textual and design-centred literacies in tandem with sociocultural forms and, latterly with new thinking on body and affect within them, through the spatial and sociomaterial literacies of writers working in education. We followed this by looking in the subsequent chapter at locations for these dynamic literacies and the production of meaning in '*third spaces*' as it related to the worlds of formal and informal education. In this chapter we would like to bring the ideas of dynamic literacies and *third spaces* together in a discussion of 'curation' which has been characterised as a new literacy practice in digital media (Potter 2012), pitched part way between a range of behaviours, skills and dispositions analogous to curating, such as cataloguing, recording, editing, exhibiting and so on.

Digital curation, as a term, and its associated skillset, digital curatorship, are both in wider and wider circulation in popular culture through social and broadcast digital media. In this explosion of use of the term and the concept, the word 'curation' itself is undergoing change from specialised definitions owned by experts in particular fields into a wider and fuzzier set of meanings owned by non-experts. In turn, at least in part, this transition

J. Potter, J. McDougall, *Digital Media, Culture and Education*,
DOI 10.1057/978-1-137-55315-7_4

in meaning has been informed by its wider use in digital culture, such that digital curation (the process) or digital curatorship (the set of skills associated with that process) are standing in as synonyms for terms such as writing, editing, and authorship when making or collecting digital content, from the blog to the social media page, from the uploaded snap to the chat and the tweet around those pictures and thoughts. Here the semantic change is evident, the tectonic plates of meaning shifting the definition away from its original source, even if not yet, that far. We will look later at how social media functions in this context.

It is worth noting that curation has also come to have a set of commercial meanings associated with food, entertainment and retail activities, so that it is no longer uncommon to see it used in, for example, music festivals (where the programming of bands who will play is curated by a musician or DJ or, as in the case below, a comedian) or in shops. The ubiquity of the term is cause for critical commentary and even some mockery and satire by some (Williams 2009). Stewart Lee, writer and comedian, has, for example, written about curation in his column for the national newspaper in the United Kingdom, the *Observer*. Invited to curate a music festival called 'All Tomorrow's Parties' in Wales in April 2016, he reflected on his role:

> 'Curating' myself into a visionary state, I saw the Prestatyn event as a pyramid-shaped sonic universe with new acts like Shopping, Trash Kit and Ex-Easter Island Head orbiting its tip, unfamiliar free jazz and folk artists floating in random gyratories, and the whole thing balanced on the back of a huge four-legged turtle, the legs representing musicians whose works are supporting pillars of postwar contemporary music; John Cale; the 13 Floor Elevators; Sun Ra Arkestra; and Giant Sand, wellspring of alt-country. A mysterious fifth vestigial leg is in the form of the proto-alternative comedian Ted Chippington, though its exact function is uncertain. This, my friends, is what 'curating' means. (Lee 2016)

Each item elaborated from the list has a reason to be there, the whole thing creaking under the weight of the pretentious use of the word, and yet the account stays true to some inner logic, even as the term is satirised. It is evident here that much more than *editing* or *choosing* is going on because each item in the list depends on its position in relation to everything else. As readers, we are also invited to interpret this account based on our knowledge of music, music festivals and Stewart Lee's column in the paper. Our shared previous experience and cultural capital comes into play as does our awareness of how Stewart Lee writes in a way that allows intertextuality to flourish; things make new meanings because they are next to each other and read in the same space. Lee operates at this meta level in everything he writes and in his performances on stage, so we should expect a curated event to be no different.

Curation Origins

The origin of the word curation lies in Latin with the word *curare*, a verb meaning to 'take care of' (Oxford 2003). Originally this meant to look after or preserve specific spaces in Rome, with the meaning changing through time, as noted below:

> In Roman times, it meant to take care of the bath houses. In medieval times, it designated the priest who cared for souls. Later, in the 18th century, it meant looking after collections of art and artefacts. (Obrist 2014)

This final definition is the one most commonly understood prior to its burgeoning usage in the digital age. So, in its most traditionally accepted meaning, curation meant the process of looking after and conserving artefacts, cultural texts and practices for present and future generations, using specific sets of skills and knowledge gained over time. This kind of process required specialist knowledge about the field in question and a means to provide access to that knowledge for the present generation and for generations to come. Exhibitions were the point at which the tacit and specific knowledge of the curator became public and open to interpretation. The role of the curator in this context means different things to different artists. For some, curators are co-designers of the whole space. In digital media, the role flips between the curation and the exhibition, the personal and the group (of which more later).

Curation, however, means much more than conservation and exhibition; it also involves creating narrative threads between artefacts, sometimes, though not always, in a temporal and linear way. An example of this would be the 2010 BBC radio series and subsequent book *A History of the World in 100 Objects* which attempted to tell the 'story' of the human race, using 100 selected artefacts from the British Museum (MacGregor 2012). In an art gallery context, it might also mean assembling a series of artworks in a particular sequence and context in order to tell a *new* story about an artistic movement or about a single artist's life and development. Curators at the Tate Modern Gallery in London a few years ago told a new story about Paul Klee by, for the first time, hanging his paintings according to the numbering he himself gave them. In this way, curation, even in its most traditional form, implies a level of storying, engagement, and informing according to new information or changing perspectives, of uncovering and revealing things previously not well understood or even deliberately covered up. Sometimes this can be politically or socially motivated as in Rozsika Parker and Griselda Pollock's *Old Mistresses* (Parker and Pollock 1995) which inspired the feminist reclaiming of women's art from more patriarchal accounts of art history. Exhibitions followed in later years in which the curators uncovered and retold stories of women artists whose work represented a much-needed feminist retelling of the story of art history.

Curation in this sense is about much more than the personal. It is about the cultural and the political. One of the criticisms levelled at this idea is this tendency towards a celebration of individual agency and of facile constructions in wider culture (Williams 2009), of which more later on. But at the political and social level it can be powerful and empowering, as in the case of the feminist art history text discussed previously. Other examples include the curated claims and counter-claims made on behalf of the various interests represented in the slavery museum in Liverpool or, in another case, the indigenous people's gallery in the Melbourne Museum, which houses a collection of cultural artefacts from indigenous tribes, a retelling in the twenty-first century of one version of the story of part of Australia, a culturally problematic and sensitive practice relating to the cultural identity of that nation.

Digital Curation

What difference, then, is suggested by the word 'digital' when applied to curation? Certainly the profusion of curation in all its many forms in new media is suggested. Digital *anything* suggests something transmissible, replicable and changed forever, by virtue of its transduction into code and bits of data. It is worth, at this stage, pointing out that for some expert archivists of modern media, *digital* curation is a process which is not too dissimilar to its analogue counterpart and quite close to the definitions outlined earlier, the expert preservation of many kinds of archives and artefacts. There is a great deal of debate over how digital media from the twentieth and twenty-first century can be preserved and whether our digital legacy will last in the same way as our printed manuscripts (see, for example, Garde-Hansen et al. 2009; Williams et al. 2009). It will depend on institutional and organisational agreements on which digital formats will be preserved and, therefore, playable on devices far into the future. Other important debates which move beyond preservation are concerned with how digital content is archived, made searchable, and how it is to be interpreted in the future as a repository of cultural memory. In this definition, digital curation has both a technical and a social dimension drawing on knowledge of how collections are managed and applying the changed arrangements and practices of digital media to them.

Using *this* definition, digital curation bears some relation to the traditional meaning of curation, but the really large shift in meaning has been away from a sole ownership of the word curation by experts, with specific sorts of scholarship and training, towards a more widespread ownership and adoption. In 2009 *The New York Times* ran a piece that suggested this explosion in other kinds of usage was away for people to announce to the world simply, 'I belong'. In this understanding of the term, the personal curation of objects, texts and artefacts is a process for making a statement about identity and belonging in a range of spheres from art to shopping to collecting (Williams 2009). Nowhere is this more evident in more recent times than in digital culture where the word curation as well as its near relatives, curate and curatorship, have taken hold in blogging, tweeting, photo/video sharing and content creation of all kinds, whether personally and individually produced or collected for group purposes.

The reflexive impulse shared by many users of social media, that they must narrate their experiences in order to story the self (Bruner 1987) or reveal and support the 'trajectory of the self' (Giddens 1991), finds its apogee in the world of social media, particularly in such sites as Facebook, Twitter, Instagram and others all over the world. These are spaces in which the audience for the curated media artefacts can be limited to family and friends but which frequently extends beyond them to other 'followers' or audiences, intentionally or unintentionally. Users of such spaces gather collections of links and media made by others, often alongside media they make themselves, and they 'share' this with the world. At the same time, they also freely share their memories and photographs as 'data' to be harvested by the corporations which lie behind those online sharing sites. Increasingly the algorithms which provide the digital data infrastructure to the corporations who own large social media spaces, are capable of arranging the artefacts for users in new ways and then suggesting them to the profile holder in a message at login. For example, Facebook gathers the photographic data from users over a number of years and sends out reminders of what the profile holder was doing on various anniversaries, suggesting that they post it. In more recent developments, Facebook offers slideshows of recent *unposted* photographs from mobile devices arranged in galleries which it suggests that the owner of the profile might like to share, including items not previously shared, reaching deep into the mobile device. In this way the social media spaces suggest ways to extend and develop the reflexivity of the space, suggesting sharing which lies outside the initial scope of the page. The use of data in this way plays into the curatorial impulse whilst the requirement to consult profile holders and end users is buried deep in the terms and conditions and ever-changing privacy settings.

But what does this collecting, displaying and sharing actually have to do with curation? The answer lies in the fact that users understand how their curated arrangements of media tell particular stories about the person, people or groups arranging them. They know this because they regularly *read* such juxtapositioning from family and friends amongst the media which is shared as consumers of it; the impulse to join in, to produce is strong. The media they put together shares references in some way with all the other things they've posted, shared and assembled. In this way skilled users of social media know how the media they display alongside each other work together to tell stories in new ways. Placing their work alongside something made by someone else changes the meaning of both texts and makes something new, as we discussed earlier in relation to Stewart Lee's notion of curation. This intertextuality shares characteristics and affordances with real world objects and texts; for example, it was on view in a 2011–2012 exhibition at the British Museum when the artist Grayson Perry was given free rein to display works from the collection alongside his own newly made work. In the programme notes, he alludes to this propensity of arranged objects to work together to produce meanings or to reinforce the self in some way:

> The British Museum holds eight million objects from every corner of the globe. Why not, I thought, make the works I am inspired to create and find objects in this vast collection that respond to them? Somewhere in its endless storerooms there must be objects that echo my concerns and styles. (Perry 2011, p. 11)

The key parallels here lie with the impulse to create and then find artefacts which echo concerns and styles. When people post images of themselves, or their affiliations they bring themselves into being in the world by curating themselves into it; the 'concerns and styles' are mirrored everywhere amongst peer groups and amongst pages which have been previously 'liked'.

Up to this point the range of tools and behaviours is very individualistic and culturally centred on Facebook. However, many of the same concerns apply to groups and organisations which are subscribers to aggregated pages of all kinds, featuring niche interest groups, everything from political affiliations through to bands and stars which are followed and pages such as 'cats on synthesisers in space' which groups together three interests into one page. In their newsfeed, users knowingly tag themselves into groups alongside their individual posts.

Although curation is sometimes reductively referred to as *editing*, as we've seen, *curating* is better described as an umbrella, meta-level activity that subsumes collecting, cataloguing, arranging and assembling for exhibition and which, to some degree, subsumes smaller editorial acts of selection within it. Individual texts within a grouping may be edited but the whole is constructed out of assembling, sorting and narrating according to predetermined criteria. And, as we have seen, the pieces of work themselves are altered into new messages and stories by the ways in which they are arranged. Put side by side, each text makes intertextual borrowings from its neighbours to make new meaning.

The other way in which curation in digital social media is different from editing is because it is usually a provisional process, not a fixed one. Changes are made to collections depending on the spaces that frame the content in question, the nature of the audience, the context of previous posts and more. Exhibitions are for years or days or only minutes long in some cases. To consider another possible criticism of this approach to curation, what does it really matter? How does this concept of (digital) curation matter beyond the audiences of the developed world? Is it simply a set of connected practices among a relatively wealthy section of the world's population essentially sharing pictures of themselves, videos of their cats and music they love, and nothing more? It matters because it goes to the heart of how meaning is made between people, between communities, using the many modes of communication in the digital age. It touches on issues of identity and community (because communities also make meaning through curation) as well as safety (because people may not always know the meaning of their curated assemblages or even that they are making them in front of hostile audiences or in unsafe spaces). It involves open, personal, and tacit knowledge about the world and our relationship to it and to each other. It matters in the same way as any of the previously discussed concepts of 'dynamic literacies' and '*third spaces*' because it is such a large part of material culture and lived experience for many people and shapes the world view of a surprising range of individuals and groups.

For those offline, not sharing, not connecting for various reasons, through poverty or by refusing in some way, there are other forms of curation, of personal stories, of personal artefacts. From anthropology and the work of Daniel Miller (2008), we learn about the ways in which our arrangements of objects and artefacts, our relationships to them, represent a way we relate to the world itself; he goes further to suggest that our relationship to our possessions and how we organise them finds a corollary in the way we relate to people. As with other social practices, the modes of digital communication make curation visible where previously it existed but was hidden or disconnected; yet it is absolutely not the only location for acts of personal curation.

Curation and Learning: Connecting to Dynamic Literacies and Third Spaces

Finally, how is this notion of curation important for learning? To an extent the answer depends very much on the perspective of the originator of the question. As for any literacy practice (and we first have to accept that it *is* a literacy practice), if we assume that the locus of control is closest to the interests, affiliations and experiences of the learner, then it is likely to be an important concept. Children and young people for whom the locus of control lies elsewhere, with the institutions of assessment for example, are not likely to see their interests or experiences represented; they will misrecognise themselves as learners, not least because those experiences of learning are not connected to their learning lives, nor are they part of the continuum which connects literacy practices to pedagogy. The consequences of this approach have been written about before. John Yandell (2014), for example, writes of an assessment experience in which school students are not merely assessed but become the number, the level itself; under such conditions, the curriculum determines many facets of the learning activity, is disconnected from wider culture and replaces it with a set of arid and mechanistic competences which, by a twist of irony are not necessarily regarded as desirable for employment in neoliberal education systems (which frequently, if emptily, cite problem solving, collaboration and other aims as desirable whilst simultaneously practising something else).

The answer to the question of the importance of curation, therefore, lies in what we consider to be of importance for *all* learning and for particular kinds of learners and is certainly worthy of further exploration and commentary. The spaces in which learners are most active and agentive may be spaces in which they are either outside school altogether or in transition between home and school, as discussed in Chapter 2. Or they may even be located in school spaces if the conditions allow for some personal agency and ownership of the activity. In *curating* their learning, it is just possible that learners would have the opportunity to put things that they make and share into new configurations alongside what they have previously achieved. Under the right conditions, this could function as a resource that they can draw on to develop new knowledge, to make new artefacts and productions. But to make such claims is to run ahead, especially in an era where it is possible for technology itself to engage with curating learning experiences, suggesting pathways through experiences based on algorithms which are determined by the software itself. If it can be done with Facebook for profile users, assisting or suggesting the curation of their photographs, then corporate control of curated learning could be an issue in the future.

The relationship of digital production to digital curation seems to be a further important factor. In youth video and authoring work we have seen in recent years, in various projects, examples of how children write, film or otherwise write themselves into being in their productions. Of how they story themselves (Bruner 1987), retelling and making the self of the moment in the production (Potter 2005, 2010), recording their learned ways of being in settings, their *habitus* (Bourdieu 1986) emerging in curated production in other words, but only under very specific pedagogical conditions, most often in '*third spaces*' as constructed metaphorically or literally. This is not simple as has been noted previously and elaborated below:

> Of course, as many have pointed out, the apparent freedom to be in control of these spaces and publishing opportunities is still shaped by corporate endeavor, albeit of a somewhat different nature to the media industries of the past;

> our utterances, pictures, and media collections are happy hunting grounds for advertisers and serve a giant, global marketplace. Notwithstanding the wider picture, at the individual level, if there is an overarching new cultural and literacy practice in the production and sharing of new media of all kinds, it is this metaphorical, meta-combination of literacies into what I' ve called a new 'curatorship of the self,' an expression of the anchored aspects of our identity and our transient affiliations and choices (Merchant 2006). These are exhibitions assembled, presented, dismantled, and reassembled for different audiences: family, friends, coworkers, employers, fellow campaigners, and so on. In each of these cases, some kind of textual design is employed, either in the components of the individual text, a video clip of some sort, or in their assembly from a range of different material and modes of production into a new whole (a page containing, e.g., favorite videos, status updates, personal productions, profile pictures, tagging on others' online spaces, etc.). In these cases, the decisions and intentions of the designers of these texts is important intertextually; that is, these texts of all kinds, markers, and modes of expression that work together to make meaning on the screen in representing the self and, at the moment they get made, the aspects of the author's own cultural capital are important. (Potter 2012, pp. 2–3)

At this point it would be useful to pause and consider examples of spaces in which curation appears to be an important construct which are drawn from recent research in the field, especially that of production in digital media. Three areas of working are offered as examples here: digital video production in a number of settings; blog postings by older students; and animations and other production by learners in a games oriented space.

Digital Video as Digital Curation

First, in a study of the digital video making practices of younger learners (Potter 2012) one salient feature was the way in which some of their already-established practices around image making were admitted into the process as markers of their cultural capital (Alanen et al. 2015) and funds of knowledge (Moll et al. 1992) which they possessed, as has been found in other studies of children making media (Parry 2013).

And yet, in their productions, they had important things to say in their pieces about formal learning that looked very much like curating their experiences; their actions became closely linked to the skill sets of curation more generally, involving such things as care for collected assets, a high degree of organisation, the opportunity to exhibit work and share it.

In the project school in the earlier study (which forms the basis of Potter 2012) the children produced 10 videos. They ranged from playful but sometimes incoherent excursions around the space of the school through to comedic, carefully edited parodies and, in one case, a quiet and reflective piece about time spent in the place and a deep friendship. All of them placed original footage alongside quotations and appropriation from favourite media, some of it on the soundtrack, some acted out for the camera. Improvisation and performance in the spaces of the school became hallmarks. Each video was a montage of modes and clips intended for reading by their classmates and families, markers of time spent in the school in different friendship groups or, in a couple of cases, as an isolated person. The idea was that they would be representing their time at primary school before leaving in whatever form they chose, over a two- to three-minute production.

Two films in the study ('Right, let's get on with the show' and 'This is where we used to sit') presented a contrasting approach to the task, one of them full of parody and comedy, the other one a tranquil and elegiac memorial to friendship on the part of the two girls. These have been written as case studies in different contexts at different times (Potter 2005, 2010) but in both cases a form of multimodal analysis was used, a derived and adapted methodology based on work which had been used to code and unlock some of the meanings inherent in the gestures and other modes in the production (Burn and Parker 2003).

Other films in the set created in this project represented a range of approaches to the task. 'Do not try this at home' was a collection of parodies, walks around the school, interviews with teachers and with children. A group of four girls, high achievers in the class, who approached the production with a clipboard, detailed notes and shooting schedules, made it. There was a degree of improvisation and play involved throughout and mildly transgressive behaviour, hurtling up and down the school hall on mats. 'Me and him are close', made by a mixed group of girls and boys was a similar collage of faces and names, including a long sequence during which each child in the leavers' classes was named alongside a spoken, off-the-cuff, biographical sketch. A favourite teacher was pursued round the school, paparazzi style looking for an interview. 'In the ball pool', made by four boys, was a chaotic journey through places in the school which featured rooms and favourite spaces which were normally out of bounds. The project gave them licence to roam with the camera into the 'ball pond', a sensory area for children with special educational needs. Once they were in there a great deal of playful anarchy ensued. 'Dance with me' made by a mixed group of boys and girls visited many of the outdoor areas of the school including an exercise trail. There was a great deal of movement of the camera, some handheld interview shots with very much younger children, recalling time spent in the spaces lower down the school. 'My walk around the school' made by one girl who started the project late, did not join a group and realised her own production was a single viewpoint representation of play in the spaces of the school and, as with 'Me and him are close' featured an extended chase of an adult around the school looking for an interview. 'On their bikes' was another solo production, also by a boy who started the project late, after the groups had formed and similar in style and feel to the one above, though less idiosyncratic. It featured clips of the 'ball pool' once again, alongside shots of children completing their cycling proficiency tests. 'The two of us' made by two of the boys was a record of friendship which had some technical difficulty over the sound in the beginning featuring the two protagonists running across the back field at the school. It went on to show a series of pratfalls and practical jokes. 'Walking in to the school' was made by four of the boys and featured the only shots which included the world outside as they approach and enter the gates and some interviews with each other which were parodies of documentary filmmaking.

In representing their identity at the moment in time in which the productions in this project were shot and edited the learners were also, in curating aspects of their lives, putting down a marker of their changing identity. This is a powerful framing of video making in school, making explicit use of the cultural capital (Bourdieu 1986) which the children were able to bring authorial structures to their practices. Active, agentive curatorship of media resources in production enabled some of these previously hidden experiences in the spaces of school around growing and changing to be represented in media remixes and reformulations. In this there is a degree of accordance with aspects of theories of identity (Goffman 1990; Giddens 1991; Merchant 2005) as well as with those of learner or student voice (Fielding 2004). The authenticity of these voices may be difficult to prove and highly contested, as perhaps in the project outlined in the previous section, but, allowing for these debates, a key aim was to find a way to analyse carefully the video productions, as well as the associated interview responses, to see if activities and artefacts close to the lived culture of the learners were permitting control and curatorship of media assets. This positioned the curatorship of media assets, self-produced (as in the actual shots in the video) or collected from other sources (the music, other images) as an active skill and disposition which bridges literacy practices and identity representation and is both evident and inherent in children's media production. To these, in more recent times we might add that these activities took place in the conjunction of bodies, spaces and literacies which were filled with the messiness of classroom life, with the material practices of living and working together in a school (Burnett and Merchant 2014; Dezuanni et al. 2015), albeit during a time set aside for negotiated, '*third space*' style activities.

Whilst, as noted above, an adapted form of multimodal analysis was used to unlock the modes in the productions (Burn and Parker 2003), there were further frameworks drawn from media literacy and socio-cultural theory (De Certeau 1984; Foucault 1984; Bourdieu 1986) which enabled a rich theoretical account to be constructed about the purposes, skills and dispositions of the learners as they represented their identity. With some of the similarities in form in evidence in the children's video productions, including parody of news and interviews, or anarchic free play interspersed with more obviously narrative forms, there were clear distinctions in terms of the successful use of expressive qualities across all of them. It was also possible to locate aspects of the NLS (see Chapter 1) across all these practices, in the children's rich and active engagement with the productions in their familiar spaces, connecting back to Chapter 2.

Some of these issues have previously been addressed specifically in relation to younger learners (Marsh 2004; Larson and Marsh 2005) in arguing for a wide and inclusive definition of, and engagement with, new literacies; which takes into account the range of practices undertaken by young people with new technologies in the home and at school, such as we have seen in these productions. Marsh (2004) also points out that the necessary inter-disciplinary engagement between these domains is still in its earliest stages, certainly where the youngest learners in the education system are concerned.

Evaluations of media production by children and associated instructional texts have sometimes focused exclusively on teaching formal aspects of narrative and editing concepts, drawn from the tradition of film language (Barrance 2004). Whilst these are vitally important elements to consider in pedagogy around the construction of meaning, it is not the only way of framing the subject for learners. In an era in which the short video form is growing rapidly, made and exchanged online, and sits alongside other media assets, readily appropriated and exchanged, we need a way of understanding children and young people's engagement with digital video as a rapidly changing social literacy practice in the experience of new media and popular culture (Tyner 1998; Marsh and Millard 2006; Gee 2004; Jenkins et al. 2006). In the view of Sefton-Green (2005) and Buckingham (2003) we further need to align this with a socialised view of creativity which is much more closely connected with group work, situated peer-review and an awareness of group roles in cultural production than with individual auteurs and the realisation of a personal expressive goal. Once again, this is a way of responding within a theory of digital curation to accusations that the focus is too much on the individual; it places curation and associated processes within the realm of the social.

It is possible that, instead, building on viewing and evaluation in the very public spaces of YouTube would allow an eliding of the process of media production with the end- product more closely. Such spaces have altered substantially the nature of the process of composition and consumption of media texts and are becoming a form in themselves, based more on cultural resonance and exchange (Burgess and Green 2009), even as they are not unproblematic or unmediated in themselves. Many of the videos in the project depended on the organisation of particular patterned communication which, in turn, reflected the children's lived social experiences up to that point; how they had found their voice and exhibited the general, performed self in the spaces of the school. To an extent this is how the children organised their short videos, intending them to be vignettes and records of their lives up to the point of boundary crossing between schools. Recording these ways of being involved a process of assembly of the resources needed to represent both the anchored and the transient forms of identity (Merchant 2006).

In this project, the autobiographical video explorations, one replicable piece of pedagogy is also the basis for research itself, namely, the finding of rich sources of data through self-representational work with younger learners in the setting which, by its nature, crosses the boundary between home and school. This finds a corollary in print literacy where thematic work around the self is often the earliest writing experience in schools but it moves this experience into an expressive mode in media with which the children are already familiar. The project pointed to a powerful and as yet largely untapped resource for moving forward with research and pedagogy at the interface between young children and their learning in the digital age. This resource is the literacy and cultural practices of the children themselves as they navigate both the boundary between home and school and the boundary between childhood, adolescence and beyond, into a world in which their curated selves will be ever present, however problematically in social media.

Pedagogy Meets Curatorial Practices

What happens when explicit modes of teaching and learning meet some of these sociocultural processes? In other words, where there is no ideal '*third space*' and the intention of the production is much more clearly engineered by research agendas or by other kinds of curricular demands, and stated as such. In other studies, where this has been the case, the curatorial impulse in the project is still strong and groups form identities around productions, with the work developing over time into something which exhibits many of the same characteristics as the '*third spaces*' described in the previous chapter. Whilst at play in those spaces something happens to the arc of completion of the project which drives the whole project back to markers of identity.

Doerr-Stevens (2015) has written about digital video production work from a small, public, New York City high school. In this case study, filmmaking was explored as an opportunity for youth engaged in the work to make visible a range of local and global affiliations, creating a sense of belonging and deeper knowing in increasingly diverse learning contexts. By using mediated discourse analysis (Norris 2004) the author explored digital production as a process of assemblage and rearrangement of different semiotic resources such as sound, image, transitions and special effects to become the objects, which are composed into scenes. These processes were discussed explicitly as acts of curatorship since these completed media texts became cultural artefacts in themselves, communicating affiliation and social position and recalling and counterpointing other work in the field on digital media and learner identity (Merchant 2005; Potter 2012). Similar issues were at stake in Dejaynes analysis of media makers in a year-long study following students in an English class in a high school in the Midwestern region of the USA. She focused on the social and multimodal 'struggle' within digital media composition as conducted in two classrooms in this ethnically diverse urban high school with over 2000 students and she invoked theories of 'cosmopolitanism' in the discussion of its relationship to curation (Dejaynes 2015).

There are further comments to be made about two studies from our own work which illustrate the curational/curatorial impulse further.

Firstly, in the study of children engaged in making computer games from stories reported on in Chapter 2, the connection to personal curated archives of procedures they had constructed, tagged and shared online outside the workshop was an important marker of success. The activity took place in the real physical space of the after-school club as well as in the virtual materials and galleries swapped between users. Learning was skilfully managed by the teachers and computer scientists running the workshop in real time, but personal agency was further enhanced by the children accessing their virtual, curated work online and articulated in the comments they made. They swapped and tagged games in the virtual, after-school spaces. Roles which were taken on in the group in the physical space of the club, expert, non-expert, computer operator, programmer, designer, storyteller, were elaborated in the curated performance of the site. The comments between people were affirmative of difference and, generally, when things were going well, appreciative of differing roles and responsibilities. Cultural touchstones from the world of games were brought into play alongside experiences from school, as frustrating as some of those had been over time in relation to game making. These curated remarks in person are backed by at least some of the experiences of online interaction on the website of Scratch, the programming language used (MIT 2016). It has some of the tropes of video sharing sites but without some of the below the line hostility and anger of the more massively popular spaces (such as YouTube). Nevertheless, curation is, here, an element of the success of the whole venture which, under the guidance of the developers, took the whole constructivist approach of learning to programme (Papert 1993) into a social – constructivist and curatorial space.

Secondly, in the study of very young children making stop-frame animations over the period of a year in distributed rural settings which was discussed in Chapter 1 (Bazalgette et al. 2011), the curation of online galleries enabled a shared bank of knowledge about the processes, trials and tribulations of stop-frame animation to be one of the main vehicles for learning in the project. The resource was both created and curated at school level and fuelled further development of the skills needed to make animated films. Children would comment on each other's animated films through the gallery spaces on http://Vimeo.com, and displays of cultural capital and funds of knowledge were both evident in the expressions of critical exchange in the curated online spaces ('How did you do that? And so on). Of course, the researchers were keen to provide caveats to any simple claims to success in the venture:

> Excitement about the uses of new social media technologies to support creative approaches to learning has burgeoned in recent years (Ito et al. 2009; Jenkins et al. 2006). Some critics have seen in these approaches a tendency to exaggerate the potential of the medium…(Buckingham 2007). Despite accepting those caveats, it was nevertheless possible also to see in the Vimeo channel some nascent characteristics of the "affinity spaces" described by Gee (2004), particularly in the idea that knowledge and practice become "tacit" when people are engaged in "guided participation" in their uses of the space. (Bazalgette et al. 2011, p. 4)

If learners have the opportunity to gather and share work in such spaces, to curate the record of their own achievements and experiences across settings, there is, of course, huge *potential* for developing and then promoting an active and engaged disposition towards learning. However, this is not a simple undertaking; it requires skilful and sensitive pedagogical implementation and an awareness of how curation itself plays out in wider culture. All curating decisions are contextual and contingent, fixed by circumstances that are sometimes well beyond the user's control. Building a portfolio, for example, is an act of curation which is common in arts education and beyond and which, in form and function, should always be negotiated between learners and teachers; this does not always happen (Yancey 2004). The success or otherwise of curated life, and the curated educational life, is founded on the ability to preserve, to narrate and to see connections between ourselves and the world. This requires some serious thinking about two concepts that make curation different. Firstly, that it is a reflexive literacy practice and a consequence of the widespread use of digital and social media, which is both materially present in culture and, of course, distributed unequally (so, whose curated experiences really 'count' in the world?). This has unresolved consequences for how we see this notion developing in future. Secondly, curation is a form of meta-authorship, implying the ability to stand apart from the single piece of work and to see the whole pattern of collection and distribution of a number of texts, artefacts, and practices, of assembling and sharing as part of identity formation throughout life. Again, this depends almost entirely on socially mitigating factors, access and support, equity and social justice. These conditions are not evenly spread throughout the world; in those areas where some of this activity is available more widely through informal spaces it could have a part to play in promoting equity and social justice.

It also depends on a pedagogical vision which is wide enough to sustain the notion of agency in educational settings. In the study of blogging mentioned in connection with the opening arguments around literacy (Barrs and Horrocks 2014), children were involved in creating writing which was framed within curatorial online contexts. The influence which this kind of writing had upon their work was to generate positive outcomes for the report which saw children's work improving across the board. However, the negotiation with formal codes of writing was not always positive and some negotiation with outside culture was essential to the outcomes for developing voice and curatorial aspects of the experience, as the following extract illustrates:

A teacher of younger pupils also felt that they did not do their best writing on the blog:

> Their work on the blog is more informal, chatty and with extra emoticons which they would never use in their books! The punctuation and sentence structure is much poorer on the blog than in the book.

But she also felt that the big difference that the blog had made was to pupils' confidence:

> I think the main improvement is their attitude to writing; they have all become so much more confident with both writing in their books and on the blog. They are less cautious about typing and publishing their work on the blog and are really starting to find their voice. In their books I think their non-fiction writing (which we have done a lot of this year) has improved, becoming more detailed, explanatory and technical. They are a knowledgeable bunch and so are very keen to tell everyone what they know! They are enjoying doing this on the blog. (Barrs and Horrocks 2014, p. 48)

Clearly these unresolved issues require focus and research in the future which builds on the growing and accumulated evidence around the tensions between experience curated more widely and that which exists in some form within the formal education system (of which more in later chapters).

Social Media Curation: The Case of an MA Module

For older learners in Higher Education, the subject of a study into acts of curation in a module on blogging (Potter and Banaji 2012), issues were similarly framed within the context of wider cultural impression management versus curriculum-based theoretical content. The background to the study of a module in which:

> All students were expected to create and maintain a blog during the course, thus becoming the agents in the study and also the self-reflexive objects of the study. Students were asked to keep the blog at least during the 10 weeks of the module, with the aim, not of studying blogging as a form, so much as using the blog as a vehicle with which to engage with the wider aspects of online social media, pedagogy and identity formation. At the end of that time, they were expected in written work to reflect on the process in the light of their experience, their posts and their exchanges with fellow students, tutors and comments from the wider Internet. They were also expected to write in the light of theoretical readings which were provided for them and/or which they located themselves. (Potter and Banaji 2012, p. 85)

This reflexivity played into the notion of curation as an active new literacy process but also invited investigation into the formal structures around the course and the relationship of the students to them. In short this became as much about identity construction as a literacy practice, echoing some of the issues raised around social media in the opening of this chapter, but overlaid with pedagogical purpose, a not entirely simple construct. It is conceivable that as learners take part in more and more online activity in the day-to-day activities of their degrees they become sensitised to these issues, how to manage identity which is fluid, hybrid and multipurpose in wider digital culture whilst simultaneously interacting and learning with others in a more constrained, assessment-driven and performative construct (which is also online, open in another tab on their screen!). In time, of course, the notion of being inside and outside of the course content but always traceable and managing online presences will be recognised as a skill, a curatorial one perhaps. Here, the theory of the self and curation begins to come up against other theories of networked learning, pulling it perhaps into new configurations (Wenger 1998; Lave and Wenger 2005). Certainly this is a theme to which we shall return in later chapters. For now, it is enough to note that there were problems with the module, and indeed with the research on the module, which were not easily resolved but which do point the way towards future research in the field:

> The notion that requiring a blog as part of an academic assessment might be less challenging than writing a traditional academic essay turned out to be quite misplaced in that most of our students were more comfortable and experienced in traditional academic formats than they were in the reflection-made-public mode required by the blog format. It requires further study to make sense of how learner and teacher identity plays out in an era in which self-curatorship is a key skill and disposition in new media. For some, certainly not all, young people, this fluid and multifaceted representational world is something they recognise as a cultural practice and as a literacy practice that they are engaging with inside and outside the classroom. It is likely that future pedagogy will need to build on the skills and dispositions of intergenerational groups in social media not least to connect with the need to develop criticality in performative space. (Banaji 2011; Potter and Banaji 2012, p. 90)

The article concludes with a call for future research to locate investigative practices with curation in the wider, productive culture within which such work resides, of which more below.

Curation and a Future Direction for Research

In some ways, then, the very definition of curation as a new literacy practice recognises that we all, adults, young people and children who have access and privilege in the developed world, are living in a space in which the media we collect and make can be organised, displayed, and re-presented time and again in ways that were not possible before. In this sense, curation is a new form of cultural production that is pitched partway between making and sharing, creating temporary collections for specific purposes, and then dismantling them again. Should we not recognise this and the skills, knowledge and dispositions which go with it as a practice and build on them informal settings for education? The answer is a qualified positive one, because curation is not simple, straightforward and celebratory as a concept. It is linked to the earlier discussions of literacy and spaces in the book where the pedagogical space itself is in a state of flux (of which more later). It is also linked to questions of power, access, equity and social justice.

It is apparent, anyway, that we need much more research in the field which demonstrates the added value of negotiated spaces of media production in pedagogy as well as acknowledging those things which do not always work. Celebratory reporting has its place but research which takes full account of the setting and tries to locate, hear and contextualise the voices of teachers and learners will be of more lasting value. Researchers can and should be partners with teachers and learners investigating productive agency with media at home, at school and in the spaces between in the era of self-curation not least because it is not a simple or celebratory construct arising out of the uses of social media or making digital video, audio, games or anything else in wider, curated culture.

CHAPTER 5

Porous Expertise and Powerful Knowledge

Is it possible to break away from the circle of powerlessness that ties the student to the explicator?

(Biesta 2012, p. 33)

He'd be in class imagining the stories he'd write when he'd get home . . .
and when the bell goes at last for the end of the day,
he's still in his own world a couple dimensions away.

(Kate Tempest 2013, p. 14)

In the twenty-first century, it is *argued* that education operates in a 'mixed economy' of schooled and informal learning (including digital). Traditional modes of delivery and standardised units of learning are threatened by MOOCS, peer networks, new 'providers' in the education 'market' and digital divides.

We repeat our consistent disclaimer here, as at the start of every chapter – for many people, this is not their experience of education. Their being outside of these developments are in some cases by virtue of being offline, for reasons of geography or economics, for others, the opportunities for blended learning are restricted in a conservative epistemology, transmitted in traditional classroom settings in schools with a strong resistance to integrating digitally enabled learning from the 'first space'.

However, for those who *are* experiencing a fusion of learning contexts, in this state of ongoing transition, whose knowledge counts?

J. Potter, J. McDougall, *Digital Media, Culture and Education*,
DOI 10.1057/978-1-137-55315-7_5

How are boundaries of expertise negotiated formally and informally across and between various knowledge domains?

In this chapter we think through what (discursively) frames these epistemological sites of struggle. We will argue that the potential for digitally mediated cultural practices to enable a more 'porous' exchange of expertise between teacher and student is 'kept in check' by the ongoing operation of power in the form of education's role in sustaining inequality. We return to Stuart Hall and the legacy of cultural studies to provide a conceptual framework for an investigation of how digital media learning is situated as a site of struggle – a 'new popular culture'. We put the CCCS approach in dialogue with the figure of the 'ignorant schoolmaster' from Ranciere (1991), a recurrent motif in accounts of 'emancipatory' pedagogy whereby knowledge is no longer a matter of knowing or not. This framework will then be applied a contemporary 'case' where we can assess how expertise is negotiated in digital *third spaces.*

> One reason why we are so interested in the take up of new technologies in classrooms is that the use of the digital, of devices, screens and connectivity, so often seems to disrupt dominant ways of doing things, and for us as researchers this disruption helps us to make strange the whole business of teaching and learning. (Merchant et al. p. 290)

In one of Zizek's many analogous stories (2013), an authoritarian father bluntly informs his child that they will be visiting grandmother at the weekend. No discussion is required, no rationale for the visit. The postmodern, liberal father, by contrast, attempts to elicit agreement that the visit is kind and that the child has a moral duty to visit the elderly relative. The point of this narrative is that the outcome is identical, the trip will happen and in most cases the child will be a reluctant visitor. However, the traditional parent is more honest, whilst his liberal counterpart is the more disingenuous through the coercion into a moral framework which is imposed on the terms of the adult. Zizek's point extends to the workings of liberal democracy with its problematic attempts to impose values regardless of material conditions. Specifically, in relation to education about textual practice, we can say that progressive teachers have been guilty of the conceit of the postmodern father, whilst government ministers and 'old school' teachers of the canon with their imposed enrichment discourse, are more open and honest about the function of textual learning, to accept that one culture – as manifested in texts and traditional literacy practices is superior to others, to what we are calling here the 'new popular culture'. These are the classic workings of cultural reproduction (Bourdieu and Passeron 1990). The point is that attempts to work in *third spaces* across the 'semi-permeable membrane' between students' mediated cultures and the culture of the classroom will be equally 'dishonest' in this way unless the epistemological frames of reference for 'what counts' as knowledge are genuinely co-constructed and this respect for variance among students' forms of textual curation is sustainable. This is virtually impossible when set against assessment regimes in formal education in the United Kingdom, but equally at odds with the competence framework for media literacy generally adopted across EU and American projects (see Frau-Meigs et al. 2016 and Mihailidis 2015).

Media (literacy) education has wrestled with this enduring ethical dilemma for many years, captured – and now a recurring motif – in Judith Williamson's comparison (1981) of her struggles with teaching her student Astrid about gender representation to Sissy Jupe's silence as 'Girl 20' in Dickens' *Hard Times*. As we attempt to provide transformative experiences for students to reflect on the negotiation of identity in their mediated lifeworlds, do we risk alienating them through an undermining of their own media cultures? As Turnbull asks, 'is it empowering to reject one's family and values?' (1998, p. 100). The same applies to the risk of discrediting the textual lives of our students as we try to engage with new media literacy practices. This precarious operation has been at the intersection of debates about literacy and digital media in this century. Staying with formal education for a moment, in this case the study of media as an examined curriculum subject in England, from where we write, at this time curricular reforms present clear and present 'challenges' (to understate the case) for the kinds of 'curational' work we account for in this book. At a broader level, the potential for immersive, virtual and networked digital media engagement to be embraced as an affordance for the 'Long Revolution' has most certainly not been harnessed. In reappraising his own project in the wake of new digital media at the turn of the century, Raymond Williams observed, hopefully:

> What is now happening, in the existing institutions, is a steady pressure from the late capitalist economy and its governments to reduce education both absolutely and in kind, steading excluding learning which offers more than a preparation for employment and an already regulated life . . . but use of the new technologies can add diversity and permanent availability to the most comprehensive institutions, above all in making them outward-looking taking their best knowledge and skills to a wider and more active society. (2015, pp. 110–111)

Third Space Shape-Shifting

Returning to Zizek's postmodern father, Ranciere and Freire have also been concerned with the arrogance and ultimately self-defeating strategies of the liberal 'emancipators' in progressive education. Freire speaks to a letter from Sao Paulo workers, sceptical about the worthy intentions of 'the ones that come looking for us to teach us that we're oppressed and exploited and to tell us what to do' (2004, p. 63). For Ranciere, the pedagogic relation itself is that which, in Foucauldian terms, exercises power in the unequal expression of expertise. Recent commentators (see Davis 2016) view student 'participation' – to which we turn later in this chapter's 'case' for analysis – as a neoliberal simulacrum and thus all the more a domination. Ridley (2016) observes the rush to the 'flipped classroom' in this way, replicating Ranciere's 'division of the sensible' in its reproduction of the explicative order – the authority of the pedagogue and the epistemological hierarchy is maintained, just 'from home'.

So, with our eyes on these axiomal politics and the division of knowing and not knowing being the target for disruption, we approach the *third space* with caution.

Bhabha (1994) describes the *third space* as an area:

> for elaborating strategies of selfhood, that initiate new signs of identity, and innovative sites of collaboration, and contestation, in the act of defining the idea of society itself. (pp. 1–2, cited in Benson 2010, p. 555)

Moje et al. (2004) extended this to classrooms, suggesting that the construction of *third spaces* involves the merger of aspects of the 'first' space of students' everyday lived experience with the 'second' space of the academic discourses students encounter in school (p.41). The various theoretical contributions to the notion of the *third space* seem to agree that the power of hybrid literacy practices in such fluid environments resides in harnessing the broader range of literacy resources and situated experiences available to students. Using a '*third space* gaze' (our wording), Benson (2010) urges us to consider the potential consequences of viewing student resistance or disinterest as an effort by the student to reclaim expertise (2010, p. 561). She states that the creation of a *third space* can

> shift the balance of power in the classroom, positioning students and teachers as co-learners and co-teachers. Such a dynamic has the potential to

> reduce student resistance because teachers and students mutually determine what knowledge and products are appropriate to meet both parties' learning goals. (Benson 2010, p. 562)

Third space theory draws upon NLS, taking a view of literacies as multiple, emergent and situated (Ivanič et al. 2007, p. 705 and Street 2012, p. 27). Like NLS, *third space* research recognises multiple literacies that vary with time, space and power relations. *Third space* accounts seek to make visible the overlapping, interwoven and hybrid nature of social learning and literacy. Fundamentally, *third spaces* are hybrid spaces where diversity is celebrated (Gutierrez, Baquedano-Lopez and Tejada 1999, p. 287).

The relationship between what Gutierrez describes as the 'counter-script' – a meaning-making space not integrated into official educational space (the First space) – and its facilitation of different kinds of engagement of enquiry in a *third space*, or how the former becomes the latter, is arguably more tangible in and around the combination of digital media practices and physical learning and teaching. Fundamentally, however, the socio-critical question posed by this is more epistemological – to do with what counts as culture and, within that, knowledge. Culture, understood in this way, is a practice – lived experience, as opposed to a static category, such as class or ethnicity. In education, rich variations and interesting complexities are generally skirted over in favour of generalising solutions, of course. (Digital) media literacy is far from exempt, as a functionalist competence model has been privileged in both European and US communities over the evidence yielded from the field of literacy research. Key also to the idea of the *third space* is the shift in how learning arises, more often from invitations to 'do' learning – imaginative, hypothetical, enquiry and scenario-based learning, organically generated in many cases. The political project, of which we are mindful, is to 'saturate' *third spaces* with rich 'local' literacy work for non-dominant students, both building on, and designed to foster, specific capabilities of such cohorts, turning capabilities into powerful literacies in this way.

For (digital) media educators, the '*third space*' is generally defined as the area between official curriculum and informal knowledge, with skills and dispositions brought in from outside culture. Sometimes this is a literal *third space*, the actual halfway house of an after-school media education or digital literacy project, a museum, gallery, youth club or media production/coding space, but in other cases this is co-located in school/college/University as a metaphorical space, negotiated through dialogue and pedagogical strategies designed to mediate expertise and challenge dominant roles and representations of knowledge. Where does powerful epistemology converge with lifeworld skills and dispositions, made tangible in the digital mediascape? As a primary objective of twenty-first century literacy education/entitlement, where can we thus far observe facilitation of such informed curational practices in the digital lifeworld? Even when we manage 'thick description' of media practices, into this rich (but awkward) mix comes the power dynamics of teacher-student, researcher-participant, which make genuine, empirically measurable engagement in the lifeworld even harder to reach:

> Young people are actively required to exercise their responsibility as citizens, yet for many the traditional markers of citizenship have been ever more difficult to achieve, and in this context, participation may not be a meaningful practice – and may even prove to be an oppressive imposition. (Buckingham et al. 2014, p. 280)

(Digital) Capabilities?

> Technology in itself is neither 'good' nor 'bad' for education. It can be both, but its value depends upon how and why it is used. And yes, it can have a significant positive impact if it is combined with broader changes in pedagogy. Yet the central issues here are not technological ones – or indeed to do with 'discipline' – but to do with learning. (Buckingham 2015b, p. http://davidbuckingham.net/2015/09/25/digital-distractions-whats-wrong-with-the-debate-about-technology-in-education/)

Techknowledge, previously 'Tablets for Schools' are an interesting 'case'. On the one hand they offer a range of examples of classroom practice to refute the 'tune out' rhetoric in the public sphere. But on the other hand, intentionally or not, their campaigning objectives might be seen as part of the problem of technological determinism. Among the '10 Golden Rules' they put forward as a result of the accumulation of their research findings in recent years are: *develop a clear strategy for roll out, appoint members of staff to act as 'champions' including leadership, IT and those experienced in using mobile devices* and *introduce professional development within the school to include pedagogy and tech use.* Samsung's Digital Classroom initiatives, in a similar field but part of their broader corporate citizenship work, employ a different methodology, drawing together Bloom's Taxonomy, OFSTED criteria and a broad model of 'Digital Literacy', similar to the cross-European criteria we have elsewhere challenged as being 'tangled' (McDougall et al. 2015). The published key findings relate to collaborative working (between teachers and students); more frequent presentation of ideas; independent learning with tablets fostering 'higher level skills' and some limited evidence of increased performance in STEM subjects (Science, Technology, Engineering and Maths) by those involved in the interventions, along with benefits to students with SEN (special educational needs). To illustrate the tensions at work here, Techknowledge have disseminated a case study on the work of TreeHouse School in supporting students with complex autism through the use of tablets. While this is more typical of 'witness testimony' than empirical research, a helpful distinction between the device as 'determinant' and a richer blend of pedagogic approach and co-design of learning, as appears to be evident in the work of Indira Ramraj:

> This project truly brought out learners' personalities, strengths, creativity and imagination. For some of our learners at TreeHouse School communication, emotion and imagination are barriers but in this project they shone in pushing those barriers to express themselves and create their own stories, visions and themes for their films. (http://techknowledge.org.uk/blog/sen-how-technology-can-prepare-students-for-the-real-world/)

A 'meta review' of classroom research by Family, Kids and Youth (Clarke et al. 2013) presented some 'success stories', including the importance of 1–1 access (to technology), the ability to personalise the learning experience, learner autonomy and metacognitive development:

> The portable nature of tablets and the ability to be connected at all times is argued to facilitate seamless learning. Pedagogical benefits identified across academic research include increased or improved communication and collaboration, increased independence, engagement and motivation among pupils, and the ability to customise learning and benefits for children with special educational needs. (2013, p. 16)

These are the kinds of 'functionings' that are increasingly being identified in education; for example, includes a range of cross-curricular pedagogic activities that are facilitated by tablets, such as creative practice, research, reflective practice, collaboration and programming. However,

Selwyn (2014) suggests that the opportunities presented by mobile technologies for learning are just as much socially structured as they are individually driven, meaning that:

> the likelihood of gaining advantage from digital education is clearly related to the resources that social groups command, therefore pointing towards the role of digital technology in the perpetuation of accumulated advantage and the reproduction of inequalities. (2014, p. 138)

Digital technologies therefore have, at the very least, the *potential* to amplify social inequality, so when grand claims for autonomy, voice and participation/co-design are made by both practitioners and policymakers, with mobile video making in particular constructed as a democratic and empowering 'articulation technology' (Haw and Hadfield 2011, p. 113), it is important to be reminded that:

> The current emphasis on youth voice and visibility is occurring at a time when young people have few opportunities for unmediated, unscrutinised expressions of culture, recreation, critique and social commentary. It also coincides with the disappearance of a genuine public sphere in which participation typically takes place. (Harris 2004, p. 149)

Crucially, all this research into the value of tablets in schools, specifically, indicates the importance of a shared pedagogic rationale for the work, but Kendall (2015) places emphasis on parental engagement, again with layers of complexity when viewed through a social literacies lens. In particular, this contribution shared one sobering observation – of a lack of transgression of degrees of the various forms of 'capital' (social, cultural, academic and digital). In other words, very often the students who thrive in '*third spaces*' are those that are successful in school already, the parents that engage with schools through social media interventions engage in traditional modes as well and successful 'community hub' initiatives are often in areas with relatively low barriers to participation, either virtual or 'real world':

> Whilst our analysis encourages us to remain enthusiastic about the potential of social media to support vibrant school/community relations we caution against 'quick fix' approaches that treat 'e-interaction' as socially and culturally neutral. Understanding an externally-facing social media strategy instead as 'digital literacy' work deeply embedded in complex socio-cultural

> relations might, we argue, yield a much richer, more dynamic level of parental and community engagement. (Kendall 2015, p. 26)

On the ongoing digital divide – ongoing simply because in a capitalist society, all divides are sustained and the rhetoric and policy surrounding 'ed-tech' has little to say about redistribution of resources – in the USA the *Opportunity for All? Technology and Learning in Lower Income Families* report (Rideout and Katz 2016) provided the following headline findings: whilst many low income families are now online, their connection speeds are basic and do not support multiple devices (this was the case with several of the families in our sample); under-connection is a major impediment to using the Internet for learning (our intervention can only address this through the provision of devices but connection standards at home were beyond our remit); and – most striking for our project – reducing Internet access to mobile devices places students at a disadvantage (this cuts against the grain of much of the 1–1 pro-tablet work). In addition, distinctions need to be made between the different '*third spaces*' in which parents feel comfortable:

> Lower-income parents were also unlikely to take advantage of community resources such as libraries in order to get connected: Just 29 percent of those without home computer access said they used computers at public libraries 'sometimes' or 'often.' Mobile-only parents were more likely to make regular use of free Wi-Fi at places such as coffee shops and restaurants. (http://blogs.edweek.org/edweek/DigitalEducation/2016/02/mobile_internet_access_low_income_parents_survey.html)

An alternative to the instrumental (deficit) model often at work in digital literacy, when research situates digital media practices in and across particular communities or contexts, richer, more nuanced insights can be drawn for the purpose of 'digital inclusivity'. Amartya Sen's (2008) concept of capability reacts against models by which the well-being of groups of people is assessed upon reductionist metrics which tend to focus on material comforts and financial security. In contrast, capability emphasises human diversity, the nature of being and the possibilities of flourishing. For Sen, (2008), the capability approach is based on a view of living as a combination of various 'doings and beings':

> The capability approach to a person's advantage is concerned with evaluating it in terms of his or her actual ability to achieve various valuable

> functionings as a part of living... Some functionings are very elementary, such as being adequately nourished, being in good health, etc., and these may be strongly valued by all, for obvious reasons. Others may be more complex, but still widely valued, such as achieving self-respect or being socially integrated. Individuals may, however, differ a good deal from each other in the weights they attach to these different functionings – valuable though they may all be – and the assessment of individual and social advantages must be alive to these variations. (2008, pp. 271–272)

The implications for (digital media) literacy are clear: networked devices, for example, are not a 'capability' in themselves, but a resource, and therefore any educational project will attempt to facilitate changes in 'functionings', beyond merely enumerating the 'new' possibilities that tablets may create, but rather to assess how valuable those possibilities are to the participants – on their terms. The developmental motive underlying this hinges on a desire to construct human lives in terms of possibilities rather than deficits, again a key shift in thinking from the majority of 'digital literacy' policy. Resisting both technological determinism *and* the ease of equating new digital practices straightforwardly with autonomous models, through, specific, situated research, a capability approach might potentially examine the ways in which students move between the worlds of home and school and how the construction of the *third space* relates to 'the real effective freedoms people have and their choice among possible bundles of functionings' (Terzi 2005, p. 450). Digital capability might be a fruitful way to take forward the socio-critical questioning of *third space* theory, providing a sensitivity to the diversity of the participants with a social justice ethos and a relational framework for understanding how individuals apply particular freedoms of choice from various capabilities.

Third Space Capability?

The two central questions we return to in each chapter are restated:

- What happens to people doing education in a (digital) *third space*?
- How do engagements in the (digital) *third space* influence practices back in the second space?

Along with these questions, a key motif in this book is the figure of the 'shape-shifting' educator, working to renegotiate spaces and relations in the hybrid contexts for learning which are partly facilitated, but never determined, by digital media. But in this chapter we are most keenly concerned with the status of knowledge and expertise in such hybridity. As Taylor et al. (2014) observe in their study of *third space* teacher education, a profoundly non-hierarchical approach to expertise is necessary to foster genuinely collaborative agency and 'blended relationships' (2014, p. 17) The latter is very important here as we will argue that the best practice in blended learning is more about those relationship shifts than the fusion of on and offline /physical and virtual engagements. Whilst this is something of a 'chicken and egg', digital outcomes whereby the power of knowledge-making is redistributed are the most fruitful. For Taylor et al., this is 'reciprocal authority', for our interests this is closely aligned with the notion of the 'post-expert'. When applied specifically to (media) literacy education, the convergence of the adolescent (first) space with the classroom is often at stake in the construction of the *third space*, grounded in principles of efficacy so that students can safely bring funds of knowledge into play with long-standing literacy practices of reflexive and *reciprocal* value, so that 'Teachers can challenge students to move this adolescent space to a *third space* that combines both their personal and academic spaces' (Dredger et al. 2010, p. 95). However, taking for granted the desire to construct *third spaces* with political desires for a public redistribution of expertise and knowledge making power is a dangerous leap of faith.

Teaching the Digital Neoliberal

Paul Mason (2015) predicts 'post-capitalist' economics, a logical episode in long wave economic theory (upturn and downturn cycles) and cites digital technology as a driver. Three elements are foregrounded – the blurring of labour with free time; the abundance of online information and the proliferation of collaborative, peer production in digital spaces. We can easily map these against specifically educational shifts – the blurring of formal education with free time (the MOOC, blended learning, enquiry-based informal learning); the endemic use of the Internet for all study in the affluent parts of the connected world and the reconstituted status of teaching from the front/the lecture/the textbook in this context; the rise of student to student exchanges in the kinds of *third spaces* that are constructed by academics and researchers and, more commonly, those developed by students. All of these are, of course, entirely against the grain of the curricular reforms at work in epistemological conservatism that pervades in the context in which we work. At the same time, the classic neoliberal 'rolling back' of state is progressed through the deregulation of school governance and administration. For these reasons, the affordances of digital media for *third spaces* defined by 'post-expertise' are fraught with contradictions. Fuchs observes such, in a critique of Mason's thesis:

> The digital law of value has created new forms of exploitation as well as contradictions that allow the creation of new spheres of non-commercial, alternative, co-operative production and a solidarity, commons-based and peer production economy outside the realm of capitalism that undermine the law of value. But the aim and tendency of destroying the law of value is not an automatism that follow from information technology. It can rather only be achieved in conscious political struggles for the decommodification of information, the economy and the world. (Fuchs 2016, p. 237)

Likewise, or rather a part of this, our 'after the expert' undermining of the law of knowledge authority in educational *third spaces* is no more an automatism arising from the mere 'affordance' of digital learning contexts. Instead, this new manifestation of popular culture is a site of political struggle for the decommodification of knowledge.

The New Popular Culture?

This is an epistemological starting point for an implementation of the '*third space*' notion of the extended classroom – to the social practices of learning in digital contexts as in themselves a 'new popular culture'. Related to this way of thinking about the intersections between media education and new (digital) literacies, we are mindful of the status of popular culture, for Williams, as not only the 'stuff' of texts but the continuing energy of people:

> in the generality of their impulses and in their intransigent attachments to human diversity and recreation, they survive, under any pressures and through whatever forms, while life itself survives, and while so many people – real if not always connected majorities – keep living and working to live beyond the routines that attempt to control and reduce them. (2015, p. 106)

So if digital media is a 'new popular culture', then (digital media) literacy education doesn't only teach about and with popular culture, rather this educational (third) space *is* popular culture. Teachers, then, are transformative intellectuals, in Giroux's terms, 'making the pedagogical more political and the political more pedagogical' (1988, p. 127).

In returning to the legacy of Stuart Hall and the Birmingham Centre for Contemporary Cultural Studies, John Clarke (Cannon and McDougall 2014), reflecting on the extraordinary 'disproportionate effects' of the Centre's impact across disciplines, identified two conditions for this possibility. First, students and teachers co-produced material as the orthodoxy (as the CCCS50 archive itself now curates), not an exception to celebrate. Second, the Centre always worked across and against disciplines, or, in Clarke's words 'they let us mess about' (2014). In the digital realm today, it is worth asking: Have we, despite ourselves, constructed some unhelpful new disciplines – media education, media literacy, digital literacy, along with maintaining the boundary between media and people and between school and home, or education and lifeworld? Working across and between spaces and classifications, with students as ethnographic partners, across and between formal education and the digital 'out there' – doing teacher-research in messy *third spaces* where things aren't *either* digital or *not*, media or something else, *this* literacy or *that* literacy, civic action versus reified consumption.

> We wanted to explore the 'common sense' that provided a basis for moral and social as well as literary and visual judgements.... We were attempting to make up, on almost a week to week basis, something that today has become widely known as 'cultural studies. (Hall, S 2014, p. 3, foreword to CCCS: 50 Years On. Birmingham: UoB /Midland Arts Centre)

Fifty years ago, Richard Hoggart established the Centre in Birmingham as a space for the serious study of 'mass culture', as weaved into the fabric of everyday life by Raymond Williams in *The Long Revolution.* (1961, 2015) In the aftermath of the recent passing of both Hoggart and Stuart Hall, culture has never been more visibly a 'site of struggle' in education as it is today. Progressive teachers of texts/culture, products of the CCCS legacy, would now seem, perhaps more than ever, to lack a space for interdisciplinary thinking and subsequent pedagogic work, about the ever-increasing textualised essence of everyday life, just when, in the 'always connected' social media zeitgeist, they need it the most, we would argue. The antidote, as was ever thus, is a more negotiated pedagogy whereby degrees of cultural capital are negotiated and exchanged in a 'porous expertise' between students and between students and teachers – closer to Ranciere's 'indiscipline' (Bowman 2011).

Situating Digital

The 'fault-lines' between literacy, new literacies, time and space based literacies, media literacy, digital literacy, transliteracies and broader 'safeguarding' objectives have 'always-already' been the subject of dispute and compromised practice. Frau-Meigs argues for transliteracy as a conduit for 'new collective dynamics' (2012, p. 22), whilst Comber reflects on decades of her own research with the disclaimer 'the impact of literacy wars and bandwagons has for too long distracted educators from the main game… that people understand how to use texts appropriately to get things done, how to make meaning and how to question the views of the world represented in texts in the interests of particular groups' (2014, p. 116). This complex configuration of (media /digital) literacy education is far more than navel-gazing among and between a clique community of practice. The increasing traverse, in the hyper-commodified, deprofessionalised education system, between research and practice, between serious enquiry into what's happening when young people learn with digital media, and the proliferation of funded programmes and projects assuming problems and solutions – threatens to undermine the credibility of the field and more importantly, leave behind children and young people who do not consume knowledge through digital media in the ways their teachers assume. A really stark example of this is in the area of media literacy for 'civic engagement', the subject of many funded projects across the European Union and in the USA in particular.

The plethora of digital media literacy projects, networks and initiatives which seek to emancipate marginalised people – usually youth – via various forms of 'civic engagement' often struggle to deal with the kinds of variance at work in the socio-critical premise of *third spaces*. As Zinck (2013) describe, marginalised and vulnerable youth have different experiences, live within distinct contexts, and have diverse needs that impact on their relative desires to engage with what we might think of as 'society'. Persistent assumptions cast marginalised (young) people either as either potential victims (themselves at risk) or as perpetrators of crime (a risk to society) or often both at the same time (Watt and Stenson 1998). Such self-fulfilling 'fold devil' representations are cyclical and impact on the relationships between the very people such well-intentioned digital literacy projects 'target' and their potential use of public space. For example, the EU funded project *Processes Influencing Democratic Ownership and Participation* (2009–2012) (PIDOP) discovered that young people often did not participate in democracy because they felt they had no voice, were ignored by politicians and/or because they lacked competencies or experience for participation.

More recent research across EU digital literacy communities has accepted that if young people are going to play a more meaningful role in democracy across the EU, they must be invited to engage not just as consumers and users of digital 'affordances', but as creators. Sustainability is only possible if young people are involved in creating mobile tools themselves. Many top-down resources available to young people today – youth forums, websites, various 'toolkits' for participatory culture – are ironically inaccessible to anyone but those youth who can 'speak the language' of official documents and institutional policies (Gerodimos 2008). At the same time, the digital tools themselves also tend to constrain agency in ways that diminish the public sphere (e.g. through 'walled garden' business models), as currently for reasons of finance and legitimation the use of online and mobile tools for civic engagement must often be balanced between the demands of civic participation and the market. Users are subsequently affected by widespread personal data mining by media and technology companies and government surveillance, along with digital rights management (DRM) and intellectual (see Boyle 2008, on how information ecology is threatened by the enclosure of private enterprise).

Therefore, the impact of 'digital civic engagement' on the terms of established civil society organisations has tended to be more constrained than that of more unstructured, short-term and ad hoc – online movements. Moreover, there is evidence from the 'dual adaptation' youth media production of Occupy and the performative 'street politics' protest movements mobilised as a response to austerity (see Kousis 2013), as well as new forms of the mediated construction of 'publics' (see Butsch and Livingstone 2014) that mobile technology combined with the lived experience of inequality can lead to an increase in civic engagement, but the renegotiation of engagement as well as the terms in which the meaning of 'civic' is made are part of the process of 'third-spacing' civics, it seems. Understood in this way, a progressive digital media education will combine addressing inequality with creating new pathways to renegotiated forms of engagement through an open, collective philosophy for both learning and the use of technology.

These calls for moments of sobering political caution are more significant than mere 'naysaying' cynicism. Returning to Fuchs' critique of Mason's 'post capitalism', and with the research-informed analyses of technology in education and young peoples' complicated 'digital capabilities' in mind, from the field of social literacies research it's essential to do serious cultural studies on the politics of the (digital) *third space*.

Digital practices are impossible to untangle from life narrative, schooled identity and, again, the power dynamics of education. Clearly, many of our contemporary 'digital literacy' interventions ignore this 'macro' level, and so doing is far more than an oversight. Rather it's a complicity in 'zombie politics' as it 'feeds off the lawlessness caused by massive inequalities in wealth, income and power' (Giroux 2014, p. 155).

Case: Co-creation

In this chapter we apply the two recurrent questions – about what happens to people in the *third space* and what difference it makes in the second space – to the case of UK higher education projects whereby teachers have designed co-creation projects with their students. Our focus here is on the potential for these interventions to disrupt epistemological power, as opposed to reproduce them in a simulacrum of participation. We are also 'zoomed in' on the role of digital media and technology in such interactions.

In 2014, record numbers of students from 'disadvantaged areas' (criteria: IDACI index), and mature students were accepted to Universities in England (source: UCAS). As this evidence indicates, the objective of widening participation is now embedded across higher education, and in particular the new University/'post-92' sub-sector. However, as the work of the Society for Research in Higher Education's Access and WP network demonstrates, widening access to enrolment to 'non-traditional' groups requires a pedagogic response in order to widen access but narrow the continuing 'achievement gap'. The UK Higher Education Funding Council (HEFCE) analysis states: 'those from the most disadvantaged areas have consistently lower HE degree outcomes than those with the same prior educational attainment from other areas' and report similar trends for BME students (see HEFCE data: Differences in Degree Outcomes 2013/2014). Such a pedagogic response, on the published evidence, almost always involves the utilisation of digital learning spaces of various kinds.

The University sector, in the United Kingdom, now places high value on students as partners, as is evidenced by the continuing debate, following the CHERI report around how to generate 'a more explicit focus on notions of learning partnerships and perceived barriers to, and effective practices in, creating cohesive learning communities'. The intention to raise the status of teaching and to 'fuse' pedagogy with research in order to address such a need for new modes of learning design is manifested across policy and practice in the recent proliferation of institutionally or sector funded projects and initiatives – again, almost always framed by 'digital literacy' activities – aiming to facilitate collaboration between students and lecturers towards the co-production of knowledge (see Trowler and Trowler, 2010; Weller and Kandiko Howson 2014). The reported outcomes of such initiatives are generally positive against one or a combination of three broad criteria: (1) raising students' confidence in working with higher education discourse/'language games' (e.g. Curzon and Millard 2013); (2) adapting pedagogy to more constructivist mode, often by utilising affordances of web 2.0 and harnessing 'digital literacies' (e.g. Kerrigan /JISC 2013); (3) increasing students' employability through public engagement (e.g. Cullum et al. 2014). For this work, the second strand is our focus.

The Higher Education Academy (2014) presents the following 'new pedagogical ideas':

Learner empowerment – actively involving students in learning development and processes of 'co-creation'
Future-facing education – enabling people to think critically, creatively and flexibly to generate alternative visions of the future
Decolonising education – extending inter-cultural understanding and experiences of students so they can be sensitive to global ways of working
Transformative capabilities – seeing capabilities not just as abilities but being able adapt a skill to be used in both familiar and unfamiliar circumstances
Crossing boundaries – to support inter-disciplinary, inter-professional and cross-sectoral learning
Social learning – developing cultures and environments for learning that harness the emancipatory power of spaces and interactions outside the formal curriculum, particularly through the use of new technologies and co-curricular activities

(HEA 2014: https://www.heacademy.ac.uk/flexible-pedagogies-new-pedagogical-ideas)

Whilst only the final element speaks explicitly to digital media, a review of the evidence of practice around the preceding five typically brings up the use of hybrid online/offline learning spaces as the norm. However, without questioning the redistributive intentions of this work, two issues are clear and present. Firstly, the lack of a theoretical rationale for the use of digital spaces and hybrid contexts for working with students. And secondly, the considerable variability in the extent to which these initiatives support 'widening participation' students, as many interventions are short-term pilot projects involving a relatively small group of volunteering students who may already possess significant academic confidence, or capital. For this reason, the extent to which digitally framed co-production initiatives have been successful in transforming non-traditional students' capabilities during higher education and after through the conversion of engagement with a more 'porous' conception of expertise into increased 'academic capital' needs to be understood. Towards this, scanning the published outcomes of the range of such digital co-creation interventions in the two years prior to writing, we can identify six cases that seem to represent various points along a continuum. This scale relates to Bernstein's work on classification:

> To see the pedagogic encounter only in terms of a range of potential voices and their relation to each other is to avoid the issue of pedagogy itself, i.e. the appropriate classification and framing modality. When this is considered, institutional, structural and interactional features are integrated into the analysis. The necessary resources (material and symbolic) can be assessed to become the site for challenges of what is and demands for what should be. (Bernstein 1996, p. 174)

The other criterion, to be placed in alignment with classification, is the extent to which expertise is negotiated, the degree of porosity.

First, a description of interventions we understand to be representative of the scale and scope of co-creation in UK higher education at this time, which is followed by illustration of the axes of classification and porosity. Our rationale for selecting these and putting Ranciere 'to work' on them is that they are all in the public domain as exemplars of good practice in co-creation, both self-identified and endorsed by such agents as the Higher Education Academy and the Society for Research into Higher Education.

An important disclaimer – we are not critical of the intentions or the outcomes of these projects. Rather, we think they are interesting 'cases' for thinking with some critical passion about the production of knowledge and how it relates to power in digital – physical hybrid spaces.

Hallet (2014) published outcomes from a co-creation project whereby History undergraduates worked ethnographically with community organisations to co-produce local history materials and activities (some digital, some 'real'). Through this blended *third space* work, students reported a constructivist approach to knowledge construction and confidence in working with both academic experts and community 'stakeholders'. Framed by the current 'public engagement' discourse, students talked of History 'in the real world', perhaps ironically given the role of digital technology as a conduit.

The broader Higher Education Academy/JISC project 'Digital Literacy in the Disciplines' (McAndrew 2014) captured student practices, via funded projects, relating to the 'new pedagogies' listed above, but crucially focused on the digital identity of and in disciplines, as opposed to between, across or even beyond these epistemological boundaries.

Susan Orr's Higher Education Academy Fellowship work, on media (digital) arts based signature pedagogy, foregrounds porosity through co-making of 'the work' and 'the learning'. Profoundly curational but still discipline bound (creative practice), this work begins to reach out across boundaries by thinking not only of learning itself as 'the work' but also of creative practice and pedagogy as forms parallel forms of research.

Other digitally 'afforded' co-creation projects situated activities entirely within an economic modality (market reports for industry, the 'Engagement Elevator', using digital spaces to blend dialogue and collaboration between academics, students and industry professionals), seeking to 'fuse' academic and corporate practices to develop new digital models for 'enterprise education', for instance. Co-creation and a non-hierarchical conception of expertise is evident here, but the notion of a 'contractual', real world client and emphasis on commercial viability imposes a horizontal/'precept' discourse which is profoundly non-permeable (or, in Zizekian terms, the economy here cannot be decoupled from ideology). Equally, 'digital engagement' itself becomes commodified, with exchange value, likewise employability in the digital economy as a 'tool', as opposed to using digital affordances for a more transgressive renegotiation of studentship or knowledge.

Weller and Kandiko-Howson's scoping study (2014) for the Society for Research into Higher Education utilised digital *third space* environments to 'reconceptualise students as participants and experts in educational change as well as partners and agents for that change'. As with many of the richer initiatives, the role of the teacher in the academy was at stake, with the institutional 'PG Cert' (a training course for academics without a formal teaching qualification) the context. The authors report that whilst academics are seen to have an expertise that is defined as essentially logico-rational, knowledge that encapsulates traditional, 'textbook', ways of knowing, related to mastery of the discipline or of pedagogic theory, student perspectives were more intuitive, emotional and experiential. Project outcomes included bearing witness in online interactions to more curational, negotiated, reflexive and interdisciplinary forms of professional practice reflexivity, moving towards porosity but stopping at the point of witnessing (on screen) the negotiation of expertise.

Cullum (2014) produced *Collabhub* – a set of collaborative History projects within community groups (History 'at work'), a more organic construction of history, utilising the curational properties of social media. We can distinguish this approach to Hallet, although working in very similar contexts – for its 'at work' negotiation of history in the community as opposed to a transfer 'of it' for employability. Curzon and Millard (2013) worked with students as authors, a collaborative digital writing project cited as a product of enhanced student engagement, with all the work written in close collaboration between students and staff (see Nygaard et al. (2013), resonating with both the CCCS tradition of students and supervisors working together on 'working papers' and Rancierian shades of 'the forcing of the will' (to be the expert, to be equal). These practices are, perhaps oddly, perhaps deliberately, absent from the undergraduate phase, either for reasons of scale and logistics or more problematically because 'co-creation' is rarely a relation of equals in real terms.

Neary's (2014) 'student as producer' project sought to 'reflect not only that students are much more than consumers of education, but to show our commitment to undergraduates as part of the academic project of the university', taking its title from an article by Walter Benjamin in Germany in the 1930s on how radical intellectuals should act in a time of social crisis. This work differs from the other projects through its material conditions for non-hierarchical ways of working, not only utilising digital spaces for co-creation but also physically located in a cooperative centre with no student fees and no *formal distinction between students and staff, a radical alternative to marketisation of higher education*, managed by its members – academics, students, administrators, educators and activists.

Finally, and probably the most 'mission central' for this work, the Disruptive/Open Media project (Shaw, Hall et al. 2015) states 'one effective way to understand higher education institutions is as sites of contestation between divergent constituencies whose needs are often incommensurate and operating on disparate timescales'. The ongoing work of the centre – as opposed to a discrete project – is at all times enabled by entirely open digital media education aligned with teaching and learning in physical spaces on campus in ways which are explicitly intended to experiment in interdisciplinary, phenomenological and curational modes. Epistemological porosity is emergent for staff and for students, on the evidence in the public domain, but the extent to which 'open' itself yields a renegotiation of expertise/knowledge in the centre's core fields (e.g. Photography) is less clear.

Plotting these co-construction projects – all funded and /or endorsed by cross-sector institutions and disseminated as good practice and all with (digital) *third space* constituents – against our criteria for 'messing about' with how knowledge gets made and what it means to be an expert – looks like this: (Table 5.1)

Table 5.1 Vertical, curational and porous co-construction

	Vertical	*Curational*	*Porous*
Discipline Bound	*History in the Real World* *Digital Literacies in the Disciplines*		*Media Arts Making Learning*
Interdisciplinary	*Engagement Elevator*	*PG Cert third space co-construction* *Collabhub*	*Students as authors* *Students as Producers*
Indisciplined		*Disruptive Open Learning*	*CCCS 'Messing About' (1980s)* *Current??*

The key finding from this review of funded and/or sector-endorsed co-creation projects exemplifying co-creation and 'new pedagogies' in various *third space* configurations returns us directly to the long-standing political battles at stake in the work of Freire, Stuart Hall, Ranciere and Raymond Williams. The more genuinely porous co-creation interventions are those with more explicit and coherent political intentions, those initiated by Curzon and Millard and Neary that situate co-creation ('shape-shifting', renegotiation of expertise) as a form of public redistribution. We found no evidence, though, of that being achieved in such a way as to completely align indiscipline with porosity, as we suggest CCCS were able to do in the pre-commodification landscape. These projects are those with the 'counter-script', with something to kick against, as opposed to those framed by discourses of 'quality' or 'employability'.

In this book generally, we want to contribute to the maturation phase of enquiry into technology, learning and literacy. In this phase we move beyond reductive opposition between emancipatory '2.0' ideas and rejectionist discourse to observe the complex interplay between democratizing, neoliberal and regulatory agencies around literacies in multimodal fields, the intersection of technologies, literacies, education and self'. The key tension at work here, always, is how digital:

> challenges an underlying assumption that learning can only be successful or take place in sanctioned, controlled spaces. The participatory nature of the internet has rendered this idea obsolete, and yet governing institutions persist in ignoring these changes rather than rethinking what teaching and learning is and can be. (Hamilton et al. 2015, p. 216)

Returning to our two core questions in the light of this 'case':

What Happens to People Doing Education in a (Digital) Third Space?

> Knowledge is no public affair, but partitioned and conserved according to positions, with access to it being regulated through selection and initiation.... The democratic struggle is precisely the struggle in which the connections (between talents/givens, occupations and positions) are disturbed that occurs when an individual group declares itself able to perform an activity that does not fit her place (according to the order). (Masschelein and Simons 2011, pp. 155–156)

When such a digital space is constructed with the effect of transgressing disciplines, power relations and traditional ideas about knowledge and expertise, the space can be 'saturated' with rich, usually curational literacy practices. When the more reciprocal kinds of 'studio work' can be reproduced in digital or hybrid spaces or when co-creation or student authorship can be liberated from the precepts of 'employability' and the vertical discourse of 'digital skills', it's clear from the field scanned in this chapter that the specific educational practices can 'shape-shift' to challenge epistemological power relations. But the key finding here is that the kinds of renegotiation at work in these digital contexts are actually quite old-school constructivist principles and take us back to the kinds of collaborative endeavour undertaken by the CCCS with their students in the 1980s – 'messing about'. For Ranciere, exemplified in his story about the French teacher Jacotot (1770–1840) – the 'ignorant schoolmaster' – the stuff of critical pedagogy is process, never content and experience, never explanation. We would expect digital technology to provide the kinds of *third spaces*, then, where we can 'reject the need for explication in favour of a community of learning between students that, on the one hand, depends on solidarity between students and, on the other, encourages students to make up their own minds about the material they are given' (Ridley 2016, p. 9). Accordingly, it's very clear that the co-creation activities in our 'case' moved closer to this ideal when the digital 'affordances' were put to work from a critical pedagogy starting point – where a desire to change the pedagogic relation was privileged above the neoliberal obligation to commodify the 'learning experience'.

How Do Engagements in the (Digital) Third Space Influence Practices Back in the Second Space?

Research into education more broadly and the small-scale action research interventions in *third spaces* discussed in this chapter bring worlds into being. However, immediately transgressive they are back in the second space, they cannot fail to cut across established pedagogic practices, if not in the short term bringing the collapse of the relationship between knowledge and the social order (as equality is always-already a deferred state), then at least attacking, or chipping away at the infantilising of society in the perpetuation of epistemological hierarchies – in this way the *third space* is less to do with location or the digital and more about wilful dispossession –

a space where we can pay 'attention to a thing in common' – a space for an 'overtaking of the self' on the part of the teacher (Cornelissen 2010, p. 26).

The kinds of well-intentioned projects reviewed in this chapter are typical of where we tend to be when it comes to using digital media for 'redistributive public intervention' (Fenton 2013). Across the UK higher education projects, the European Union /UNESCO digital literacy network, the American media for civic engagement work and the school interventions from technology providers in the name of what we are calling 'Digital Capability', a relatively small group of students, often volunteering and sometimes already demonstrating high levels of academic capital, usually benefit from a small funded study. Evidence of up-scaling to whole institution or beyond, back in the 'second space' is usually harder to find. Likewise, much of the work here – history 'out there' on the one hand or more Vygotskian work with SEN learners on the other – is entirely at odds with the conservative assessment modalities to which students are obliged to return. However, it's clear that students – and teachers /researchers – will inevitably take back to the second space rich experiences that disrupt apparently neutral functional and economic discourses about what learning in digital spaces is *for*, as opposed to *what* is learned. Thus, it's unlikely that any educational encounter in the kinds of digitally mediated *third spaces* that start out from a radical pedagogy stance – towards 'democratic indiscipline' – would fail to bring to the surface questions of entitlements, rights, ethics and voice in 'everyday' pedagogy on the part of all the social actors involved.

CHAPTER 6

The Networked Educator and Open Learning

This chapter will assess the research evidence (not the conjecture) that supports the view that the social (digital) network is a powerful agent in contemporary education. The focus here is on the networked educator and thus on learning by proxy/extension. Our specific 'cases' under scrutiny here will be Teachmeets, thqe Open/Disruptive Education movement, MOOCs and *third space* networks circulating in and from protest camps. Having analysed these 'found' cases, the chapter will move on to new research capturing the networking practices of a group of teachers. The strategy for this exercise is to mirror 'The Class' (Livingstone and Sefton-Green 2016) with 'The Department', albeit a smaller scale investigation.

In each case, both aspects of ANT and recent theories of connectivity – specifically the development of an 'activist thought collective' in and for education – will be deployed to evaluate the place of the 'affordance' in the educational landscape and the degree to which validation is present, on what terms and how best to understand human and non-human agency. Keeping our focus on how the *third space* impacts the second space, we'll look for evidence of how a network can disturb 'either or' models of learning and teaching from within the educational mainstream, in favour of 'either and' disruptions which problematise conditions of possibility for expertise, discipline boundaries and the commodification of learning, whilst existing in the same space as profoundly neoliberal 'providers'. Crucially, the extent to which each network operates within a *pedagogic*

J. Potter, J. McDougall, *Digital Media, Culture and Education*,
DOI 10.1057/978-1-137-55315-7_6

rationale – as opposed to a mere repository of 'stuff' – will be explored, from the perspectives of providers and users (terms used under erasure). Observing as historical trajectory 'the transformation from networked communication to platformed sociality and from a participatory culture to a culture of connectivity' (Van Dijk 2013, pp. 4–5) and asserting that networks represent a 'dominant cultural logic' (Varnelis 2010) may be valid, but the research suggests that digital networks tend not to make *much* difference to existing, partly spatial, boundaries between inside, margins and outside or between home and school or work and home, or to transcend social framings of gender, class and ethnicity:

> Put bluntly, it still matters very much who one is. The social disadvantages of being black, female, poor and /or of having a physical or intellectual disability do not simply disappear when one learns through the internet. (Selwyn 2014, p. 45)

In essence, any online network 'enables us to reconfigure relationships without the constraints of the present and the face to face' (Alleyne 2015 p. 116). Relationships are, of course, central to learning. When such a network can facilitate the development of a community of practice, a collective resource which would be impossible in physical space and real time, then educators look for Wenger (1998) full participation. When these virtual spaces can be a hub for, or start to generate passion and affinity, then we can apply ideas from Henry Jenkins and James Gee (Jenkins et al. 2006; Gee 2004) about transmedia literacy practices. Whether or not the digital spaces are driving the passion or just providing a more visible archive for human beings' innate desires to make and connect is at the heart of David Gauntlett's work (Gauntlett 2015). Finally, when the digital space works to converge an 'analogue' learning setting with the lifeworld – across our 'semi-permeable membrane', then we can invoke notions of the '*third space*'.

This book is a sociocultural and political analysis of technology, media and education, but we start out from our situated histories in media education/media literacy. Networks have a particular status in this genealogy and a particular discourse clash is at a key moment at the time of writing. Digital media networks have been appropriated for both the 'voice discourse' and the 'entrepreneurial discourse' in rationales for digital media literacy for many years. Many of us have become adept and working across and between them, for pragmatic ends, but they are undoubtedly in conflict (see De Abreu et al. 2017, in press). As Blum-Ross and Livingstone observe:

> Although at present the discourses appear to co-exist, the considerable resources being provided to support entrepreneurial approaches to digital media learning threaten to obscure and undermine the social justice imaginary that originally inspired this field. (Blum-Ross and Livingstone 2016, p. 1)

Systemworld Networks

At the time of writing, there are some clear and present challenges to the notion that digital networks transgress cultural and geographical borders. Geopolitics is still largely a matter of terrain (even when reconfigured as digital space), conflict and constraint, so that 'although we have broken free from the shackles of gravity, we are still imprisoned in our own minds, confined by our suspicion of "the other" and thus our primal competition for resources' (Marshall 2015, p. 283). Furthermore, recent events in Britain and the USA, Brexit and the Trump candidacy respectively, present an unexpected kind of 'border imaginary' among publics, desiring walls to fence off territory, a very different way of thinking to the global neoliberal:

> The craven language of scarcity that seeks to guide our aggression and restrict our immigration policies can be diffused only when we understand that there are different priorities here and there. Travel, then, is not merely a luxury or an educational strategy, but a moral imperative for those that have the means for it. It is a corrective lens that helps focus the earth's blurred reality. (Solomon 2016, p. 3)

The relationship between virtual networking and travel, or the extent to which 'digital travel' can facilitate this empathetic imperative, must be considered.

Our lens here is not a wholesale critical theory of online connectivity or a cultural history of digital sharing. It's primarily about people being at work when they are not physically 'in the building' and, then, it's about attempts to blur boundaries for students (in the broadest sense) between being in school (or college or University) and being at home/somewhere else. What all the research shows is that the first part is abundant, simply because it helps not all, but many, professional adults juggle the demands of their lives if we can be in a *third space* which is both home and work. But the second part if much less straightforward as young people in education quite understandably want, not always but often, to keep bits of the lifeworld away from the Systemworld. Put bluntly, and with some middle-aged resignation, they still have the choice after all! It's also very important to situate the adoption of blended working practices through a class lens, as Melissa Gregg reminds us in her thick description of the sociology of online labour, 'the most successful online platforms of recent years, social networking sites, build on the deliberate confusion of work and friendship that have been the hallmark of middle-class office cultures for decades' (Gregg 2011, p. 6).

In the theoretical 'meta', we can think about networks with ideas from Deleuze and Guattari (1993). Networks decentre, destabilise and disrupt; they confound the oppressively singular order exercised in hierarchy. So whilst a network is any set of connections bringing together discrete elements, a network has radical potential when they disrupt power relations. Often, networks reinforce those. So in this book we are not celebrating networks in themselves. Whilst networks have been observed to be culturally significant in general (see Castells and Cardoso 2005; Fuchs 2012) and long-standing as a human technology – again, often for the circulation of power, by empires most profoundly (Mann 2005). Going back and further 'zooming' out, we can see society itself as a network of networks. But our concern here is with networks that open possibilities for teaching to do something radical for learning. And we are mindful to resist an unhelpful opposition of open, democratic network to closed, hierarchical forms:

> When it comes to the relationship between wholes and networks, it is not always clear which form will dominate. Some networks can be contained, others thwart containment.... networks and enclosures are constantly meeting, sometimes sustaining and reinforcing one another, at other times creating threats and obstacles. Neither form has the final organizing word – neither always regulates the other. (Levine 2015, pp. 118–119)

In histories of 'at work' networks, the analyses of Wright Mills (1956) and William H Whyte (1956) are often cited for their observation of the 'cheques and balances' of white-collar (male) professionals taking work home or being on call outside of the 9–5 office day. Liu (2004) traces the departure from meritocracy or company loyalty in an application of a similar approach to working practices – the 'affect' in the online age and Gregg (ibid.) takes this further in her study of how the ontological bearings of fear and anxiety identified by Wright Mills are traced through to the contemporary 'presence bleed' around networking technology. Later in the chapter, we'll compare Gregg's findings – and crucially how gender, class and domestic/familial habits make a difference to 'work's intimacy' to Livingstone and Sefton-Green's ethnography of the digital learning and networking practices of secondary school students in a London school. In both accounts, the importance of avoiding assumption and generalisation when dealing with networking 'affordances' chime with Selwyn's (2014) antidotes to network evangelism, reminding us of the divisions that networks tend to reproduce:

> These include inequalities of income and resources, social networks and relationships, pressures of time, health, family demands and working conditions. These also include less tangible differences in the extent to which individuals benefit from equal rights and are fulfilled in terms of basic human needs for care, love and solidarity. Clearly, there is much here that will not be addressed through online courses. (2014, p. 51)

Indeed. So hopefully it is clear this chapter won't be a celebration of the emancipated networked educator, and her newly participating students, but will rather be a considered and more nuanced critique of how teachers' choices of whether/how to network always go back to other – and bigger – aspects of who we are.

Network theory as a whole (as it were) posits that in a network we can find clusters, hubs or nodes, some more coherently or closely linked than others. The potential for narrative to be increasingly networked by digital affordances is of great interest to new learning theories concerned with curation, but again we are reminded that 'spreadable' narrative is nothing new. Levine cites Dickens as an exponent, his stories hinging on the reader's acceptance that 'our knowledge of social interconnections can only be partial: we may intuit the overwhelmingly complex webs of social interconnections in glimpses and hints, but the networks that connect rich and poor, city and world, the dead and the living, are never fully present to consciousness' (2015, p. 129). The BBC's recent Dickensian project appears to add weight, as his own canon of characters is networked across the boundaries of each text. Finally, for this setting out of the territory, we are also mindful that teachers and learners are always already in networks and '*third spaces*' must be read as being an attachment to, not a replacement for, the classroom as a networked space:

> While networks and other flows circulate through the teacher's practices, her own actions, desires and so on are not determined by the network, but by emerge through the myriad translations that are negotiated among all the movements, talk, materials, emotions and discourses making the classroom's everyday encounters. (Fenwick and Edwards 2010, p. xvi)

Networked Activism

Van Dijk (2013) bears witness to the complexity of how public sphere rhetorics are appropriated into corporate strategy and how profoundly the coding of human connections 'monetises' the emancipatory logic of the web. The operational logic of social media platforms is shown to be vulnerable; Twitter's 'precarious choreography', the dance between ambient utility and information network and how connectivity is paradoxical, subject to axes of engagement, autonomy and boundaries – configurations of locking in, fencing off, opting out. The language of struggle pervades and casts the operational logic of connectivity as the site of power and exploitation rather than neutral evolution. The (rapid) progression from 'platformed' sociality to participatory culture to a culture of connectivity, wherein hitherto casual speech acts are inscribed in the public domain and where human connections are coded is not simply moulded by historical contingency but engineered. Furthermore, the utopian notion of 'watchful caretakers and diverse gardeners' in the web 2.0 ecosystem cuts against a responsive colonisation of pioneer non-profits by corporations.

The interplay between the network as a counter-commodifying space of resistance (the Digital Commons, for example) and the hegemonic control of networks coincides with the two other main conflicts discussed here – the 'double edged' flexibility of blended professional lives and the tug of war between critical pedagogues and both children and parents' conservative positions over the politics of digital learning in the lifeworld. Whilst perhaps it is still reasonable to say, as commentators did at the advent of 'the online age' that non-hierarchical arrangements on the Internet are very different to capitalist impositions of control and enclosure, it is sobering to reflect at this time that the empire has struck back pretty well in profiting from 'the dialectic between autonomy and exploitation' (Wittel 2016, p. 59). Wittel, writing about educational labour, offers a similar political economy of professional networks to Gregg (2011), who we turn to shortly, seeing a 'Fordism 2.0' in the new forms of subjectivity 'in which the academic worker becomes an entrepreneurial self that is at the same time subject and object of the new cultures of auditing' (2016, pp. 81–82). However, some rich sites for conflict are presented in this dialectical space with radical opportunities in each for teachers and academics – the open source web; the 'Free Culture' movement; new publishing modes (and associated activism against the commodifying, metric hierarchy corporate practices of Academic and ResearchGate); the Digital Commons, financial activism (e.g. the Global Debt Amnesty) and alternative education movements. Networks, in this taxonomy, are understood as 'thought collectives', of which two are in clear opposition. On one side, the neoliberal hegemony, itself a network of ideology, reliant on a first-order acceptance of the market and second-order state policy of opening everything up to it – in Zizek's terms, the market *as* ideology. On the other side, the commons, a contribution economy, whereby we give to one another our progressive ideas and resources (in our context, for teaching) and accept that some give more than others (as opposed to a gift economy, which requires reciprocal exchange). The commons, for the second thought collective, is given priority over the market as a 'natural order':

> The network of the activist thought collective needs spaces to meet and to talk. It will be another challenge to make these gatherings possible. We need them regularly, we need them on a global scale and we need them to be funded. We also need these gatherings to be free from the usual constraints of academic conferences, which are designed not to foster but to hinder the free circulation of ideas. (p. 85)

In an optimistic presentation of research into youth activism mobilised 'by any media necessary' Jenkins (2016) offers another hopeful lens for seeing 'networked publics' as productively disruptive:

> These models push against the individuality of personalizing logics of neoliberalism. Networked publics depend on social connections among participants and often demand that we care about the plight of others. (2016, p. 269)

However, many of the movements studied in the collection might be considered mile wide, inch deep in the sense of being short-term 'crash and burn' impacts on the order of things, which returns to equilibrium having allowed sufficient resistance for the centre to hold. I'm mindful of the current Momentum campaign around Jeremy Corbyn in the United Kingdom, most definitely charged with network capital, and the politics of which are seductive to us – 'welcome to the mass movement of giving a toss about stuff' – but with an absence of powerful hybridity as the activist impulses of the Labour movement are increasingly decoupled from the parliamentary party. This is a quite different form of hegemony to the co-option of networking practices by the political mainstream, however, which Jenkins observes in the USA as no surprise, given 'these new kinds of civic cultures are developing a new repertoire of mobilization tactics, communication practices and rhetorical genres'. In this sense the (popular) cultural sphere is the transition point (gateway, in Jenkins' terms) to the political/civic sphere – 'by any media necessary'. We might, here, return to the notion of the social media network *as* popular culture, from Hall's call to arms, or look ahead to Chapter 6, where we engage with cultural studies directly again. Soep concludes 'By Any Media' with a set of directions for travel for networked activist learning, whereby learning is understood as a (Freirian) mode of cross-community; cross-platform activism in itself:

> How can we continue to broaden the range of genres through which young people share their school-sanctioned civic and political knowledge to include community performances and social media conversations to experimental digital displays? (2016, p. 308)

The *third space* can be generated in the second space. The networked virtual world Minecraft has been the subject of much educational research and gamification/simulation interventions in recent years, but the more interesting work for our focus here is that which explores the interweaving of in world, embodied and social/performative literacy practices. Regarding ANT, to which we turn shortly, it would seem reasonable to propose that children building worlds collaboratively in Minecraft are working across technical, imaginative and social domains, with the machinery (software and hardware), objects (blocks) and human beings in the network equally subject to translations and temporary black boxing to make the in-world community coherent. The Minecraft actant is an interface between a human in the network, cultural context and technology. Whether Minecraft itself is black boxed or members of the network black box the object of their own world within the world depends on the strength of translation. For the researcher, the imposition of power lies in where we 'cut' the network to analyse it and which actants to follow. Whilst distinct from ANT, Chris Bailey's year-long ethnography of an after school Minecraft club includes a rich, similarly micro-semiotic critical incident whereby the researcher observed club members performing mimetic 'free flow vocalising', creating and performing songs whilst playing that offered another layer of partial critique of in world practices, with the research exploring:

> how they managed to put song into Minecraft, in the formation of the text but also, critically, through its enactment. In this context, performance was used for recruiting, regrouping, uniting and opposing in multiple locations – reflecting the fluid grouping present during the club itself. (Bailey 2016, p. 70)

The 10- to11-year-old children were in a classroom, but after school, playing Minecraft in a hybrid network context, but brought to the situation a further extension of the hybridity, by performing songs that both related to the in-world practices and offered a reflexive and parodic commentary in the physical space. Resources from the game, the social experience of being in the group and other experiences, were integrated and adapted organically but no elements were abstracted from the others, rather 'they were networked and dependent on each other in a number of complex ways' (p. 70).

Returning specifically to our focus here, professional working practices, the sobering reality from empirical research appears to be that inequalities in network capital (and /or aptitude) among the workforce limit the potential for the more impactful 'repertoire extension' we've spent some time on above.

Gregg's enquiry brought up both the importance of, and labour required to maintain 'network capital', going beyond the more obvious application of Goffman to social media identity curation to ask more searching questions about Fordist enfranchisement – a 'new form of presence' and 'register of intimacy' (2011, p. 173). Gregg avoids bold claims for networks and dystopian 'dataveillance' concerns equally, instead offering research findings that bring to light the pervading middle-class occupation of the network space:

> The choice to engage in long hours of sacrificial labour in generally enjoyable jobs stands in stark contrast to the forms of coercion and surveillance suffered by many of the world poorest workers. These include the legions of employees whose job it is to assemble the devices that deliver so-called flexibility to the wealthy workers of the West. (171)

Working with Actor Network Theory

ANT emerged in the 1980s (notably from Latour 2005) and has been taken up by social scientists, including educational researchers, who are energised by its potential to disrupt epistemology, ontology and the social order through attention to how 'socio-material' relations bring the world into being. For education, this means looking at how processes, people and objects work together, particularly around educational change, including the introduction and adoption of new technologies. For example, Nespor explores the ways in which different kinds of digital devices, when used for learning, 'ask us to reconsider where artefacts begin and end in time – the temporalities of associations and translations' (2012, p. 19). Seeing the world as a network of hybrid (social /technological) actants, ANT asserts that we can investigate people and technologies on an equal footing and thus observe more keenly how the social and technological are mutually co-embedded. In very simple terms, ANT provides a methodology for looking more deeply into the complexities beneath observations of hybridity (sometimes *third spaces*) such as Grayson Perry here:

> It seems that, in the digital age, people are keener than ever to visit art galleries, to be in the presence of the actual unique object (and take a selfie in front of it, natch, to post on Twitter), and there are more artists, dealers, collectors and curators than ever. (2015, p. 134)

So here we can think about a network that includes the art object – itself the outcome of a combination of human actions and tools and materials, curated in a physical space among other objects and artefacts – the gallery – networked both within the curational narrative and externally in 'the art world', visited by a human actant and captured through a machine and then shared with a social network, itself a combination of other humans, cultural arrangements, devices and algorithmic categorisations.

Recent educational ideas about curation help us make a bridge between Perry's 'pleasant surprise' observation of young people still embracing art but in a digitally mediated way of being around it and the micro-semiotic methodological labour of doing ANT on such hybrid sociocultural practices. Putting a selfie of yourself with an art object into the social network is to express curational agency in self-reflexive and mimetic, even transgressive ways. In creating and then disassembling and then reassembling the image of oneself in the exhibition for exhibition, we are expressing, knowingly, 'ways of being active in gathering together and assembling the resources needed to represent both the anchored and the transient forms of identity in a variety of spaces for difference purposes and audiences' (Potter 2012, p. 222). But the point of ANT is that it helps us realise first, and then discern second, how the actant posting the selfie is immersed in relational power with the human/non-human gallery spaces and the human/non-human network – the network is never just 'in use' for us.

ANT follows the movements of actants and moments where things happen that develop the network in various, never neutral ways – these are 'obligatory passage points' which necessitate 'translations' of the complex into the orderly for pragmatic purposes. This process of articulation involves building and reproducing, extending or disrupting power relations. The terminology of ANT always speaks to these operations of power – *problematisation* (creating the figured world for the network), *interessement* (stabilising the network, creating hierarchies, usually discursive), *enrolment* (initiation of actants to perform their identities in particular ways necessary to the network), mobilisation – the crucial stage where a minority come to represent the crowd in a process of reification in which things are 'black boxed' so the network can function, despite outside of the box it's ontology being infinite. ANT is, then, potentially and powerfully critical of educational network developments, particularly when the result is, as so often, reform:

> When policy is presented as a rational process, ANT interprets this as a power play in its own right. (Hamilton 2012, p. 56)

So, to be clear for our purposes here, ANT provides a conceptual framework for looking at machines, people, objects and texts in relational power networks. Importantly, the actors do not use the network for power, they are dependent on it. Seeing power this way as never held but always exercised is Foucauldian and in that sense the relativist impulse in ANT is similarly criticised, along with its most controversial assertion – that humans are quasi-subjects and non-humans quasi-objects, neither has a pure distinction from the other. However, the ANT lens has influenced the more obviously political social materiality theory, in the field of literacies, for example and ANT proponents do not claim the equity of people and things as an ethics, merely a methodology:

> Power is considered to be relational in so far as actors gain their powers through the sets of relations they construct with other actors and therefore are an affect or outcome of these sets of relations. (Jackson 2015, p. 34)

In this chapter we are concerned with the possibilities for digital networks to provide *third space* transformations for teachers, and subsequently people who are learning. Nespor (2012) offers an ANT exploration of the adoption of digital devices for educational change and observes a familiar unfolding progression of 'junctions' from

> the translation of some immediate, situated activity in itself not yet or obviously productive (devices like interactive video) into a contingent future (a university offering computer-mediated courses) that might in turn be translated into legislative policy (a less expensive university system). (2013, p. 9)

New Public Spaces

> Emerging networked publics and the related tools to support accountability, social movement building and democracy are important developments for schools to consider for three reasons. First, these spaces constitute a new site for citizenship. Secondly, such tools offer new resources to enable schools themselves to effect change. Finally, schools themselves are places in which students learn what it means to 'do democracy'. (Facer 2011, pp. 89–90)

Working broadly within this framework – publics, change and democracy, this chapter is concerned with the difference digital networks might make to these things to teachers and then to students. But it's important to take a step back and think carefully about the assumptions we might make about not only 'digital natives' but their civic predispositions.

As part of a comparative media literacy project with the United Kingdom Literacy Association (McDougall et al. 2015), a group of Media students in a sixth form college (pre-University, 16–19 years old) were asked to undertake a creative task, which involved making something with an explicit agenda of civic participation, putting it online and attempting to engage an audience. They were shown some short extracts from a range of 'issue based' videos by other young people, ranging from simple webcam pieces to vox pops and more sophisticated edited videos. They were told that their work did not have to use video as a format and that if they wished to use a 'private' online space such as *Facebook*, they could send us screengrabs of audience responses, rather than giving us full access. They were given three weeks from the date of the interview and were incentivised to complete the process.

The majority used video, one an audio piece and one wrote a short blog post. The blog writer was the only participant to gain feedback. Topics included the death penalty, the global water crisis, the cost of public transport for youth, feminism, teen female body image (twice), or the need for politics to be taught in schools and football (twice). One participant already had her own *Tumblr* but opted to set up a *Blogspot* in order to share her short written post on the death penalty. Her feedback amounted to responses from three friends via *Whatsapp*. There was no visual content, no links to other sites or any attempt to move beyond a traditional 'mini-essay' style format. Similarly, a very brief podcast on the cost of public transport provided little evidence of multimodal creativity, with the audio content comprising a complaint about older people having it easier than the young with their free bus passes. The author largely relied upon her own experience of having to get a lift from her parents or pay £4 for the bus rather than walk a mile. It was not placed online nor did it generate any audience response. The one non-media student to make a video claimed that she did not have the facility to upload it to the web: 'I have no hosting sites to add my video onto as I do not have internet access on my laptop at home, I have took a video from my phone of the video I made on movie maker on my laptop so I could attach it here for you'. Her video about the water crisis comprised stills, captions and music and was reminiscent of charity appeals.

A 'Politics in school' piece began and ended with a piece to camera about the creator's own experience, framing a series of vox pops with fellow students which served to demonstrate their own ignorance of politics. Each vox pop concluded with a freezeframe, which seemed to offer the audience pause for thought each time. At the time of writing, the video had 60 views, but no responses. Another video, 'The tyranny of slenderness' largely comprises shots of fashion and makeup in shops with voiceovers from different girls about their response to the body image expected of women. It features a range of shots from close up to wide, tracking shots, edits and some stylish titles designed to reflect the theme. This piece clearly speaks to its audience and adopts a style of documentary where the pictures are reinforced by the commentary. This participant did show that she had shared the link on her *Facebook, Twitter* and *Tumblr* accounts, though, again, there was no evidence of any audience engagement. Overall, none of the participants made any attempt to engage an audience online beyond a small circle of friends either due to reluctance or inability.

This finding is in keeping with the longitudinal, ethnographic observations from 'The Class', to which we turn in detail shortly. Whilst the young people here are strongly networked and there are some overlaps between college and lifeworld connections, there remains a great deal of insulation between personal and educational networking and a significant absence of civic engagement with any 'new public spaces'.

A Fourth Space?

The two central questions we return to in each chapter are restated:

- What happens to people doing education in a (digital) *third space*?
- How do engagements in the (digital) *third space* influence practices back in the second space?

To recap but also focus in on the concerns of this chapter, the first space (self, home, community) is already 'invaded' by the second space in the form of homework and, in middle class homes, what we might call the 'pedagogising' of everyday life. This does not constitute a *third space* if 'schooled' learning merely travels outwards, to home or other first space contexts. The two figured worlds of home/school are not connected in this way by a 'semi-permeable membrane' (Potter 2011), instead the fund of knowledge accumulated outside of school remains outside but is added to or even reconstituted by the fund of knowledge and the epistemological order from the second space. When people are able to meaningfully blend lived experience with academic knowledge in ways that bolster identities, then hitherto competing discourses and 'ways of being' can be positively integrated with reflexive outcomes for both learners and educators. Utilising the affordances of digital media doesn't necessarily have to only be in a virtual space in between the first and third, as the Minecraft research discussed earlier shows us. But for such initiatives to count as meaningful here, there does have to be a transformation with redistributive outcomes for people. These might be reflexive outcomes for teachers, curriculum shifts, new forms of assessment even, or for people finding rich opportunities to understand their identities around learning, as people with stories to tell and experiences to share and as generators of new knowledge. And on redistribution, we're talking unashamedly about the various aspects of dispossession that make up working class – in the various ways of being so at this point in history (see Hanley 2016) – alienation from the flow of academic capital, accepting that education has, far from resolving inequality through social mobility, been mobilised as an apparatus for the exacerbation of social stratification, something digital networks threaten to amplify yet further despite evangelical claims to the contrary:

> A society as technologically advanced as ours, as rich in natural resources and wealth, could and should be committed to providing all children with the best possible start in life, not just a handpicked few. In a selective education system, even in a relatively affluent society, the education of the majority will be under-resourced, precisely because the ruling elite ascribe very little value to the work that the majority are being equipped to do. (Todd 2015, p. 391)

We must be mindful, then, of how networked learning that's more bespoke and personal is most beneficial to those are who 'well positioned to be nimble, nomadic and to act generally in the "flexible" manner we are told is advantageous in the digital age' (Selwyn 2014, p. 76). And thinly veiled corporate interests lie beneath the deregulated economy of many investments in networked reforms, with starkly different agendas and objectives to those associated with public education for the greater good of the whole of society. Perhaps many *third space* interventions have begun to mobilise in this redistributive sense, but within limitations of funding and scale – the nature of the 'perennial pilot' study. But, more optimistically, it's also possible that the work we talk about in this chapter might help us extend this to consider the idea of a fourth space.

We are thinking broadly about home/lifeworld as the first space, the educational institution as the second and the porous membrane of a pedagogically charged, rich either/and space converging the first and second as the *third space*. Then we ask how the second space might be transformed by encounters in the third. If this happens, and it's rare and very difficult in the 'current climate', of course, then can we imagine an accredited, 'mainstreamed' version of the *third space* back in the second? And if this could genuinely be socially transformative, celebrate difference and be resistant to neoliberal hegemonic co-option of the network, if it could disrupt the 'trade off' that Livingstone and Sefton-Green observe in young peoples' thinking, so that school itself became a different kind of networked experience for the pursuit of radical pedagogy and social justice, could we call this a fourth space? Or does the numerical and spatial metaphor break at this point because the disruptive neither/both connotations of the *third space* /third way are at odds (or evens?) with the 'squaring off' implications of a fourth point?

Case 1 – Teachmeets: De-scripting CPD?

Teachmeets have been in operation for almost a decade, at the time of writing. They demonstrate 'counterscript' tendencies in so much as they are grassroots, collective and non-hierarchical, informed by the concept of the 'unconference' and open space values of organic, fluid, reflective and spontaneous collaboration between professionals, an antidote to the school improvement/performance management discourse that pervades within and between institutions. The 'Teachmeet bounce' is attributed by participants more to well-being than 'development'. Teachers take away ideas for teaching – a form of 'spreadable' teaching, and indirectly learning. 'The digital' comes into play when this spreading out can be achieved through a combination of physical meetings and an online network, or when the latter stands in for the former entirely – our interest here is on the Teachmeet as either/and these entities, thus another *third space*, potentially.

According to the emerging genealogy, Teachmeets first appeared in Scotland, the earliest record being of a meeting hosted in a pub. Conventions of Teachmeets which have been widely adopted include short presentations, acceptance of members 'dipping in and out' and using devices during meetings, the presence of children so members can manage work and life together and the prolific use of social media to spread the ideas live and ask questions of speakers and other members of the network during the meeting – the prominence of the 'back channel'. According to the official Teachmeet site:

> The idea is to create a space for educators to come together and talk shop with the goal of innovating, improving practice and student engagement. Teachmeets can be held in pubs, parks, restaurants, museums, food courts... whatever space is accessible and will accommodate your participants. TeachMeets have a very simple framework: Introduction – go around the table and share your name, workplace, and interest; Sharing Time – go around again and offer each participant two uninterrupted minutes to share; Response Time – offer three minutes for quick questions; Conversation Time. (http://www.teachmeet.org.uk/)

Applying aspects of ANT to Teachmeets, we can say that the conversation time is mobilisation, whereby the actants with proposals for implementation/transfer to other actants' situations, via translation, will come to speak for the many and the Teachmeet is black boxed. Where particular forms of reification take place, where policy is 're-rationalised' through the pragmatic enrolment of participants, the key question for ANT will be whether the 'free range' networking of the Teachmeet process disrupts the relational power flowing from policy to pedagogy. Whether Teachmeet as a macro network – as opposed to local devolution – is a form of 'activist thought collective' – will also depend on the extent to which professional practices in the second space are transformed via the 'network ontology' to create opportunities for resistance via 'safety in numbers', as opposed to a collective interessement of the 'what works' discourse.

Case 2 – Open, Massive, Disruptive

> There's no sense of open being necessarily a mode of resistance, it depends on what you are doing with it and how you're working with it. (Hall, quoted in McDougall, 2015)

The Open Education Movement, a network convened around the Disruptive Media Learning Lab and, clearly, an activist thought collective, seeks to critically engage with the big questions, from John Henry Newman to Collini about the role of the University in the digital age. 'Open' can, though, mean many things, in this case arising from a departmental open media strategy (at Coventry University), broadly to develop open educational resources. Core objectives included tactical about use of mobile technologies in media education to connect staff and students in working together visibly in new ways, encouraging engagement through staff's own media practices and their teaching, developing new transgressive learning communities and challenging the classroom boundary, to reach people outside the institution in audience communities and creative practitioner networks. Institutionally, the centre was looking for new ways of becoming sustainable in the context of the 'employability' driver in the climate of recession.

Open Media courses from the centre make learning experiences and resources freely available, and link participants to a number of networks and communities of specialists, practitioners and mentors, but this open activity is connected synchronously with classroom 'delivery' of courses at the University:

> In our own particular hybrid take on 'blended learning', classes on these courses are open online to anyone, anywhere, to participate in, add to the discussions and even rip remix and mash-up. This applies to the schedule, lectures, lesson content, exercises and assignments, recommended reading, recorded talks and interviews with visiting speakers (audio and video), RSS feeds, tag clouds and blog post archive, as well as a number of practical 'how to' videos, all of which are available under a CC-BY-SA license. The use of blogs, Vimeo, Flickr, Twitter and other social media platforms means that participants – both the in class ('atoms-based'), accredited, fee paying participants and those taking these classes for free remotely – can interact and contribute through discussion, feedback, suggestions etc. In this way the syllabus becomes a 'co-authored script', curated by the academic team 'but produced by the collective exchange and effort of the learning community. (Van Mourik Broekman et al. 2014, p. 99)

The work is not presented as a utopian or evangelical 'democracy 2.0' celebration, rather the authors account for the neoliberal assault on higher education and the instrumental and economic threats attendant to MOOCS and open source 'delivery' – 'Open Education's explicit (and often deliberate) fusion of conservative, liberal, neoliberal and more radical tendencies and discourses is undoubtedly an important element in this somewhat contradictory picture' (ibid, p. 24). Going further with this theme of contradiction and conflict, it might seem inevitable that taking open educational practice towards some sense of its more disruptive conclusion might lead inevitably to a 'deschooling'? For example, a statement like 'one effective way to understand HEIs is as sites of contestation between divergent constituencies whose needs are often incommensurate and operating on disparate timescales' (ibid, px) which is presented early on in the text as part of a contextual scene setting for the intervention made by open specifically in higher education might seem to leave a very narrow space for more modest, careful disruption as opposed to a more self-destructive 'endgame' for HE practitioners. On the other hand, this version of the Open movement appears to offer a theorised and politicised reaction to the threat/opportunity discourse around MOOCs. Equally, the Disruptive Media 'version' of Open is keen to engage with discipline politics and the kinds of epistemological power we considered in Chapter 2:

> The idea of 'either and' is intriguing. What's happening in photography is that a medium invented to capture motion has become determined by its status as a commercial product and what's happening now is at a subject it's revisiting its birth and the plurality associated with that and the joy when something is fresh and trying to understand its place. I come at this as a practitioner rather than an academic as such, so I had to learn how to be the academic. But the relationship these days is more the academic back into the practitioner and adopting the mechanisms from my photographic practice in the University. Collaborating across boundaries, it feels like a modelling of that experience, and this perhaps gives us different kinds of insight, we're more comfortable with the disruptive or distributed nature of knowledge, when things are more dispersed, how do you work, how do you move to a more curational, conversational stance as opposed to assuming a voice of authority? (Shaw, quoted in McDougall, 2015)

Turning to a case within the case, collaborating with the *Journal of Media Practice*, the Disruptive Media /Open Education group 'occupied' a disruptive special issue to experiment with how media practice, in rethinking research as practice, could also disrupt the way academics mediate this research through various formal and informal scholarly forms (http://journal.disruptivemedia.org.uk/). The project considered a number of existential questions – how can a journal of media practice extend from a speculative focus on what media practice as research could be to an exploration of the alternative forms of communication and circulation it could enable? How is media practice disruptive of and reperforming the way we do scholarly communication and education? How can a journal reconfigure (the politics of) its own practice and what should a disruptive 'journal' look/sound/feel like? To provide an alternative to the standard journal article, the editors structured the issue around a selection of conversations to emphasise the evolving and collaborative nature of research. The submissions were multimodal, text-based or hybrid; articles, blog posts or books. The conversations openly evolved (from 'drafts' to 'final versions' and beyond) incorporating peer commentary and reviews from invited media practitioners and the audience at large, using hypothesis. The topics of conversation invited were multimodal research (how can we explore criticality with or via media forms?); practice-based methodologies (what methods are most suited to creative practice as research?); performative research (how do the media we use perform their content and vice versa, how we can bring together and align more closely the material form of a publication with its content, what is the agency of our media, and how are we entangled with the media we use?); debating publishing (what could a journal be in a digital environment, what kind of inhibitions do the politics and economics of publishing pose?) and processual research (from iterative publications to evolving scholarship).

MOOCs (Massive Open Online Courses) offer arguably the biggest change in educational practice since the Open University appeared in 1968. MOOCs often report huge registration numbers, but there is considerable debate about business models, assessment, accreditation, completion and quality assurance, and a distinction has emerged between more constructivist, 'disruptive' MOOCs with peer pedagogies and assessments and those that mainly provide digital resources from universities. MOOCs that are in keeping with some of the *third space* network traits under review here include synchronous events, peer-to-peer assessment, crowd sourced content, organic structures, co-constructed and learner-led curricular, with reflective and reflexive learning given prominence.

> Perhaps in a world of bottom-up, with Valve and Steam transforming gaming, eBay and Amazon transforming retail, YouTube and Vine redefining mass broadcasting and so on, the new role for HE might start to look like a vehicle for peer review, an aggregator and a membership based set of diverse communities, rather than the top down QAAed oligopoly that it currently is. (Heppell, 2014)

'Connectivism and Connective Knowledge' was the title of the MOOC usually credited with being the first, in 2008. This combined a cohort paying fees with open access to anyone, as in the DML case above. The proliferation of MOOCs in the near-decade since has developed along two lines, those that emphasise progressive, constructivist modes of learning, closer to our *third space* interests, and those offering mainly a repository for course materials with some conventional interactive aspects. In both trajectories, MOOCs are often developed by well-financed institutions who can use them as a recruitment tool for traditional courses, with international fee-paying students the target market. Variants include distributed open collaborative courses, foregrounding feminist pedagogies, private online courses (free but restricted, selective enrolment) and hybrid MOOCs (see Ross et al. 2014) offering competing models to MOOCs.

The increasing variants of MOOCs among both traditional distance institutions and contact

> institutions have created an urgency to revisit the concept of MOOCs with the view to understanding MOOCs not merely as a disruptive practice, but its potential as a practice for educational transformation in the 21st century. One of the dilemmas regarding MOOCs is that while being a potential tool for democratisation of knowledge, they also present a threat to higher education institutions. MOOCs do have the potential to be disruptive, but generally it is only elite institutions that are financially viable who can consider offering them in the first place, as they are generally expensive to run, especially if conducted in pedagogically sound ways. The two questions these institutions face is about what the future holds for them and whether it will be possible for such poor institutions and MOOCs to coexist. If so, would MOOCs redefine new roles for institutions? (Ng'ambi 2015, p. 452)

Futurelearn, an Open University platform, is a dominant player in the current 'MOOC economy', operating a social learning model. Most courses offered (by accredited providers, often Universities) give participants a series of staged activities, enabled for mobile use, usually with the option for comments but not a shared peer forum as such. Social media networking emerges from participation, but is not a driver. Users requiring certification pay £40, with a new option to take an exam accredited by Pearson for a larger fee. Futurelearn distinguish between active learners (pressing the 'mark as complete' button after finishing a stage), returning learners (continuing and marking more stages as complete) and fully participating learners – completing the assessment (Futurelearn report 15% of participants are in this category). Demographically, a diverse mix of age, gender and educational profiles are enrolling for these MOOCs. However, the nature of participation is less *socially* networked:

> We believe that social learning is really important and we're happy to see that on average 34% of learners are posting comments. Many more will be viewing and learning from those comments. Naturally the level of conversation varies from course to course with the least social ones seeing 24% of learners posting and the most social featuring a very talkative 45%. (Simon Nelson, CEO of Futurelearn, 2014: https://about.futurelearn.com/blog/measuring-our-first-eight-courses/)

Analysis of MOOCs needs to move to a maturation phase, currently our scrutiny does provide rich evidence of some *third space* practices (peer pedagogy, asynchronous 'membraning' between academy knowledge and storytelling from 'publics'), but the majority of interaction is between the student, the technology and the course materials, with less evidence of the rich dialectic that the more progressive pedagogic rationales for MOOCs desire. A productive strand of MOOC activity appears, perhaps unsurprisingly, to be the alternative model of professional development, given the obvious benefits for scale and access among practitioners:

> Educators can use their MOOC experiences to improve their on-campus, blended and mobile teaching by design and by the continuing provision of resources, share and apply knowledge in their own networks. This is authentic, experiential academic development for the future. (Salmon et al. 2015, p. 553)

However, whether this kind of digital third-spacing is transformative or redistribute in the second space depends on the same dynamics as the Teachmeet, the tension between sharing good practice, framed by the existing order of things and the empty signifier of 'the student experience' and changing the relational power dynamics of 'practice' itself.

Case 3 – Learning in/from the Protest Camp

In protest camp media, from Feigenbaum's research (2014) a 'dual adaption' arises in both the use of media and the representational/pedagogic methods at work. The adoption of mainstream media practices is required for visibility, whilst at the same time camps rework media conventions to facilitate voice and diversity. Protest camps appear to fit with *third space* rhetoric since they are either/and, at once 'front and back stage' spaces, protest sites, 'work' and home. In the conceptual framework of ANT, whereby the physical shelter and media hardware are in relational power flows with protestor actants/residents/educators, in acts of translation common definitions and meanings are constructed and representations of the network are negotiated internally and externally. The negotiation of the space itself for both everyday life and a symbolic act requires sustainable and ephemeral infrastructure, as a camp generally co-locates educational spaces with sanitation, communal kitchens, performance areas, medical resources and media production. Media, politics and education are all embodied processes in a network. However, pinning down (as it were) the nature of a protest network and how it differs from some of the other forms of 'open' is important, because protest camps need to balance a tension between open networking and organisational requirements, and so can rarely be entirely horizontal. Ahrne and Brunsson call this 'partial organisation' (2011) and attribute this to the way that camps have both physical space boundaries and open networking impulses.

As a thought collective, the network of physical and digital spaces, whereby these social and cultural politics are circulated, effect those voices that are heard and how. The network spans community spaces, 'squatted' social centres, university campuses, public squares, homes, outdoor camps, union offices and online conferences. These spaces in which political conversation and performative praxes are mobilised are networked as a '*third space* of citizenship':

> While movements have always shared knowledge, in an age of digitally networked communication and high-speed travel, this knowledge now spreads and circulates quickly. As social movement participants and protest campers alike pass on, share, learn from and adapt past experiences, they modify their communication, action, governance and re-creation practices. (Feigenbaum et al. 2014, p. 62)

It is quite straightforward to put ANT to work on protest camps, given the very visible co-relation of people and objects and their networked circulation of sustainability and action. The processes of collaborating to form and maintain the site of protest and the profoundly pedagogic function of negotiating and renegotiating the camp as an entity and an extended (digital) network are in keeping with ANT's focus on how particular relations are formed and configured organically. For learning, how occupants rethink and rearticulate their identities and how they engage with space, framing, and mediated representation both inside and to the outside has great potential to inform constructivist approaches to classroom dynamics, albeit a 'hard sell' to current policymakers.

Case 4 – The Class versus the Department

'The Class' was discussed in Chapter 2 but is a more detailed case in this chapter, so to recap – the project, subsequently published as a book (Livingstone and Sefton-Green 2016) was an ethnography of a group of 13- to 14-year-old secondary school students in a London neighbourhood. The researchers reported on the various ways in which the lives of the participants were/are shaped by pressures of individualisation and how schools, families and the young people themselves attempt to negotiate the meaning of education in the contexts of digital networks and increasing competition. The project was far broader than the use of digital networks, and yet this provides a conduit for many of the other themes addressed – social stratification, globalisation and consumerism, uncertainties about the future, crises of confidence in the family, contested visions of educational goals, anxieties about norms and values:

> By prioritizing links over nodes, the network metaphor offers an alternative to research focused either on particular places (such as the small social worlds of home or school or neighbourhood) or on particular individuals. Mapping the networks within and beyond the class also allows us to see the class not as a mere aggregate of individuals or a collection of girls or boys or wealthy or poor children but as a mesh of interconnections. (Livingstone and Sefton-Green 2016, p. 61)

Findings reveal the use of popular (digital) media culture at school as a way of creating forms of shared and common experiences across a diverse population. At home, the project demonstrated how media are used in the domestic context both to create moments of togetherness but simultaneously to allow for family fragmentation and separateness. The participants were active and engaged users of social media, online gaming and mobile phones, mainly to make face-to-face contact or to stay in touch with friends or to download and consume entertainment. However, little connection between after-school media use and school-defined ('schooled') learning was apparent.

Analysing the networks at work in the participants' lives, as related to their learning, the researchers found the participants' 'ego networks' to be divided between a core group, cliques and a periphery aligned in various ways to networks of migration, with each student's configuration of these clusters being unique. Speculative generalising from the data can suggest this to be a microcosm of contemporary UK society, perhaps more broadly across the connected West – 'they were embedded, more or less securely, within rather tight networks – experienced as coherent small worlds – centred on home, school, locale and diaspora' (p. 83). The digital networks engaged with served, in the main, to reinforce rather than create or disrupt relations of popularity and marginalisation. Energy was being put into maintaining multiple networks and interconnecting social worlds, but there was no evidence that networked digital media was diversifying or deepening connections. Returning to our interest in the first and second spaces, this research is sobering in its account of the lack of *third space* activity, with the schooled concept of learning being profoundly disconnected from everyday life and this being accepted as the order of things by the participants and their parents or carers, the writers being surprised by 'the effort that the school and family put into resisting moves to connect learning across sites' (p. 240) as 'both teachers and young people have a lot invested in keeping their spheres of interest and identity separate and away from the scrutiny of the other' (p. 235).

Summarising the attitudes of the class as 'connected, conservative and competitive', Livingstone and Sefton-Green's key implication for the digital *third space* is the lack of interest by either the school or parents to look beyond their 'immediate gaze', coupled with rich ethnographic observations of how digital mediations of being together in the home were managed to maintain fragile family bonds and bearing witness to the place of the digital in the 'risk society', in terms of both corporate interests in networked learning and the dangers of 'opening the door' to social inequalities. Regarding the *third space* and our 'semi permeable membrane' this risk lies in ignoring the ways in which the physical classroom insists on civility and diversity, to an extent, whilst the network enables hierarchies to pervade or be reconstructed. Following a social network analysis, generating a whole group mapping by eliciting key information from a series of questions about connections and networks, the participants then provided mapping diagrams representing their 'ego networks'.

These served to reveal 'how the seemingly equivalent links in the network had very different qualities' (p. 69). The diagrams enabled attention to different versions of each self and to ways in which participants took different roles within different sub-networks depending on domestic and social circumstances, as well as eliciting critical incidents and micro-narratives, as in this example (NB pseudonym used by the authors):

> Although Aiden's story is really a sadly familiar one of social disadvantage reproducing itself across generations and across sites, the digital media have complicated matters – on the one hand, creating s new space for at times rapid-fire transgressive peer interaction, while on the other hand, undermining long-established boundaries of authority dividing home and school in ways that can become troubling for all concerned. (p. 101)

To start to think about how a similar approach might be used to explore teachers' relationships with professional, personal, social and blended networks, we asked a secondary school department to provide network diagrams and answer a similar suite of questions to those put to 'The Class'. We've attempted something similar, working the media educators – with a different lens each time – for several previous projects, and in each case the potential, as far as it is ever prudent, to generalise out from the findings has been obscured from the 'hyper-intertextual' and 'very digital' identity work encountered among this community. So for this work, we recruited a Physical Education department for two reasons:

1. Because there is an assumption that, whilst this discipline makes considerable use of technology (e.g. for sports science, performance simulation, recording physical activity for assessment), the social practices of PE are reasonably likely to be distinct from popular culture/text-based/screen-based learning
2. Because the role of PE teacher in a secondary school includes a substantial 'out of hours' commitment and duty of care that might make the discipline more obviously 'network-friendly'

As such, our uninitiated entry point to this research was an interest in how the PE department might be well networked but very differently so to our own community of practice (Figs. 6.1 and 6.2)

As with the class, our initial department mapping suggested a fairly consistent profile of institutional and subject discipline relationships and

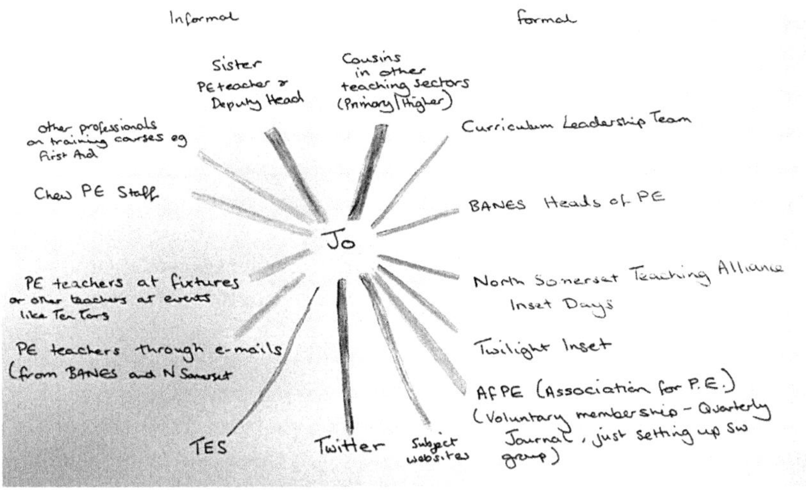

Fig. 6.1 Jo

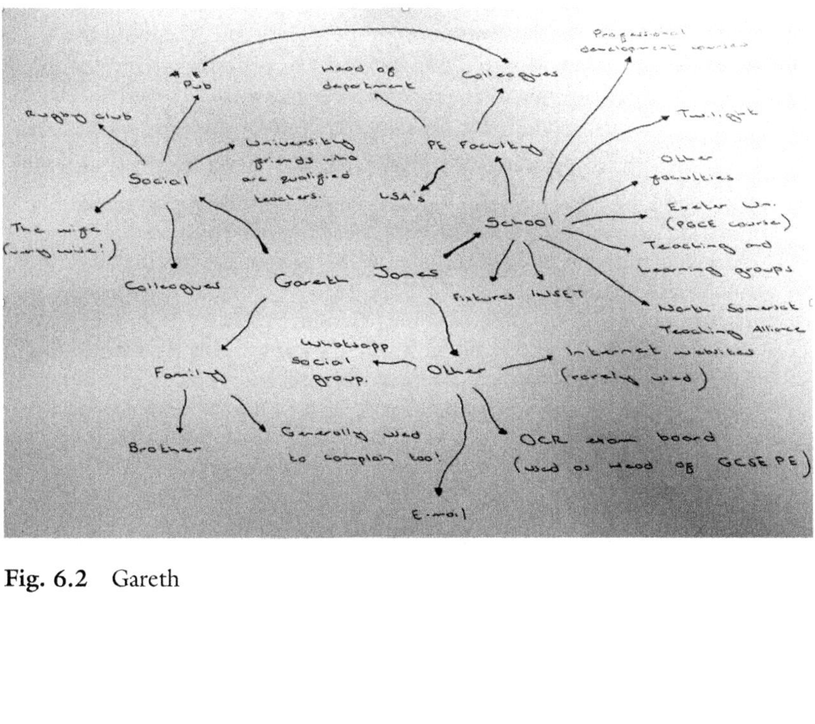

Fig. 6.2 Gareth

network connections, but the individual diagrams provided richer complexity and, as with the younger people, the importance of family connections in managing professional identity. The distinction between home life and school /working life were much more readily, even happily, blurred, than for the students in Livingstone and Sefton-Green's account, but there was scarce evidence of hybrid pedagogy, with a generally clear distinction between functional use of digital resources – either for subject information, exam board updates or using apps to demonstrate skills from viral material, and a different, personal use networks for conversations – 'family and networking overlap due to family sports background. All appear in the real world; none are digital/online.' As with much research of this kind, at times the insulation between the two domains were as much a factor of the school firewall than any habits or strategies for identity performance.

The time-intensive demands of organising and managing team fixtures emerged as a physical world networking opportunity for many, with this often blended across conversations at fixtures and subsequent digital interactions, but rarely was this a coherent network, more often one to one correspondence – participants gave examples of learning about other schools' enrichment activities and helping other departments beginning to teach new qualifications. Where participants were engaged in their own individual professional development or postgraduate research, the most obvious evidence of productive networking was presented, for example:

> I've been looking at the impact of students being withdrawn from normal lessons to go to additional literacy and maths lessons and my cousin who works in HE has sent me some links to networks to help with the theory behind the two sides of the argument. Online/digital world are twitter and TES online and subject websites. The AfPE website has specific areas for members only but they also send out a quarterly journal that has excellent articles in but isn't always practical for practising teachers. Recently I have attended a Regional meeting of AfPE where I was the only PE teacher and the others were mainly academics or retired academics. This is an area that will become more real life as we try to set up a regional committee to spread the information across the SW. This in turn may end up being more digital purely due to the massive area that the SW region has to cover.

Whilst the students in 'The Class' maintained, or accepted, hierarchies in digital networks that had appeared 'flattened' in the classroom, this teacher here observes distinctions between domains and communities – the

HE professional in the family is a resource for accessing new networks, however the professional journal's material reproduces a perceived boundary between theory and practice. This participant, despite holding two postgraduate qualifications, running a large, very successful PE department and now embarking on doctoral research, separates herself from 'academics'. Finally, the affordance of 'the digital' for the regional network is at this point to do with time and space.

The main distinction between the department and the class was around how the professional and the personal/familial is more blurred with much less work being put into keeping these distinct. This is hardly surprising, since a vocation is at the heart of the lifeworld for these participants, and their life-stage and professional status makes such laboured insulation less important and, if it were, far less viable. But that said the family patterning was marked, with every participant reporting significant others in the same profession and in most cases, the same subject area or broader community (i.e. PE teachers, athletes or in other areas of sporting employment).

There was no evidence of any members of the department ever having attended a Teachmeet and an air of scepticism about whether finding the time to do so was possible for a PE teacher doing their fair share of sports fixtures.

The most striking evidence of the 'networked educator' related to physical attendance at an event in London with regional sub-networks, engagement with this group 'allows me to network and speak to teachers from this area and then to present the information to the department with clarity and authority and this in turn helped us to create an assessment package that really focussed on learning and progress, not just putting a label on a child'. However, the network functioning here was largely 'old school', attending an event, meeting people, sharing ideas and applying new approaches through 'cascading' and implementation, accompanied by, but not driven by or reliant on, digital connections. However, evidence of 'blending' arose more around the 'border crossing' nature of educational discourse and the subsequent greater engagement with a multitude of voices:

> social media is online but when the conversations I have with students and colleagues are a result of a "Tweet" the social network, I suppose, becomes the "real world". I think there is no restriction in the networks – at any time they can overlap and interlink. For example, the use of social media can cross over to PE, pastoral, professional discussion etc. Social media makes me more aware of the teaching world and to some degree society. I have learned to be more empathetic with pupils.

Discussion: Not Net Neutral

Disclaimers/justifications – this book is written in the United Kingdom at a particular moment in history and the theoretical preoccupations, political frameworks and cases for discussion are generally located in this particular context. In this chapter, that might be a bigger issue since many of the bolder claims for networks relate to their trans-cultural, border-crossing affordances. This is clearly abundant in new literacy research (see Williams and Zenger 2012) and it's apparent that in many developing countries, networks offer rich resources of hope for students, for example:

> Nepalese youth seem to find the virtual space on the net both an escape from and a better substitute for a frustratingly outmoded educational system, hopeless political crisis and a conservative society. (Sharma and Sharma 2012, p. 161)

and, from Lebanon:

> The student protest video is a literary performance that appropriates globally (networked) available sources and uses them to locate the student population both in relation to a geographical region and in relation to the students of the same university in history – 'AUBites'. (Zenger 2012, p. 38)

Equally, closer to home, there are many rich, productive networks for media literacy *educators* and all offer digital spaces for exchange and collaboration – the United Kingdom Literacy Association, Media Education Association, British Film Institute, Northern Ireland Screen, Creative Scotland, Media Literacy Wales, the English and Media Centre, empirical evidence of either national or cross-cultural educator networks offering *third space* resistance to nation-state policy, ways of being at the contemporary, highly regulated and performative 'chalkface' or the conventions of 'local' classroom practice, are harder to find.

In the section on MOOCs, some notable international players are conspicuously ignored, but for a different reason. Most obviously, we pay no attention to Khan Academy, and skirt around Pearson.

Networks can have transformative power for educators, can form activist thought collectives, can foster *third space* exchanges and ultimately impact on the second space towards a radical fourth space (term used 'under erasure'). The stories media educators have told and the narratives woven by the community about the discipline as a project (see Bolas 2009; Jolls 2011; Lopez 2014; Hobbs 2016, Berger et al. 2015), even a campaign in the case of media literacy, generally give prominence to networking as a vital element in such horizontal discourse formation (Bernstein 1996). But whilst networking as a 'game changer' is social and cultural rather than technological, ANT reminds us that the digital tools and devices for networking are never merely at our service, but are actants with relational power:

> Without forgetting that people are networked, far from equilibrium systems, we can understand some organizational changes, whatever the public narratives used to legitimize them, as emergent in a back and forth process in which the devices we make, becoming elements of our environments and articulations with the world, remake us. (Nespor 2012, p. 20)

On the one hand, the rhetoric of transmedia networked education is compelling, especially when aligned with a 'maker culture' pedagogy and practiced in liminal (third) spaces, as partly exemplified by the Lego creativity network, which participants testify 'strikes a balance between being guided by disciplinary instructions and inspired by the new creative new possibilities discovered by thinking across traditional boundaries and objects of study' (Mittell 2015, p. 272), as does the lead protagonist in the *Lego Movie*, who comes to balance 'instruction manual conformity and freeform creative practice' (ibid).

But on the other hand, a decade on, we're still 'waiting for the revolution' (Buckingham 2007). In his 'Beyond Technology', Buckingham's reflections still chime with those of Selwyn (2014) as the nouns (tools) have changed but the verbs (ways of being) and the structural forces around us have not. His parting call, related to McLuhan, on the potential for networks to produce different arrangements of social power, was that 'we need to stop thinking merely in terms of technology, and start thinking afresh about learning, communication and culture' (2007, p. 183). This is what we're doing in this book, but our narrative turning full circle back here is telling.

More of a concern is the lack of a sophisticated, nuanced discourse for talking about the 'use value' of technology for learning and the sociological illiteracy that pervades public sphere discussion of the 'digital divide'. 2016 OECD research (see Coughlan 2016), presenting data from 40 countries in Europe, Asia and South America found that in many countries wealthy and poor students spent similar amounts of time online, but more affluent teenagers 'were much more likely to use the internet for learning rather than games', with the criteria for 'educational use' being 'gathering information and reading news'. As gaming is more likely to be connected, networked engagement and under this criteria, educational use appears more solitary and related to 'pull media (1.0)' this OECD approach appears to be entirely disconnected from the field of educational research into participatory culture, affinity, new civics and transmedia literacy practices.

Returning to our key lines of enquiry – what evidence have we found here of networks in the (digital) *third space* fostering networking literacies towards radical pedagogic and, ultimately, redistributive outcomes? Activist thought collectives are potentially mobilised around Teachmeets, in MOOC spaces and in the feedback loop from negotiated, constructivist protest epistemologies. In all cases the fluid hybridity of these blended networks – people, physical spaces, interaction, machines and devices, objects, virtual spaces and asynchronous sharing – can we well-judged through the lens of ANT. But no network in itself is transformative. Whilst it's no surprise that the powerful will use networks to reproduce relations of inequality and hierarchies, a recurring, and sobering, finding here is that our 'networked publics' actually put a great deal more effort than we might think into keeping things apart and as they are. As always, it's complicated, and it depends.

> A local male carrier can weaken a centralized network of imperial power by superimposing another, more local network, and a woman poet can retreat to the boundaries of her bedroom to block the encroachment of some very tiresome social networks in favour of a richer, more expansive world. (Levine 2015, p. 131)

CHAPTER 7

Cultural Studies Goes to Not-School: Digital Struggles

The disagreements about education's emancipatory possibilities have largely been contained within an assumption about the basic validity of the modern project of progress. The distinction facing education in the postmodern moment is the oppressiveness of the humanism and rationality which legitimise educational practices. In other words, the parameters of the debate are questioned and the very possibility of education providing its espoused goals are thrown into doubt.

(Usher and Edwards 1994, p. 226)

This third space involves a simultaneous coming and going in a borderland zone between different modes of action. A prerequisite for this is that we must believe that we can inhabit these different sites, making each a space of relative comfort. To do so will require inventing creative ways to cross perceived and real 'borders'. The third space is thus a place of invention and transformational encounters, a dynamic in-between space that is imbued with the traces, relays, ambivalences, ambiguities and contradictions, with the feelings and practices of both sites, to fashion something different, unexpected.

(Bhabha 1994, p. 406)

What digitally enabled frameworks of education are negotiating different ways to make meaning and how are these informed by *third space* principles in 'not-school' contexts? Is not-school a *third space*, and if so how

J. Potter, J. McDougall, *Digital Media, Culture and Education*,
DOI 10.1057/978-1-137-55315-7_7

does 'the digital' transform its focus from the local to, potentially, the global? This chapter will provide a theoretical lens to assess digital media education's impact on the broader not-school project as a social practice of 'horizontal' meaning making rather than a 'vertical' regime of value/legitimation. This chapter will be framed by a consideration of the implications of digital networks and *third spaces* for the explicitly pedagogic legacy of the Birmingham Contemporary Centre for Cultural Studies, its development in the 'seminal' *Cultural Studies Goes to School* (Buckingham and Sefton-Green (eds) and recent revisiting of these approaches in an NLS context but also with a conviction to recast a political lens, towards not only the usual suspects – technological determinism and reductive functional notions of literacies and deficits – but towards a deeper awakening from the tendencies of what Adam Curtis has termed the dream-state of 'hyper-normalisation': *Over the past forty years, politicians, financiers and technological utopians, rather than face up to the real complexities of the world, retreated. Instead, they constructed a simpler version of the world, in order to hang on to power. And as this fake world grew, all of us went along with it, because the simplicity was reassuring.* (Curtis, BBC 2016)

NOT-SCHOOL (ANALOGUE)

The term 'not-school' is misleading in the sense that it's often not really 'not'. Not-school education is typically funded and provided by accredited professionals in either out of school (but related to) or community youth provision or after-school as 'enrichment' – in other words, in extension to, as opposed to alternative to the mainstream curriculum, especially in the case of the latter which usually happen in the school, just outside of the mandatory timetabled hours and thus act as hybrid of education and childcare for working parents. Learning contexts are often arts, media or sports related and as such in the United Kingdom at least, fill a gap where these areas have been structurally marginalised in the national curriculum. The sustainability question clearly arises when we consider that many not-school projects are grant-funded and a distinction between provision in the United Kingdom, the USA and the EU emerges:

> From an international perspective, that this divergence and diversity of funding and organization exists within the local ecologies of educational programs is startling, and there are very few, if any, comparative international studies and thus very little understanding of what might comprise the key elements in any

> structural analysis. In addition, by definition, funders (private, philanthropic, and public) often have aims, ambitions, and obligations both to their stakeholders and to the young people they may be supporting.... One major source of tension is about initiatives that are led and developed as bottom-up projects – those that have been initiated through grassroots efforts but have then sought funding from funders who may have different agendas from the project's founders and who seek to impose these more formal metrics of achievement. The fact that organizations are 'not-school' however much they operate as an image of mainstream schools in terms of system, structure, and discipline doesn't of course give them coherence as a sector or homogeneity in institutional form or scope. (Sefton-Green 2013, pp. 7–8)

The historical objectives of not-school have involved in-between news and a focus on subjectivity aligned with civic virtues, often assumed to be facilitated by radical social pedagogies (although there is insufficient evidence of this). Whilst organic, community-based models for success and evaluation are put in opposition to formal school-based grading and metrics, there is often crossover between. Pre-Internet, the kinds of not-school projects accounted for in accounts of formative work tend to have been organised in youth centres, arts venues, public and civic sector contexts, and in cultural studies' frame of reference, can be pulled together around the theme of a reflexive 'symbolic creativity', from Paul Willis – 'it is here, in this interlocking of human beings and cultural codes and of forms, that there is the possibility of "being surprised"' (Willis 1980, p. 92). Learning is organised around community, civic activity or from interests, as opposed to specific ages or sectors, or 'local ecologies' in the physical, pre-digital phase. The pedagogic attitude, combining Vygotskian and Papertian approaches in the main, pervading across the diverse provision is resistant to any deficit model of youth, in not-school, identity work, often semiotic, facilitates critical reflection. Converged conceptions of multiple literacies, a horizontal discourse of collaborative pedagogies and the valuing of public sphere authenticity – as opposed to more contrived 'real world' school projects – as highly legitimate learning – all align not-school with the *third space*.

Hip-hop provides a seemingly tangential, even indulgent, 'case' which justifiably provides a more lateral example of a not-school *third space* – 'Rappers and MCs had this sense that they were teachers, that they were schooling you. Here is what they never taught you in school. Here is who we are, here is where we come from. The idea that music can give you a sense of consciousness and root you in a sense of self' (Rodney P, BBC 2016).

Hip-hop culture, operating for many of its advocates as a belief-system offering identity negotiation and resistance to dominant and oppressive ideologies, consists of five elements, of which one is epistemological (Graffiti Art, Turntablism, Breakdancing, MC-ing, Knowledge). The fifth element is made up of knowledge, history and culture. (see https://hiphoped4youth.com/2016/08/19/5-elements-of-hip-hop/), in this way being a person in hip-hop culture fits with Bhabha's (1994) conception of the *Third space* in post-colonial education, it's primary purpose being 'For elaborating strategies of selfhood, that initiates new signs of identity, and innovative sites of collaboration, and contestation, in the act of defining the idea of society itself' *(p. 1–2, cited in* Benson 2010, *p. 555).*

That Hip-Hop Education has a sustained presence in the American not-school genealogy is clear, often framed by preventative and rehabilitative civic objectives for urban black youth. However, the pedagogic status *of* hip-hop, as opposed to the use of hip-hop as a context for informal and community-based education, presents a compelling, lesser stated case, for understanding hip-hop textual practice *itself* as a *third space*:

> Hip Hop is a site of Pedagogy is to live in this dialogic space between dangers and possibilities. It is here that resides a 'pedagogy of jouissance', which is introduced as a 'third ear' (Lacou-Labarthe 1989) as mattering map and a pedagogical framework that links Hip Hop, identity investment, the process of critical teaching and learning. (Ibrahim, in Alim, Ibrahim and Pennycook 2009, p. 242)

In keeping with our premise in this book that learning in and through digital media is itself a form of popular culture, and thus subverting the cultural studies insulation of the discipline practices from the textual 'matter', proponents of *third space* hip-hop practices converge hip-hop as popular culture with its utility as a discourse community with intersections for academic and critical literacies and the hegemonic interplay between hip-hop and education (see Au 2005):

The distinction between co-opting hip-hop 'funds of knowledge' *into* the semi-permeable space of the progressive *third space* and understanding the hip-hop culture as always-already a *third space* in itself, is key:

> Hip Hop as cultural discourse constitutes one of the principal social communities that have points of convergence for the teacher and student, thereby serving as a discursive field for (re)negotiating meaning and participation in the lived spaces of school. The fifth element of knowledge of self,

> speaks to a Freirean critical consciousness of the social conditions of the oppressed and how one is historically located, with the liberatory goal of positive social transformation. (Hafner 2012, p. 49)

Of course, we acknowledge that the idea of hip-hop – and other subcultural manifestations of *third space* – only work as a neat and tidy case if we operate with a binary between the spaces which is always under erasure:

> Although we have chosen to align the concept of first space with that of the everyday world that is close to or common to people, the naming of what counts as first or second space is arbitrary; one could easily reverse these labels to suggest that first space is often that space which is privileged or dominant in social interaction, whereas second space is that which is marginalized. What is critical to our position is the sense that these spaces can be reconstructed to form a third, different or alternative, space of knowledges and discourses. (Moje et al. 2004, p.41)

Along with creative/media contexts for not-school, other negotiated modalities for mentoring and engagement include sport as a catalyst for tacking disaffection (Deuchar 2009). In Glasgow, initiatives across and between the two major football clubs, the City Council, careers services and the Princes Trust provides an example of the multiagency angle often operating around not-school, which we discuss later with regard to 'beyond school' and in terms of broader notions of capability from earlier chapters, converging efficacy, social capital as 'communal'. It is too early to say yet, but we'd anticipate similar arrangements of *third space* – whether utilising sports or media production, or both – being put to work to support people arriving in the United Kingdom from Calais' 'The Jungle', in particular unaccompanied children, towards 'increasing both personal and communal forms of social capital, strengthening trust and reciprocity between young citizens and their civic institutions and promoting shared cultural values' (Deuchar 2009, p. 137).

Where the transition from more 'old school' creative arts and media production contexts for not-school to the digital, networked phase is clearest is in the focus on voice and efficacy. Arguably, for our immediate interests in this book, the proliferation of media production and arts enquiry-based learning in UK schools and colleges in recent decades is an example of the *third space* of not-school informing the second space of formal education, as opposed to a hegemonic incorporation. However, the grounding of both civic engagement, reflective identity work and well-being of the self, achieved through prominence of relational pedagogy – the bonds between students, adults and peers – might be at risk in digital not-school where the pedagogic rationale is obscured by more instrumental network practices and working with the self in the community is undermined by a more neoliberal idea of the global individual. For discussion.

Of course, the transition from analogue to digital not-school is contested. It is perhaps in this reconfiguration of *third spaces* that we can see an interesting, but from our perspective worrying attempt by parents to regain the kinds of cultural control in the first space which have arguably been eroded in the second space in the 'digital age', as 'the school is no longer in control of the socialization and enculturation of children – if indeed it ever was. For better or rose, new popular cultural practices have come more and more to challenge the legitimacy of schooling, and hence its claim to sustain established forms of social power' (Buckingham 2007, p. 97).

In the primary phase, many schools are enlisting the extended 'wrap-around' services of community hubs, where members of a 'busy parents network' offer peer-to-peer support and a range of workshops with parents and children working together. Whereas the kinds of Digital Families community work described elsewhere in this book look towards a kind of holistic 'digital capability', others – often in more affluent areas where more conservative values about parenting and academic activity may pervade – operate with more of a 'tune out' discourse, with emphasis on controlling 'screen time': *The good news is that we can get back in charge as parents in this area so that screen activity becomes a positive activity rather than a negative element in family life* (Mullen 2016, p. 11 and see; Janis-Norton 2015 – this text appears to be influential in this kind of contemporary not-school space, whereas the research-informed work on the same topic by; Livingstone (LES 2016) which advises parents to move beyond the obsolete concept of 'screen time' altogether, which we might observe as indicative of the kind of dream-like simplicity addressed at the outset of this chapter, is ignored. There is a great irony here, as it can be argued that the foundational non-school 'templates' from its emerging genealogy are often framed by forms of media production that may have been analogue/early digital, as opposed to networked-screen-based, but nonetheless carry more apparent crossover into digital community learning than the 'tune out' methodology understands. As well as hip-hop and Soep's community radio work (which appears in accounts of both 'old school not-school' and digital *third space*), Steven Goodman's pioneering youth media work in New York (2003), manifestly and strategically alternative to what he termed the 'factory system' of American schooling, despite being entirely framed by watching, analysing, making and producing stories for screens, is heralded as hugely successful and influential mode for 'third arena' work between school and family:

> Policymakers, practitioners and philanthropists see such programs as an effective way to accomplish a variety of goals, including meeting children's needs for safe and environments and supervision from caring adults, bolstering academic achievement; supporting overall youth development; and supporting youth engagement in community development. (Goodman 2003, p. 102)

These objectives would appear to be paradoxically very similar to those of the 'tune out' version of not-school currently proliferating in suburban *third spaces.*

Digital Not-school

In the USA, a range of digitally networked media activism is claimed (Jenkins 2016) as a kind of civic pedagogy in itself that, whilst never labelled 'not-school' appears to offer a sense of transition of symbolic creativity work from the analogue. The cultural is not only the gateway to the political but, perhaps indirectly, to the educational. Learning arises from culturally relevant critical pedagogy combined with digital transmedia production and reflexive, imaginative participation of individuals in communities in practice – learning as participation. Combining Willis on symbolic creativity (or 'common culture') with Couldry on the material conditions for voice (2010), the digital *third space* is where personal storytelling connects with civic action in a mode of (bigger) community participation which certainly echoes the pedagogic objectives of not-school.

A justification for converging not-school and this new digital mode of informal civic learning is offered by Soep (2016), whose community radio work is offered as a not-school case study by Sefton-Green (2013) and also in Jenkins' collection. For Soep, the 'business of figuring out' (291) is shared by analogue media projects and digital networks across both modes of what we are calling the *third space*. However, and importantly in avoiding the 'naïve advocacy' Sefton-Green warns against, new risks are abundant:

> We don't yet know enough about how to practice culturally relevant critical pedagogy from a precarious position, where self-disclosure, expression and

> community inquiry can be high-risk activities, and when 'context collapse' can leave makers ill prepared to face life-altering consequences (e.g. deportation) and possible backlash (e.g. waves of cruel online comments). (Soep 2016, p. 308)

As not-school attempts, with difficulty, to disentangle its modes of learning and relational practices from schooled learning and attendant metrics for progress, so does the contemporary manifestation of this in transmedia participation seek, also with difficulties, to challenge the version of participation at work in corporate discourses:

> Critics of participatory politics often see participation as simply another term for co-optation, implying that participating in a neoliberal economy only empowers corporate forces controlling the pipelines through which these new messages flow. Rather, we describe participation in terms of the ability to forge a sense of collective voice and efficacy through larger networks that work together to bring about change. (Jenkins et al. 2016, p. 41)

A series of shared approaches bring together these examples of current not-school as digital activism (we are claiming these here whether formally pedagogical or by our inference). Narrative circulation for a kind of voice hitherto excluded; transmedia ways of learning, talking and sharing across modes; the notion of a 'civic imagination' whereby key stakeholders facilitate the ability to project how change would happen, look like, feel like; enabling devices to enable 'lifeworld' skills to cross the membrane into the public sphere (similar to the curational pedagogy we discuss elsewhere in this book) and the explicit connecting of the educational to the political – converging the 'media strategies, creative vision, organizational activities and informal learning practices through which American youth are conducting politics in the early 21st century' (2016, p. 56).

Case studies in circulation are captured by Jenkins' authors but already in the public domain. Invisible Children/Kony 2012 is reframed here as a *third space* (our words) between digital circulation and subsequent 'real world' actions. The Harry Potter Alliance, Imagine Better and Nerdfighters are spoken to with regard to the affordances of fan activism as *third space* between schooled literacy and the shared but more plural languages of popular culture as they translate into 'fannish civics' through 'cultural acupuncture' (57). At the time of writing, as Donald Trump remains a potential US President, American Muslim Youth offers a compelling example of a more precarious *third space* between authentic voice as counter-script to mainstream media representation and digital surveillance. The DREAM Act, a campaign to bring undocumented youth into formal education offers perhaps the clearest version of the in-between, transitional mode of not-school, except that the drive to become educationally 'official' is entirely grassroots, so in this sense this is the opposite of the formal school culture reaching the disengaged, exclusion from education due to legal status is translated into a learning motivation, a further paradox:

> Inequalities in digital media literacy and access to digital technologies have raised concern that the 'digital divide' is widening, especially among racial and lower income communities. On the other hand, there is growing evidence that members of marginalized communities – especially youth – are adopting digital media tools and skills to empower themselves, build social movements, and participate politically. (Gamber-Thompson and Zimmerman 2016, p. 193)

Likewise, Students for Liberty offers a rich case for the 'digital not-school *third space*', on the one hand echoing community activist principles for symbolic creativity as a political, educational and cultural mode for political action, but at the same time making use of social media 'against the grain'.

In the United Kingdom, one quite different manifestation of Not-school as a discrete digital intervention has origins in Ultralab (Heppell 2014) and arose from the recognition that substantial numbers of young students are excluded from institutional education (school refusals, school phobics, school exclusions, children in long-term hospital care, profoundly physically impaired resident at home); the cost of these students and their fragmentary support structures is vast and, typically, their loss to the economy is even more expensive and the potential of on-line learning communities to be viable, social and effective. The first model relied on the recruitment of retired teachers to contribute, part time and online from their own homes. This early prototype of 'virtual learning' sought to combine social justice objectives with economic efficiency and to explore:

The extent to which we can bring children back into mainstream learning by the employment or HE stage, or provide an alternative route to, for example, non-standard HE delivery or employment (Fig. 7.1)

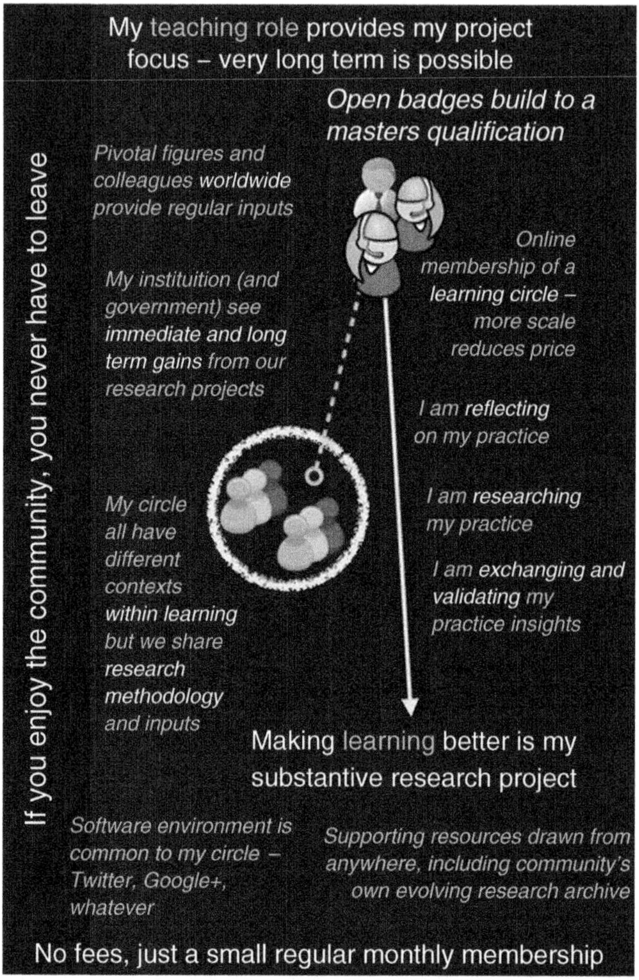

Fig. 7.1 Masters diagram (Stephen Heppell)

The extent to which we can use technology to offer multiple media types so that our learners are not just text driven (since we might assume that their exclusion has been reflected in impaired textual prowess).

A careful and honest analysis of the model of cost and returns with a view to illustrating viability.

> The extent to which the different communities that our students would be drawn from can make progress through the virtual nature of the school where they could not progress with a conventional institution, for whatever reasons.
>
> (source: http://history.notschool.net/origins.html)

Fast forward 30 years and the first architects of Not-school are developing a model for a digital professional development community (Fig 7.1) which works at Master's degree level but without an end point, using the analogy of a gym membership with a monthly fee. The comparison is rich, as the Not-school cohort are at the furthest point in the engagement continuum to the target membership of Learnology, given that the latter are described as being enthusiastic educational professionals seeking an online community for 'in work' R&D, many of whom already hold postgraduate qualifications (Fig. 7.1):

> This has been a long journey. My first B.Ed. degree programme for the many professionals in the 80s coming into schools from the computing industry ended up as an on-line community because 'they could' and because they all got jobs so quickly that they needed to move away for work. Later, after many other on-line communities, we put a large cohort of 21,000 UK headteachers on-line. The collegiality, the exchanges, the parity of esteem of contribution, were all pretty seductive. It worked reaffirmingly well. But so many learning professionals on courses leading to postgraduate qualifications kept saying 'I don't want it to stop', or 'I've learned so much alongside my peers that I don't think I could be as good at work without their cameraderie', and so on. And now we have: the technology, very obvious need, the sense that so many value learning; it seemed like the perfect time to rethink professional development and learning professionals' research wherever they are.
>
> (Heppell 2016, source: http://rubble.heppell.net/learnology/index.html)

The Learnology community is intended to be at the same time a Master's degree and an online community characterised by peer support and open badged recognition for continual progress. Over time (not constrained by registration periods), the badges accumulate to the accredited postgraduate qualification. In a sense, this potentially infinite community is the flipside to 'Not-school', transcending and transgressing institutional borders, not to 're-engage' the disconnected but to extend engagement of the already connected. Students (in this case professionals) will be a member of a learning circle, using different software platforms to collaborate ('some maybe through Google, some a mix of blog and Twitter, some might share a Sharepoint on-line world'). These circles are strategically diverse, bringing together members from two or more distinct contexts.

This is far from an organic, bottom up intervention, indeed the same deregulated economy that enables the 'free school' is adopted for the creation of a neither an arguably hegemonic sub-set of formal education or a radical counter-script version of 'anti-school' but instead another layer of 'in-between' education, albeit in a very different, seemingly apolitical frame. The community's participants are profoundly on the *inside* (of formal education), but at the same time the design of learning clusters, 'free range' mix of contexts, use of organic, hybrid spaces and the inference of identity objectives for a broader socialization experience for community members appear to share aspects of the *third space*. It's complicated.

The University of the Third Age is on the one hand difficult to conceptualise as a *third space*, since its students are retired and thus in most cases entirely operating in a first space, but on the other hand, the way in which it's pedagogic and informally academic hierarchies are negotiated is framed entirely by the ghost of, or past lived experience of the second space. Uo3A is, like many not-school cases, a movement rather than a curriculum, international and offering both physical, virtual and blended models with an organic, peer-to-peer approach to learning design and distinctions between dominant models emerging in different countries. In the United Kingdom, engagement is framed by participants being their 'third age', after the second age of full employment/parenting. So any direct parallel between *third space* and third age is problematic, since *third space* is an in-between membrane between first and second whereas third age is after first and second. But on closer scrutiny, participant accounts consistently observe first age/second space (schooled) knowledge and cultural capital hierarchies emerging in the process of deciding on curriculum, who teaches and 'what counts' as legitimate/peripheral participation in the pedagogic process. The model of the learning circle or cooperative is profoundly *third space*, even the use of the term 'university' is derived here from the medieval definition of a gathering or co-operative, where 'everyone teaches and everyone learns'. However, according to participant accounts, the vast majority – and in some Uo3As all – of teaching is done by members with either a teaching background, degree level academic capital or other forms of cultural capital – for example published authors, exhibiting artists, trained accountants – or employment/ professional experience. There is very little evidence of a more transgressive 'knowledge exchange' in the Rancierian sense. Writing about Uo3A in Poland, Marcinkiewicz (2011) describes:

> Undeniably the University of the Third Age significantly affects the quality of life of its students. The U3A activates them all intellectually, socially and physically affecting their ability to cope in difficult situations, thus minimizing the danger of social exclusion. Nevertheless, if the university wants to better counteract marginalization it should effectively impact on society by changing the image of an elderly person. This effect can be achieved by the organization of conferences, publication of scientific and popular work, volunteering, or working with the local community. Please also note that most people who attend to the U3A are of sound physique and educated, so are the intellectual elite of the older generation. Therefore, activities should focus on ways to reach out to the rest of Polish seniors, because only in this way you can talk about really counteracting marginalization among the elderly. One solution is the creation of the Third Age Universities in small towns and villages.

Like many of the co-creation projects discussed in previous chapters and in keeping with some of the configurations of 'not-school' under review here, the social and educational objectives of Uo3A appear to be inclusive as a response to marginalisation but limited in their capacity to transgress more far-reaching and systemic hierarchies around knowledge, efficacy and representation of people in relation to learning, more successful in extending the second space – in this case by age rather than stratification – than disrupting its order of things. Uo3A is justifiably celebrated as a neo-Freirian model of *Critical Educational Gerontology* (Formosa 2000) and yet Freirian notions of 'banking education' are often undermined by the relatively exclusive nature of the participation:

> It is true that the U3E can be attended by any older person. But what's the use of attending university lectures if one does not have the necessary background? You have to remember that a large percentage of older persons are illiterate. A larger percentage are illiterate in the English language. It is impossible for such older persons to participate fully in the U3E. Non-educated older persons would find it very difficult to understand the lectures. (Male U3E member, cited in Formosa 2000, p. 323)

Two obstacles are presented here, the more straightforward perception – accurate or not – of a language barrier, but also the 'habitus clash' encountered by those lacking 'the necessary background'.

So does digital offer a way out of this paradox for Uo3A?

The Virtual University of the Third Age is also open to anyone but aims to reach in particular those with engagement by necessity (e.g. health or other access issues) rather than learning preference. The stated pedagogic principle is participative learning and each learning group is organised by a voluntary interest groups 'coordinator' or 'moderator'. There is some compelling evidence that the 'second spaced' hierarchies from the face-to-face Uo3A cases are less consistently carried over to the virtual networks for two reasons. Firstly, the presence of some 'technophobia' means the model of expertise required to co-ordinate is a hybrid of epistemology and technical confidence, so peer learners are more relaxed about conventional pedagogic 'entitlements', and secondly the participants in virtual Uo3A communities are often carrying less cultural capital and therefore may be less equipped to judge the credentials of co-ordinators. The micro-politics of this are, of course complex, whether the virtual space is offering a more transgressive, Wengerian/Freirian model or a lower-capital modality will depend on each case, but there does appear to be a richer digitally enabled shift in the pedagogic relation between the two modes than in the other not-school cases or the MOOCs we reviewed in earlier chapters. Interestingly, rather than a tidy 'habitus transfer', complexity and idiosyncratic preferences around technology and ways of working appear to be embraced by participants in virtual Uo3A, as this co-ordinator illustrates:

> In the past ten years I have become interested in the social consequences of computing, especially in the impact of the Internet. And here I find that there is a divide in people's attitudes to it, although not always in ways I would have expected. I am especially interested in the reactions of people in our age group. Audrey and I have met people whose attitudes range from gleeful enthusiasm, almost addiction, to: 'We have one, but don't use it much'. And: 'I wouldn't have one in the house'. The strange thing is that the viewpoints have no pattern to them. We know couples where the woman is the keen surfer and the man is not – and the other way round. We have friends whose backgrounds would have made them naturals but who aren't, and others whose unexpected keenness and knowledge bowls us over. You could argue that this is just a social observation, and of not much consequence. But I believe that it is important. Although the focus of new technology is on people half or even a third of our ages, it is clear that (a)

> the Third Agers are a group to be reckoned with, and (b) there is too much happening in the wired, or indeed wireless world for us to miss out. (Carpenter 2006, p. 6)

Prison education appears to be an obvious and unique *third space* 'case' – in that when the institution is permanently 'home', the first and second spaces are inevitably collapsed (although a precise modelling of this would need to take into account the length of sentence and therefore the significance of the remembered/deferred first space, and also the predominance of reoffending and institutionalisation of prisoners). However, attempts to reconfigure this in the digital/virtual domain have been less successful than we might expect. On the one hand, the technological barrier in some countries, including the United Kingdom, that denies prisoners access to the Internet, along with funding restrictions:

> As a system, it might seem tailor-made for people stuck in a cell for hours every day but, according to Jones, a host of barriers must be overcome for a prisoner to have any chance of success. Even to apply to study at level 3 or above, she says, prisoners must first get permission from everyone in the prison involved in their daily routine, and the course must fit with their personal development plan. Once accepted – and having managed to secure funding – prison restrictions can frustrate even the most motivated learner. (Tickle 2012, p. 1)

On the other hand, the pedagogic model underpinning 'real world' prison education has been variably translated into virtual practice. The Virtual Campus project (Kendall and Hughes 2011) invited teachers and tutors from prisons in five UK regions to work collaboratively to produce a new suite of tutor produced, sector-specific and context-tested resources; to train up Virtual Pedagogy Champions to cascade experience and expertise and build across the regions; to establish regional Pedagogy Champion network groups; develop an e-resource to support and sustain connectivity beyond the lifetime of the project; develop a bespoke, context-specific content authoring tool and a teacher-led framework for working effectively with the virtual campus. Some collaborative pedagogies were harnessed, for example co-created storyboarding for managing the learning design process and thinking through the stages of the learning to include assessment for learning. However, an interesting 'about take' emerged in the conclusion that the translation of conventional learning plans into virtual activities was much less representative of progressive 'third spacing' for prisoners than a seemingly more orthodox Reading Plan intervention in prisons, commissioned by the Sutton Trust (Hopkins and Kendall 2017). The Reading Plan is a peer-delivered programme through which prisoners support and mentor other prisoners to improve their reading, usually outside the formal structures of 'Education' or offender learning services and without the intervention of professional teachers. The kind of space prison provides for literacy is, of course, unique and this situates prisoners, as well as other members of the community, in very particular ways. Prison ethnographer Anita Wilson has applied our pivotal concept – *third space literacy* – along with 'educentricity' to map prisoners' relationships with literacies and education to the prison context:

> On the one hand, prison tries to push prisoners into an institutional space which prioritizes institutional literacy, while, on the other hand, prisoners resist by defending their personal space with contextualized literacies that carry the traces of outside world practices and activities. From what appears to be a no-win situation, the tension is resolved by the selective amalgamation and colonization of institutional space and situated literacy/ies which both constitute and are constitutive of a third space. (Wilson 2000, p. 70)

The focus of the reading scheme was twofold, firstly, to provide change orientations, prisoner participants acquiring gains in relation to a variety of reading practices, including both those that enable them to navigate prison life more successfully (reading canteen menus, legal letters and information leaflets) and those that support links with the outside (reading letters from friends and relatives). Secondly, to move on to opening up opportunities for reflection on being (*who am I?*) and doing (*how do I want to be in the world?*) which in turn lead to new possibilities for action: being more independent, exercising agency through decision making, working towards a future goal. This resonates with the capability model we explored previously in this book:

> Whilst these new capacities will not solve the structural relations that will inevitably continue to position Learners and Mentors in social and material ways on release they may have the potential to support greater resilience, the beginnings of desistence identity building and a re-adjusted educentricity. (Hopkins and Kendall 2017, p. 91)

In working across both the virtual campus and the reading plan projects, Kendall observes that, perhaps surprisingly, both *third space* literacies – and adopting Wilson's term, the 'educentric turn' – were enabled more in the 'fixed second space' (our words) of prison classrooms than in a virtual environment. The face-to-face reading mentorship scheme enabled prisoners to build new social identities that were meaningful and useful, whereas the virtual translation of conventional learning activities lacked this 'educentric' potential.

> Where education in the conventional sense – a serious business, intent of raising standards, core curriculum and identifiable outcomes – moves to a place where 'teachers treat you like individuals'... 'where I can blether with my mates'... and as a place 'to get away from cockroaches'. It has less to do with learning and more to do with the maintenance of a social identity. (Wilson 2000, p. 199)

Gerodimos and Mihailidis, within an over-arching account of civic media (Gordon and Mihailidis 2016), spend time working through the pedagogic approach used at the Salzburg Academy on Media and Global Change. Since 2007, the academy has gathered more than 600 young people and 100 scholars, educators and practitioners from around the world to engage in the development and implementation of projects that advocate for social change in local communities across the world and adopts approaches from multimedia storytelling and comparative research to model the teaching and learning of media as an act of civic engagement:

> Over the past ten years, we have seen our case studies implemented in rural schools in sub-Saharan Africa, and we have led media action projects in rural communities in Mexico and in the buffer zone of Cyprus. We have implemented active storytelling projects in Slovakia, used games for development in Egypt, and launched a project on digital literacy and human rights in Beirut. Out of this work we have identified a framework that guides a pedagogy of civic media. (2016, p. 383)

This framework moves learners through three steps – (1) Listen: *how do citizens encounter and make sense of diverse voices? And how do they process stimuli so as to develop their identities and open up to change?* (b) Share: *how can young people articulate their voices so as to reach out to the community and make an impact?* (c) Act: *in what ways and through which means can citizens take meaningful action to address problems of inequality, injustice, and lack of freedom?*

The key distinction with this framework is that digital media is not the platform for civics but instead civic digital media is the action, the means of production, with the Salzburg workshops as an incubation, but as the participants are in 'summer school' mode, they are also in a *third space* between the more commodified educational context of their 'second school' university studies and their 'first space' desire for social justice, perhaps. On the other hand, a substantial disclaimer is that participation is via second space scholarships – reliant on 'good standing' or outstanding performance, in either case an ambassadorial identity is constructed – or via self-financing, in which case these change agents are far from the margins and a philanthropic discourse may pervade.

Laing (2010) proposes alternative model to the use of virtual not-school learning to connect people across sociocultural boundaries by advocating a virtual learning solution for black male students in the USA that would cut across geographical and structural barriers but be bound by gender and ethnicity, in order to foster efficacy and learning potential against the grain of alienating schooled practices. However, of greatest interest here is the transparent negotiation of the legal/governance contexts for such an intervention:

> What are the legal issues for an all-black boys' virtual learning space that will be run through a public or private school? If the central organization of the virtual learning space is public with federal funds, it will be subjected to laws and policies by the government, including the Civil Rights Act. If, however, the virtual learning space is run privately, then it will be subject to relatively less scrutiny and oversight. I therefore propose that the virtual learning space be a hybrid and run through either a summer bridge program or community based organization that is not fully public. This way, this type of environment will not be subjected to strict laws set forth by the federal government relating to how funds could be used, what student membership would look like, and how it will be run. The potential benefits of having a virtual learning space /classroom that is combined public and private will not be fully restricted; and membership, albeit online, could be made up of all-black males, meeting the objective of helping to improve their public education. Once this virtual space has been tested thoroughly, the environment can then be extended to other marginalized groups of students. (Laing 2010, p. 224)

So far we've reviewed a range of analogue and digital examples of a very broad, mixed economy of what we think about when we talk about not-school. The theoretical approach to this has been a loose fusion of *third space* educational theory and sociocultural and political analysis of each 'case' as transgressive and redistributive in relation to schooled learning and literacy practices. Now we will apply a more specific cultural studies lens on this landscape.

Doing Cultural Studies

The two central questions we return to in each chapter are restated:

- What happens to people doing education in a (digital) *third space*?
- How do engagements in the (digital) *third space* influence practices back in the second space?

Here, these recurrent lines of enquiry are fused with these key theoretical questions, derived from formative CCCS studies, put to work on the various digital modes of 'not-school' are

- How are 'not-schools' digitally encoded and decoded by their 'users'?
- If we work with the notion of negotiated readings of education by its audiences, can we see 'not-school' opening up transformative discursive spaces when combined with digital media?
- How can the engagement driver for digitally mediated 'not-school' be reflexively attentive to sociocultural and sub-cultural framings of resistance to education?
- How is 'not-school' in digital contexts situated in and by the neoliberal social order and how are class, gender, sexuality and ethnicity performed and negotiated in its exchanges?

How 'not-school' is situated in the intersections between education, democracy, power and progressive/redistributive politics is, as always, complex. Crucially, the hinge point must be the extent to which 'alternative' forms of education are sustainable for the less privileged, beyond the mere value of what they are not. On the other hand, if we can agree that the powerless are routinely denied access to the arts (Neelands 2013), then the more curational, permeable modes of learning made possible by digital media and facilitated in *third spaces can* be celebrated as a site of resistance. Likewise, not-school is, by its configuration, more conducive to the interaction of disciplines, to the collision and juxtaposition of ways of learning, to more reflective, experiential relationships between teachers as cultural workers (Freire 1970) and learning identities, whether or not this is despite of and against the grain of its external drivers.

Still, at first glance, readers with a healthy cynical gaze on all things 'digi-ed' will be likely to look awry from 'not-school' as reframed in the ed-tech 'Pearson age'. However, there is a perhaps unlikely parallel here with the notion of the 'working class novel and the 'classic' critical theory debate over form and ideology. From *Love on the Dole* via *The Ragged Trousered Philanthropist to Saturday Night and Sunday Morning, Billy Liar* to *Fish Tank*, the 'working class novel' and the burgeoning adapted genre of 'social realism' in film has failed to provide an expression of any 'common culture' of the disadvantaged. No transgression of bourgeois culture is evident because the forms are so powerfully reproductive of the (cultural) order of things. In the genealogy of British social realism, across media and genre, the creative focus of those working with bourgeois forms has tended to be on the 'worthy poor'. Reflective understanding of the 'living wage' worker's own situation is underscored – from Arthur Seaton at his lathe to Kate Tempest's Becky (2014): *Some don't understand, But I'm happiest when struggling.* At the time of writing, Sleaford Mods articulate an alternative representation – as 'austerity dogs', it appears, living embodiments of 'Broken Britain':

> Gaping-wound-raw poetry about the spirit-crushing minutiae of a working life lived at the behest of middle management, the bleak landscape of broken down pubs, and the commodification of counter-culture, it's been dubbed the soundtrack to our fractured society. (Gush 2015)

In their 'year zero' commentary on the symbolic and material violence done to the poor, might we understand Sleaford Mods' 'not-politics' as being *more* political than any attempts to represent austerity in culture hitherto? On the other hand, the bourgeois mythology of proletariat vulnerability to xenophobia, the rise of neo-fascism explained away as 'divide and rule' of the dispossessed, must be challenged as, at the time of writing, we mark the anniversary of Cable Street:

> Working class people, black and white, have repeatedly organised and fought against oppression. There is a long history of working class anti-racist struggles, from Cable Street in 1933 to Lewisham in 1977 and contemporary mobilisations against fascist organisations, which complicate the image of a liberal, tolerant middle class desperately trying to hose down the frothing racism of the working class hordes. (Ginsburgh 2012: http://isj.org.uk/chavs-class-and-representation/)

This may appear another digression but this parallel with the 'working class novel' returns us to a fundamental question about the '*third space*' in digital contexts – is education a profoundly bourgeois form and, if so, and therefore the idea of a 'working class education' must construct and negotiate an alternative gaze, how the digital *third space* speaks to the analogue second space must be more of a counter-script than a mere 're-engaging' of the margins with the centre. So, relating this to digital 'not-school', the interesting question that arises is this:

Can the neoliberal project of deregulation manifested in 'digital age' not-school be used against the grain to open up spaces for a meaningful, powerful resistance to education's bourgeois frame?

Terms and Conditions Apply

> There is nothing about neoliberalism that is deserving of our respect, and so in concert with a prefigurative politics of creation, my message is quite simply 'fuck it'. Fuck the hold that it has on our political imaginations. Fuck the violence it engenders. Fuck the inequality it extols as a virtue. Fuck the way it has ravaged the environment. Fuck the endless cycle of accumulation and the cult of growth ...... Fuck the ever-intensifying move towards metrics and the failure to appreciate that not everything that counts can be counted. Fuck the desire for profit over the needs of community. Fuck absolutely everything neoliberalism stands for, and fuck the Trojan horse that it rode in on! (Springer 2016, p. 288)

So, to what extent is the digital not-school such a Trojan Horse for the crassest forms of neoliberal, commodified 'learning' in the Pearson, air bnb, Uber mode?

The attempt here is to lay bare the ontological politics often at work beneath the surface of 'youth engagement'. The questions seek a return to the objective of cultural agency as opposed to fetishising 'voice' as a seemingly neutral category within neoliberal framing. The lines of enquiry attempt to move beyond youth voice to other markers of power and exclusion:

> The question is not so much about the construction of 'youth' in isolation, but about the motivations and the consequences of mobilizing this category in combination with others – or alternatively, in order to exclude others that for various reasons might prove more difficult to address. When and why, in these neoliberal times, do we speak about 'youth' as distinct from (or in combination with) gender, class, or ethnicity, or any other category of social difference? What kinds of arguments and practices does the addition of 'youth' support or justify – and what does it exclude or prevent? (Bragg, Buckingham and Kehily 2014, p. 276)

By using cultural studies lens to view the research about what happens when informal learning meets digital networks and potentially creates *third spaces*, we hope to avoid the paradox described by Sefton-Green (2013, 19):

> as scholars research, describe, analyse, and categorize varieties of in-formal and non-formal learning, they in effect formalize that learning and thus run the risk of destroying the very quality of difference that distinguishes non- and in-formal learning from their inverse. This academic concern is mirrored in the administrative and policy uses of the not-school sector – the more we develop complex programs out of school, the more we have to face the challenge of not turning not-schools into schools. Visibility and recognition are double-edged kinds of affirmation.

Here there is no judgement of not-school against criteria for affirmation, but instead an attempt to work through, in relation to digital not-schooling, the central concerns raised by cultural studies in 'going to school' back in the day, namely the critical questioning of judgements about the value of culture and the making of meanings around texts; the extent to which digital not-school facilitates negotiations of expertise by drawing on learners' literacy repertoires and funds of knowledge from the lifeworld and the complex interplay between everyday mediation and scaffolded articulation of critical discourse. In keeping with the approach taken in 'Cultural Studies Goes to School', then, this analysis will view, whether intended this way or not, each not-school case as an action research intervention and look for evidence of 'significant change' (Dart and Davies 2003) in these areas, as opposed to conventional 'schooled' learning outcomes, qualifications or paradoxical notions of 'engagement'.

Culture, (Digital) Media, Language

> Richard Hoggart's book *The Uses of Literacy* was a foundational influence on the work of the Centre for Contemporary Cultural Studies. It was an attempt to examine the changes that were taking place in working-class communities such as that is Hunslet, Leeds, where Hoggart himself grew up. Hoggart wanted to avoid romanticizing life in these areas, but he was also clear that the changes that were taking place in them – particularly the impact of new forms of media and entertainment on more traditional ways of life – required serious attention. (Connell and Hilton 2014, p. 9)

From its inception under Richard Hoggart in 1964, and subsequently under Stuart Hall, both recently deceased, the Centre for Contemporary Cultural Studies ruptured traditional university mores by embracing non-hierarchical and innovative approaches to pedagogy; unflinching political critique; commitment to local and global dialogue and interdisciplinary engagement within the academy, all of which constituted cultural studies' unique strength as much as its institutional fragility.

These indeterminate and interlocking dimensions formed the backbone of panel discussion at the CCCS50 conference in 2014. Present were a cross section of former tutors and alumni, including Richard Johnson, Ann Gray, Geoff Ely, John Clark, Paul Gilroy, David Morley, Jackie Stacey, Iain Chambers, Mikko Lehtonen, Larry Grossberg, Angela McRobbie, Dick Hebdige, Dorothy Hobson and Isaac Julien (Stuart Hall's absence lent a melancholic tone to much of the proceedings, though his presence was felt throughout). Whether cultural studies in other modes has already moved beyond the 'Hallian' era, or indeed 'won' in its interdisciplinary manifestations, were recurrent points of earnest debate.

The Birmingham Centre's analysis of youth culture, mass media representations and the relationship between the two was set in the context of class and race hegemony (arguably privileged over gender and sexuality to the detriment of the centre's legacy), theorised by attention to reception and meaning making. The methods employed by the centre's agents, both as researchers and pedagogically, embraced new approaches to the dialogue between the self, culture, knowledge and education. For our interests in this book, the Centre's focus on social relations and cultural movement is important: *As a main object of study we must take the systems of culturally mediated social relations between classes and their internal cultural resources and repertoires* (Johnson, in Hall et al. 1980, p. 48). Likewise, the dynamic approach to the decoding of cultural material as the 'politics of signification', we want to extend to thinking about digital media education as being encoded and decoded in this same way:

> The process requires, at the production end, its material instruments – its 'means' – as well as its own sets of social (production) relations – the organisation and combination of practices within media apparatuses. But it is in the discursive form that the circulation of the product takes place, as well as its distribution to different audiences. Once accomplished, the discourse must then be translated – transformed, again – into social practices if the circuit is to be complete and effective. If no 'meaning' is taken, there can be no 'consumption'. If the meaning is not articulated in practice, it has no effect. (Hall et al. 1980, p. 129)

So we can think of the negotiation of learning in digital '*third space*' contexts as being a discursive circulation, in the same way, but with an added interest in the more potentially porous relations between production and meaning-making, compared to the more straightforwardly analogue/mass media modalities of the school (second) space.

In *Cultural Studies Goes to School* (1994) Buckingham and Sefton-Green explicitly accounted for ways in which young people *in schools* were able to explore the politics of identity through various pedagogic strategies aimed at 'making sense of the media'. Here, then, was a range of examples of the integration of cultural studies and media education, English and interventions as responses to 'mass' culture. The main argument made is for a removal of the insulations and classifications surrounding categories of culture and textuality (see the *Doing Text* project as a recent extension of this premise – McDougall 2016). Pre-Internet, 'Goes to School' includes an account of research conducted with students in London comprehensive engaging, through media production work, with theories of stereotyping set against the creation of positive images of minority groups. This echoes with our *third space* hip-hop case above. However, the students' refusal to engage in 'serious' academic discussion of their own highly parodic work (Slutmo) in relation to theories of gender representation by disclaiming it as 'having a laugh' (1994, p. 190) is a central discussion point in the account.

The female student (Zerrin) who constructs, and accounts for in a highly personal evaluation, '*Slutmopolitan*' is too complicated for the academic insulations that frame her work to articulate. Here we can reconnect with our earlier discussion of form and subjectivity around the idea of the 'working class novel' and whether the frames of reference of formal education, even when informed by the ethnographic principles of the teacher-research mode at the more enquiry-led end of the Media/Cultural Studies paradigm, can accommodate more 'troubling' reflexive literacies. This problem was captured in Judith Williamson's comparison (Williamson 1981) of her struggles with teaching her student Astrid about gender representation to Sissy Jupe's silence as 'Girl 20' in Dickens' *Hard Times*. As we attempt to provide transformative experiences for students to reflect on the negotiation of identity in their mediated lifeworlds, we risk alienating them through an undermining of their own media cultures. As Turnbull asks, 'is it empowering to reject one's family and values?' (Turnbull 1998, p. 100 & see; McDougall 2016, for a contemporary reappraisal).

> If Zerrin cannot disentangle the levels of parody and power explicitly in her own writing, what can one claim for the educational value of the activity? Of course, this question raises a secondary one: the educational value for *whom*? (Buckingham and Sefton-Green 1994, pp. 198–199).

In the end these researchers were forced to distinguish between empowerment at the level of the energy students showed in engaging with questions of identity and the ability of formal education to allow this to 'make any difference' – in the sense that cultural studies was mobilised for social and political change. It seems clear that ideas, from the cultural studies inventory, of textuality, encoding and decoding and media representation and the compulsion to account for creative, playful and highly parodic activity in relation to this rather narrow idea (that 'the media' represents people and things in particular ways and that students can choose to 'reinforce or challenge' this through their own) was problematic.

Twenty years on, Sefton-Green and Rowsell (2014) revisited aspects of 'Goes to School' and other situated literacies research, reconnecting with participants, using elements of ethnographic reflexive revisiting (Buraway 2003). In some cases, authors found it more difficult to revisit 'touchstone studies' such as Paul Willis as the manufacturing labour context no longer exists, but nonetheless the question of how the cultural identity of an educated person is constructed over time and how participants in the original 'Goes to School' research had performed and were performing their 'media educated' identities were explored. Whilst there was little evidence of media education providing social mobility, there was a recurrent marker of distinction in the experiential benefits:

> The quality and nature of a reflexive mode of media consumption, of participating in digital culture and of having experienced a qualitatively different kind of curricula to their peers seems to have been an important part of their current identities. (Sefton-Green and Rowsell 2014, p. 58)

Also more recently, Butsch and Livingstone (2014) have located the idea of audience as socioculturally framed in/as discourse, written by discourses of power, representation and regulation in specific sociohistoric contexts. In applying a cultural studies approach to thinking of not-school education as text, encoded and decoded in reception, then we must equally consider its 'end-users' (students) as audiences, constructed and negotiated in these ways. Morley's original/'classic' CS contribution to audience reception theory proposed:

> The discourses mobilized by 'readers' in relation to any 'text' cannot be treated as the effect of a direct relation between 'discourses' and 'the real'. It must be analysed, instead, in terms of the effects of social relations and structures (the extra-discursive) on the structuring of the discursive space – that is, of the 'interdiscourse'. These structured relations cannot produce a 'reading' (and no other) in any specific instance. But they do exercise a limit on (that is, they 'determine') the formation of the discursive space, which in turn has a determinate effect on the practice of readings at the level of particular text-reader encounters. (Morley, in Hall et al. 1980, p. 173)

True also for discourses mobilised by 'learners' in relation to any 'education'. However, if the discursive framing of audience is understood as a means of control, often imposing Western conceptions of 'publics' in the idioms of enlightenment democracy rhetorics, then the implications of this for not only media audience research but also educational research are apparent. Butsch and Livingstone draw the observation that more strongly governed societies demonstrate more ideologically driven and 'official' representations of media audiences, dividing audiences into elites and 'masses', whereas they are careful to avoid the polarisation of either emancipation or governance, but rather to explore the tensions between these competing discourses, when assessing Internet communities as audiences.

> We now call on other teacher educators and social studies teachers to provide critical readings of the past and a reflexive understanding of how technology, consumerism, knowledge and media merge together at the present to form the 'society of the spectacle. This will resuscitate social studies education, untangling the discipline from perpetuating the status quo. It will finally become a pedagogical cornerstone of guiding youths to become agents of change and social transformation. (Porfilio 2010, pp. 134–135)

Cultural study, to recap, is concerned with a broad concept of culture and rejects value hierarchies between different cultural forms. It emphasises both difference in cultural activity and reflexivity in our understanding of ourselves as culturally mediated. Culture is dynamic and contingent, a process, and extends to everyone and all aspects of lived experience in and as culture. Cultural studies is, therefore, necessarily interdisciplinary and 'horizontal' in order to account for this idea of culture itself. (see Jenks 1993, p. 212)

Thus, if there is now a culture of connection, in accounts of its short history, a language of struggle pervades – the 'battle over information control' casts the operational logic of connectivity as the site of power and exploitation rather than neutral evolution and hinges on the argument that the (rapid) progression from 'platformed' sociality to participatory culture to a culture of connectivity is not simply moulded by historical contingency but engineered. Furthermore, the utopian notion of 'watchful caretakers and diverse gardeners' in the web 2.0 ecosystem cuts against a responsive colonisation of pioneer non-profits by corporations:

> The footprints of early communitarian ideals are visible in many corners of platformed society where small platforms have procured their spaces. Among the moguls, these footprints too often serve merely as strategic and effectual reminders of the original settlers' utopian spirit." (Van Dijck 2013, p. 165) It is in school where, arguably mind meets matter.... Matter intervenes. Capitalism meets democracy. Capital dominates. The relationship of schools to society where schools are, for the most part, capitalist schools is a reality ignored by liberal and even radical educators. (Gibson 2010, p. 44)

If digital not-school and the broader *third space* are examples of digital media education as (popular) culture, then our 'ways of looking' at it must include attention to these spaces as sites of cultural struggle. If the continuum at stake here is between at the one end a fully realised 'participatory culture' for learning and at the other the foreclosing of open participation at the hands of a neoliberal commodification of learning as competence, skill and hyper-regulatory compliance, then whether we can situate early Media Studies in English schools (the cultural studies 'version' researched by Buckingham and Sefton-Green in the early 1990s) as a kind of 'not-school within school' is for debate. Either way, we can draw out the key themes from both these key texts in the intersection between cultural studies, media education and literacies which we want to carry over to the digital context, and align them with our preoccupation with the *third space*. The meeting point is presented here as a framework of questions to pose when digital media enabled networks enable different ways to make meaning, to a greater or lesser extent informed by *third space* principles in 'not-school' contexts: (Table 7.1)

Table 7.1 Cultural studies: the digital, not-school and the *third space*

Cultural Studies	*Digital media, not-school, third space*
What happens to the Cultural Studies hypothesis that validating and exploring popular cultural engagement can develop efficacy, the sociological imagination, political identities and broader/deeper forms of engagement in 'the digital'?	How are 'not-schools' digitally encoded and decoded by their 'users'? How is 'not-school' in digital contexts situated in and by the neoliberal social order and how are class, gender, sexuality and ethnicity performed and negotiated in its exchanges?
How is it possible to use Cultural Studies as a model for such agentive explorations and identity formation in and with digital networks to compensate for the institutional framing (including digital) of school?	How can the engagement driver for digitally mediated 'not-school' be reflexively attentive to sociocultural and sub-cultural framings of resistance to education?
Which pedagogical approaches today are enabling young people to participate in the radically different social and cultural worlds foreseen by the researchers in 1994, and how is such participation politically framed?	If we work with the notion of negotiated readings of education by its audiences, can we see 'not-school' opening up transformative discursive spaces when combined with digital media?

CHAPTER 8

Afterword – An Exchange with Cathy Burnett, Neil Selwyn and Others

This concluding 'afterword' chapter is intentionally unorthodox. We might even claim it as a *third space* in itself, in so much as it takes the form of a kind of published 'viva' on our own work but within the work itself. We start by examining ourselves, asking one another to 'defend our thesis' and then we extend the conversation to seek the insights and provocations of two formative 'agents' in our fields of enquiry, Cathy Burnett and Neil Selwyn, before concluding with extracts from a recording of a workshop we convened on the key themes of this book at the Media Education Summit. So a *third space*, perhaps, because it is neither part of the book nor an 'external' review and neither a live symposium on the themes nor a retrospective account of it. It's a kind of working out/working through of our findings with both experts in the field we are working in and the community of practice we want to talk to.

Julian – looking back through these chapters, *third space* is a big idea but we, inevitably I suppose, speak to that concept in multiple ways. If we need to pin it down, what are we talking about when we talk about *third spaces*?

John – We're talking about negotiated spaces I think. The spaces where meanings are made and shared. In an educational context I think we are talking about any space in which attention is paid to the habitus, or learned and practised way of being, of the other party in any communicative act, which is why we've often spoken about it in the context of porous expertise. But Bhabha implied it was a space through which all utterances needed to

J. Potter, J. McDougall, *Digital Media, Culture and Education*,
DOI 10.1057/978-1-137-55315-7_8

pass before meaning inheres between the social actors in that space. So it's important to think of it in that way because it is not, therefore, an actual physical location; it is not necessarily an after school club or a museum education space or an art studio. That way of being around learning and knowledge is associated with those spaces which are neither home nor school because of the effect on the negotiated meanings in those spaces, the ways in which hierarchies are changed. The signature pedagogies in those after school clubs and spaces are qualitatively different because they exist in a *third space* which demands that the values and the culture of the participants feature in the space. But they can be created maybe in school as much as out of school. So what we are talking about – I suppose – is negotiated space. *Third spaces* are contested, negotiated and political.

How do you see them? And in particular how do you see their relationship to porous expertise and powerful knowledge?

Julian – you finished with 'political' and I think we've put down that marker pretty consistently throughout the book, in a way that reminds me of Prensky's distinction between nouns and verbs during that very problematic 'Media 2.0' debate. Whilst his 'digital natives' is something we've moved (far) away from, his distinguishing between the technology (nouns) and the human ways of working it enables (verbs) was far more helpful during that period when media educators were oscillating wildly around a before and after, either/or discourse about new media and the Internet. With *third spaces*, it's the same idea, at the most reductive level a *third space* can just be a thing, a place in between two other things, but in the political sense it's a verb, an active site of powerful negotiation of being a person in education, and I think we've drawn that line pretty clearly. We've written about those *third spaces* which look like they are making a difference to the second space, often by taking back to that space a different way of thinking about knowledge and also those that seem just to extend it – for example several of the 'not school' cases. The notion that this reconfiguration of the second space could be a 'fourth space' seemed like we were stretching the metaphor too far, but with regard to new literacies in prison education, that's already been thought about – the educational encounter is a creative site at the heart of the renegotiations of inside and outside and formal and informal and the potential gateway to both a new inside (reflexive) and a new outside (literally, after prison). Margaret Wilson, though, writes about prison education as one element of *third space*, not as an extra space. But again she gives prominence to education which acknowledges the fine line between institutions and identities and between its 'pedagogical and carceral parameters'. In this sense, education always situates people as learners and something else – prisoners, women, 'disengaged youth', migrants or the future Cabinet if its PPE at Oxbridge and the kinds of political *third space* education we see as enabling rich, powerful media literacies work is that which really offers a space for resistance to power, at its most simple, in media education it is the difference between observing power and 'fight the power' – the difference between a question such as *How might we need to think the traditional categories of learning: reading and writing, speaking and listening?* and something like *How have these categories previously stopped people having a voice, how will YOU thinking differently about literacy to include digital media lead to a redistribution of cultural capital?*

Neil – Language is clearly important here… in particular the terms used to convey the essence of these issues and ideas to broader educational audiences. So, I'm left wondering whether it might be reasonable to conclude a book about 'theorising *third space* literacy' with the suggestion that we need to think of more direct ways of conveying our concerns with politics, power/resistance, exclusion and so on? So what would you be calling these practices/sites if you hadn't read Bhabha? How might we more crudely (but perhaps more successfully) rebrand '*Third Spaces*' in a way that conveys everything that you've just outlined – that is that these are sites of ongoing political struggle and negotiation. I am often struck by how the field of education can take quite powerful and politically astute concepts and neutralise them to the point of banality. Think of how an initially powerful concept such as 'Communities of Practice' now gets bandied around in the most banal terms of "people doing stuff" together in groups. Or 'Affordances' gets reduced to 'things that you can do with something'. Or the ways in which activity theory is used in many educational contexts. Given these precedents, I am worried that the important ways in which you are outlining *third spaces* might get lost in translation into wider educational use. As Julian points out, these are 'not' places or physical locations, but that is precisely how I fear the term is already beginning to be used in education. So what are the verbs (rather than nouns) that we might use in order to get the concept across… or am I worrying unnecessarily? Perhaps I should have more trust in how these ideas and arguments will travel! These are important ideas that stretch well beyond reaffirming the educational potential of libraries and Makerspaces.

Cathy – Yes – I share concerns about how the idea of *third space* gets translated in practice. I worry it gets seen simply in terms of special projects or not school activities; *third space* becomes an add-on – or enhancement – which deflects from more radical reworkings of education and the role of digital media ('you can have a go at *third space* once you've done your real work'). I think the emphasis on thinking in terms of verbs not nouns is really useful and agree with Neil that it's worth exploring what these might be. I'd like to add though a point about the slipperiness of spaces. I'm interested in how activities/tasks/projects and so on assemble with other stuff as they unfold: with the histories and imaginings of groups and individuals; with established practices for doing school, doing media, doing literacy, doing friendship, teaching, learning and so on; and with other objects and memories lingering in the sites where they happen. What do media literacies become as they assemble with other stuff, and how does this shift as projects move along? For me spaces are always socially produced and as such always fluid and hybrid, and I find it difficult to accommodate the *third space* metaphor with this view. (While the *third space* idea is essentially about hybridity, for me it implies that there are spaces that aren't fluid and hybrid which I find difficult.) In my work I'm interested in what gets produced as teachers and children (I'll refer to children as my work is mainly in primary schools) take up rather mundane classroom activities. Often, unsurprisingly in the current climate, this rarely seems 'contested, negotiated and political' in the way you imply, but sometimes I think it really is. I worry that in working for a *third space* we may miss some of the ways that children and teachers improvise with the stuff they have to do, overlayering it with other things for example, or finding new pathways through it or ways of being together. Of course I'm not suggesting here that we shouldn't be looking to radically rework what happens in education, or that we shouldn't be looking at those sites where people are doing things that feel radically different to most classrooms, but maybe I am suggesting that in thinking about verbs not nouns, it's perhaps also useful to look in unexpected places.

John – That's really helpful I think. Thank you Cathy and Neil. Firstly, I agree that language is important here and the way there is a semantic shift as a concept gets worn away by the easy way in which terminology is thrown around, sometimes by well-meaning people, sometimes by commercial interests. I remember a government education agency a few years ago talking about creating a 'Community of Practice' by collecting names for a mailing list. Maybe that would be a CoP and maybe it wouldn't. Martin Oliver has a great paper on the way affordances is or isn't working in the world. I encounter 'affordance' all the time as a substitute for software 'design'. And 'multimodal' is another term which sometimes stands in when people really mean 'multimedia' or just 'media'; it has a different provenance as a study of how meaning is made and comes from social semiotics. Sometimes things sound interesting or new when a term gets used and commercially viable and easily appropriated. There is a company which pairs children in primary schools with maths tutors in the Indian subcontinent for learning concepts they are finding difficult. Soon they will be doing this for literacy lessons. It's not actually a '*third space*' as we mean it at all. It's something else. But language is malleable and shifts and belongs in the meaning that is made at the time. Turning to Cathy's point about the difficulty of defining *third spaces* as something hybrid and fluid and thereby implying that there are spaces which are not is really interesting. I think the way it's conceived here in the book is to think about the social production of possible spaces. In this way '*third spaces*' become more generalised and diffuse expressions of agency, of the qualitatively different possibilities of hybridity and fluidity. So maybe all spaces are as such but some can involve qualitatively different exchanges of cultural capital between the social actors involved. Neil's right I think to say that it is certainly not all about affirming the importance of libraries, museums or makerspaces. We need to stop and think about these terms from time to time in order, perhaps, to recast or reclaim them as part of a wider debate about what education is for and why.

Julian – Both contributions resonate with other sections of the book where we talk about 'not school' and various flavours of 'co-creation', in these cases the same risk arises, that we write a book that celebrates marginal activity that involves a small number of volunteers or selected participants, those who probably already possess an abundance of cultural/academic capital. So we've tried very hard not to do that, by always asking the question – does what happens in the *third space* transform things for a larger number of people back in the second space? Sticking with 'the verbs', a big one for us in the book, and building on John's previous work, is curation/curating. John, I know you'd have plenty to say about curation as a literacy practice, but how does curation scale and translate, in the ways that Cathy and Neil are thinking about – in other words, does it already get reduced and neutralised in the second space and also can it be agentive in the contested, political sense within but against the grain of that mundane everyday classroom work?

John – Of all the terms in the book the one which is slipperiest and most open to misunderstanding is possibly 'curation' and its associated skill-set, 'curatorship'.

The first time I used 'curation' in relation to media and new literacy practices in a conference I was told it might not work because it sounded like a theory of everything and everywhere which would just end up being too diffuse and disappear.

And I think this is the big problem with Julian's challenge for it to scale and translate. Because when that happens it runs the risk of losing every kind of nuance in the argument and emerges as a way of simply describing collecting and exhibiting things, an easily made bridge between practices in digital spaces, social media and theory. It runs the risk of becoming observational and celebratory at scale and this wasn't the prime motivation behind trying to use and develop the term. It was a term that grew out of a lot of thinking about social and cultural theory around identity and trying to meld this with what I thought I was seeing in digital media practices around production; aspects of the process which really were different and not adequately accounted for by metaphors around writing, editing or even sharing. A further criticism has been its focus on the individual, though I never intended it to be limited this way and always saw it as being about one or more social actors engaging in the process, individually or collectively. I think I – and many others – have tried subsequently to refine all of this a little bit, problematise it more and to explain that the word is metaphorical in origin and needs more work! As a term it has resonated with a lot of people in different sectors in education, different spaces but what we need is indeed a way of taking it forward in a more contested sense.

Neil and Cathy – what do you think are the possible challenges and opportunities of curation as a term to apply to digital/social media production practices – by groups or individuals?

Neil – 'Curation' is definitely a useful term to keep hold of and work with – it certainly resonates with people when talking about the digital. I have found it less readily co-opted and de-contextualised than some of the other terms that we have discussed. This is perhaps because most people do not readily align themselves with being curators (whereas they feel more comfortable with the idea of being in a 'community' or engaging in 'practice'). It is not a word that is part of the familiar lexicon of education, and as a result tends to pique people's interest. So curation is a useful term as it jolts people out of their comfort zone and makes them think otherwise. This is perhaps because of the obvious pre-digital connotations of the term. I like the sense of deliberation and intent that it conveys. I also like the thoughts that the term provokes regarding the consequences of one's curating practices (i.e. the sense that curation usually involves things being engaged with by others).

So we need to keep persisting with 'curation' (even 'though it is yet another 'C' word). In doing this, there is certainly scope to encourage the widespread use of the term in suitably nuanced ways. The idea of 'co-curation' seems to have taken hold in some quarters, as might wider discussion of what it means to be 'curated'... making the distinction between one's ability to 'do' curation, as opposed to have curation 'done to' them.

Cathy – OK, so curation is another slippery word (and we haven't even mentioned literacy yet)... I'm not sure I have much to add to Neil's defence of curation, except that I like it too. While I understand our concerns, John, I can also understand why people use it in celebratory terms – I think celebration is no bad thing sometimes, particularly when teasing out the complexity of practices that are often derided or seen as problematic, although of course we need to be wary of the overly positive accounts that are so common in accounts of digital media projects and practices. I think questions about curation as an ongoing process are really useful ones: about how we curate ourselves and others, how we are curated and by who (and maybe what), and what happens with and around what we curate (Fig. 8.1).

I also like the way the concept of curation highlights aspects of children and young people's media production that might otherwise go unnoticed. I'm thinking here, John, of your article exploring how two girls created a film of their soon-to-be left primary school, taking the chance to linger again in places that held memories for them, and exploring their particular experience of being there. I like the way a focus on this process as one of curation helps us interrogate what's going on here, and foregrounds how personal resonance and experience gets explored and renegotiated through digital media, things that get written out of dominant educational discourse.

Thinking about co-curation – I've heard this term used a little like co-production, when artists, teachers and so on have worked to help produce media artefacts with children and young people. I'm more interested in how the idea of co-curation (if we want to use that term) might help in getting at how (third???) spaces are negotiated, and all the different players – human and non-human that might contribute to this process.

Fig. 8.1 A picture of someone taking a picture

John – I agree that curation is something that needs to be preserved as a term which is useful, but also complex and nuanced in the context of digital media and learning. I think we try to keep its potential for addressing new literacy practices alive. We have another term which we think might be useful in considering some of these processes and that is the subject of our final question to put to you. We use the term 'Dynamic literacies' in the book to outline a series of literacy theories and practices which are responsive to change of all kinds: societal, semantic and pedagogical. So, it definitely links to both '*third space*' and 'curation' and the way our conversation has gone. These kinds of theories are those derived from the NLS but are also present in emergent work around sociomateriality (like yours, Cathy), and we try to show how these stand in contrast to notions of 'literacy' which are static and autonomous. We also want to connect literacy theory to pedagogy because we recognise that they are inextricably linked anyway, sometimes even by statute, but almost always by regulatory procedures and by performative assessments of the social actors involved (teachers, children, carers). So, static systems somehow impede the use – or otherwise – of more fluid and dynamic notions of what it is to be literate, to make and share meaning.

What we'd like to ask is: How do we conceive of a way of learning which is responsive to much wider definitions of literacy than currently pertain in many countries which have a narrow and even static focus? Or, in other words: How do we design an education system which can work with ideological as opposed to autonomous versions of literacy?

Neil – It's nice to finish off with an easy question! There are two responses to this kind of challenge. On the one hand you can read it as 'How do we design a "better" system?' (which implies suggestions of large-scale reform). On the other hand, you can read it as 'How do we support educators to work along these lines in the system that we have?' (which implies suggestions of small-scale tactics of resistance). From the first perspective, the answer I fear probably lies in revisiting (yet again) what it might mean to have forms of curriculum, assessment, pedagogy and expectations of time/place/space that are dynamic. fluid and fully predicated around notions of shared meaning-making. I think that literacy scholars probably know already what these might be... and they also know why these changes are unlikely to occur as long as the neoliberal project remains dominant.

So I'd be tempted to think in terms of the second perspective – that is working with what we have. There are plenty of educators already doing what you imply (despite the system in which they work), so there are plenty of examples that we can learn from. Thus is perhaps useful to position the 'static' forms of literacy that are currently served up in formal education as a something that teachers and students need to critically engage with and critically act against. This is not just a case of critical reflection. Instead teachers need to explore possibilities for critical conduct – these can be indirect (e.g. work-to-rule) as well as the occasional critical actions (e.g. direct intervention, subversion, insurrection). Yet these actions need to take place in appropriately pragmatic ways. Stephen Ball (2016) has talked recently of 'strategic skirmishes' that reflect 'a recognition of and engagement with relations of power' (p. 1131). This also relates to Miranda Matthews' notion of 'negotiated autonomy' in schools. This sees teachers and students navigating power networks – responding to some impositions in a polite (and perhaps subservient manner), while pursuing other avenues of lively resistance elsewhere. Formal schooling (and therefore formal notions of a static school 'literacy') is not something that is fully rejected or fully acquiesced to. Instead, autonomy and agency in what one does with dynamic forms of 'literacy' is an ongoing process of navigation and negotiation.

Cathy – Earlier in this exchange, Julian, you mentioned how you've tried to use the ideas and practices explored in this book to talk back to education more broadly, and specifically I think the school system. It's not surprising that some of the most provocative and inspiring works in literacy education focus on not school sites given the ever more hostile policy context in schools. I do get concerned though when the most interesting debate happens mainly outside schools amongst likeminded individuals and groups. So I think we do need to both continually imagine how things might be otherwise in terms of school systems – and try and position ourselves to work for shifts in policy and practice however unlikely these may be – as well as supporting and highlighting 'lively acts of resistance' in schools. There are two points I want to add to Neil's about resistance, based on reflecting on an ongoing project with Guy Merchant, which involves working with groups of primary teachers to generate collaborative digital media projects that manage to work alongside existing curriculum requirements. One of the striking things about our meetings is the hilarity; the laughter as we talk about ourselves, our practices and thoughts, and the sometimes absurd contexts we find ourselves in. There is something about this that allows us to have better conversations about how digital media might enter classrooms and what this might mean for literacy and for education more broadly, and somehow helps to buoy us all up to try things out. Guy and I have been using Jane Bennett's idea of enchantment of a way of thinking about this kind of playful disruption. Enchantment maybe evokes a rather naïve and overly romantic way of thinking about classrooms, but in the current context it starts to feel a bit more radical (as Bennett intends): approaching practice through enchantment, we're thinking, helps us engage with things like generosity, ephemerality, improvisation and emergence, all the stuff that doesn't count for much in the neoliberal discourse.

Leading on from this, we've started writing stories about the process of working together, and rather tentatively sharing these with the teachers we're working with. These stories allow us to give very personal accounts of our meetings that focus on things like objects, feelings and memories. And sharing these stories again seems to lead us into interesting conversations where it's OK to talk about things other than levels, or objectives or standards. We're only just now grappling with what's going on here and how this process may be useful – if indeed it is – but it does make a point about how research methods assemble with practice. If the mainly binary assumptions generated through the 'evidence based practice' movement help sustain the closed circle of accountability that holds in place static conceptualisations of literacy, then it's worth thinking more about the work that research methods do at local level, and about the contribution that playful research methods might make in celebrating, interrogating and maybe generating, lively acts of resistance.

Triangulation

In addition to our virtual conversation with Neil and Cathy, we shared the same three key themes – *third spaces*, curation and dynamic literacies – with a group of media education and media literacy practitioners at the Media Education Summit in Rome in November 2016. The four-way email exchange was reaching its final phase so the two discussions were happening at the same time, but we didn't connect the two directly. Discussions during the workshop were recorded, with the informed consent of the participants, and here we offer some transcribed extracts by way of triangulation – between what we've written about these key concepts in the book, what our critical friend scholars said to us by email and what the practitioners 'in the patch' shared with us at the workshop.

The workshop participants were media education practitioners, including higher education lecturers, teacher trainers and school or college teachers, but by virtue of their being at the conference and choosing to take part in the particular workshop, all also engaged in research, in some cases working on doctoral projects, at the other end of the scale one of the most prominent figures in media literacy research was in the room. To risk reproducing the 'banalisation' of the term Neil observes above, they are a representative cross section of the community of practice we hope will read this book. We spent a few minutes (with just a few slides, and some pictures of cats and Luton Airport) rehearsing the key themes from the book, consistent with the interactions with our discussants above, and were joined by Michelle Cannon and Fiona Scott, who each shared examples of their own work (Cannon 2016; Scott 2016) by way of applications of our three key themes, and then each of the themes was opened up to the group for discussion, with a discussion prompt in each case. Each of the three framings is here followed by extracts from the discussion.

Should we recognise the skills, knowledge and dispositions which go with curation as a practice and build on them in education? How can we do this? What conditions are necessary for this to succeed?

Participants

It reminds me of library science and classifications, people taking a three decimal system over to tagging, in Texas we call it 'tag wrangling', managing the tags. It's a form of curation in that you're naming things but also giving them priorities, these intertexts, and giving value to these objects. And taste and value definitely come into it.

I'm interested in the things that have been purely facilitated by curation. Like being a geo-cacher, it is a digital treasure hunt. So you go out and find boxes, using your phone with GPS to do that. Some people would have no interest in that if it were not for the digital technology, so it's a properly outdoor activity that is only really made possible by the interaction with an app on a phone, which is slightly different to storifying photos or curating videos, but it's a curation, with sharing online, but it's more the case with this that the technology makes the activity itself possible (rather than just using the tech to curate).

Clearly the technology is part and parcel, but as you were talking the things that came to mind were the curation that takes place in performance, the 'shelf' of performance, going back to the Goffmanesque performance of self. So I am hearing curation as curation /the performance of curation and I don't think you can separate those, even if you are curating for an audience of one but also it's a performance to self as well as of self. We may have been privileging the technology too much, there is a caution there, it's about whether it's explicitly digital curation.

But with social media, the fact that young people are routinely counselled by career advisors to refine their curation of self, to expunge it, to redo it with respect to the audience, it's not something anyone ever said to them about the shelf in their bedroom.

John – This thing of the digital making hidden processes visible, so with this in mind, do we need more by the way of theory than Goffman, who was writing about industry, and particularly the advertising industry and how people present themselves at work and then go back home to be. Whereas social media, if we're saying at least a version of it is now synonymous with curation, raises the question of what other things are important apart from this front and back stage, what other theories do we need?

Dynamic Literacies – How might literacy events which take place on and off screen, between social actors and artefacts in a range of locations become part of the pedagogical frame?

Participants

It's the question of how are we going to use these new 24/7 experiences and competences in education, it's not by chance that we are all working on this idea, and I think the answers are in understanding how the structures we already have can respond to these new points of experiences in the digital world.

But this is the history of literacy and it's NOT different, it's not about the devices and it's not about the texts. It's about the institutional control of the definition of literacy which equals power. And that's what we miss, because we keep focusing on the steps to literacy and how we do the pedagogy for this device or that device. Languages are dialects with an army. It's about power. So how can we give social capital to our students, and how can we make the classroom a place where media education can maybe unlock those handcuffs?

John – in the book we make an argument which traces the story of literacy in that way, from its origin, in a step-by-step way to gain knowledge of the letters, in order to be able to read, to perform and to be economically successful and we end up with a political and ideological position which is there is no media literacy as such, there is (just) literacy and it's dynamic, and the media artefacts, texts and practices are part of what we all do every day.

Participant

I think between us we've thrown around ideas that we use literacies as something to 'bandwagon off of', particularly in the UK. But we get confused and distracted by talking about digital, I get the spirit of where you are heading, but it feels a bit like going around in circles, literacy confers status on everything that comes before it (e.g. media, digital), so is it just the same with dynamic?

Julian – there's a clear political position in the book which is that the institutional power dynamics at work render most people, if not illiterate, then outside of literacy in one way or another. It's an old idea that the schooled version of literacy alienates more people than it includes, but the book doesn't just say that and leave it, in every chapter we try to work through case study examples and examples of research which do seem to be shape-shifting what counts as literacy, who gets to speak, what counts as knowledge.

When digital media is used to create a *third space* with the effect of transgressing disciplines and traditional ideas about knowledge and expertise, can educational practices 'shape-shift' to challenge epistemological power relations?

Participants

The thing I worry about here is the fact that there are influential people in our own community who are instrumental, narrowing down particular types of knowledge that will benefit you and there are academics in our field presenting that view of literacy and I worry that there has to be route to take those people on in some way.

It's not a functional model, it's dysfunctional. We should write a book about the failure of literacy. If this is political, for example play – it's not just that play is purposely excluded, it is, because it doesn't fit the systemic, institutional version of education. But if it's political, there are a couple of ways, one way is to go 'full tilt, bandwagon' and the other is incrementalism. Building a solid base, step by step, if you have a strategy. I would go incremental and find the opportunities, be successful, disseminate it, find new ways to work.

John – it's the problem of the institutional model of literacy being chronically unambitious for 2016, and then being on the front foot. This is an increment, this room.

Participants

The front foot can just be 'fuck neoliberalism' (referring to Springer 2016). *Calling it when we see it. Not worrying about upsetting the people we don't want to upset.*

It seems to me that actually unless you still want to be in the game of let's educate the workers so we can move them from the school gate to the factory gate, you have to add emotional literacy, the question of what's the point and why do we care?

John – we try to talk about the two arms of literacy, the text and the affect, aesthetic engagements and judgements, but two sides of the same coin, literacy and pedagogy in this push and pull. How you define your literacy in a society is how you define your pedagogy, bounded by either talking only on texts and the design of social futures or how you talk about social futures in terms of affects and sociomateriality, the artefacts and the bodies and the objects in the classroom.

End Note

Our concluding observation in difficult times for anyone with frames of reference which contrast sharply with those operating in performative and punitive systems is that the curriculum, the classroom and, ultimately, the institutional framings of literacy are unlikely to be shape-shifting any time soon if the political objectives of the powers that be are reflected, as they have always been, in the epistemological configuration of formal education.

To paraphrase and adapt Billy Bragg (1985), for sure, 'writing books is not enough in days like these'. So to what end, a publication like this?

In one of his hyper-satirical, layers upon layers, conversations with Chris Morris, also 'afterwords', at the end of each episode of his BBC 'Comedy Vehicle' TV series, the comedian Stewart Lee, reflecting on the value of his art, offers the rationale 'something happened, and then it ended, and nobody can dispute that'. We hope this book has done something more than merely existing for a number of pages and then ending, and this *third space* chapter is intended to close our contribution in a more reflexive and self-aware mode, but we concede the danger is to unravel any sense of having said anything! The cliché 'more questions than answers' isn't really good enough when we have asked readers to spend time with a book, but to posit this text as anything more than an increment would be at odds with the more sensitive and nuanced, evidence-based, we hope, account of digital media education and its attendant 'uses of literacy' we want to think we've written. So yes. An increment. Onwards.

References

Aarsand, P. (2015). *PED8009 dynamic literacies* [Online]. Trondheim: University of Trondheim. Available: https://www.ntnu.edu/studies/courses/PED8009-tab=omEmnet. Accessed 11.07.16.

Alanen, L., Brooker, L., & Mayall, B. (eds.). (2015). *Childhood with Bourdieu*. Basingstoke: Palgrave MacMillan.

Alim, H., Ibrahim, A., & Pennycook, A. (eds.). (2009). *Global linguistic flows: Hip Hop cultures, youth identities and the politics of language*. New York: Routledge.

Alleyne, B. (2015). *Narrative networks: Storied approaches in a digital age*. London: Sage.

Ahrne, G., & Brunsson, N. (2011). Organization outside organizations: The significance of partial organization. *Organization 18*(1).

Au, W. (2005). Fresh out of school: Rap music's discursive battle with education. *Journal of Negro Education*, *74*(3), 210.

Bailey, C. (2016). Free the Sheep: Improvised song and performance in and around a minecraft community. *Literacy*, *50*(2), 62–71.

Ball, S. (2016). Subjectivity as a site of struggle: Refusing neoliberalism? *British Journal of Sociology of Education*, 37(8), 1129–1146.

Banaji, S. (2011). Disempowering by assumption: How the rhetoric of 'digital natives' affects young people and influences civic organisations working with them. In M. Thomas (eds.), *Deconstructing Digital Natives*. London: Routledge.

Banaji, A., Buckingham, D., Van Zoonen, L., & Hirzalla, F. (2009). *Civicweb report: Synthesis of results and policy outcomes*. European Union.

Barrance, T. (2004). *Making movies make sense*. Cardiff: Media Education Wales.

J. Potter, J. McDougall, *Digital Media, Culture and Education*,
DOI 10.1057/978-1-137-55315-7

Barrs, M., & Horrocks, S. (2014). *Educational blogs and their effects on pupil's writing*. Reading: CfBT Education Trust.

Bazalgette, C. (eds.). (1989). *Primary media education: A curriculum statement*. London: British Film Institute.

Bazalgette, C. (2000). A stitch in time: Skills for the new literacy. *English in Education, 34*(1), 42–49.

Bazalgette, C. (2010). *Report on the persistence of vision project* [Online]. London. Available: http://themea.org/pov/volume-3-issue-2/persistence-of-vision/report/. Accessed 24.04.12.

Bazalgette, C., Parry, B., & Potter, J. (2011). 'Creative, cultural and critical: Media literacy theory in the priary school classroom'. *Creative Engagements 7*. Mansfield College, Oxford University.

BBC. (2016): *The Hip Hop world news*. London: BBC.

Bearne, E. (2009). Multimodality, literacy and texts: Developing a discourse. *Journal of Early Childhood Literacy, 9*, 156–187.

Belshaw, D. (2014). *The essential elements of digital literacies*. Self-published.

Bennett, P., & McDougall, J. (2016). *Doing text: Media after the subject*. Columbia: Columbia University Press.

Benson, S. (2010). 'I Don't Know If That'd Be English or Not': Third space theory and literacy instruction. *Journal of Adolescent & Adult Literacy, 53*(7), 555–563.

Berger, R., Hobbs, R., McDougall, J., & Mihailidis, P. (2015). We're in this Together: building a global community for media education research. *Media Education Research Journal*, 5.2, 5–10 and *Journal of Media Literacy Education, 7*(1), 1–3.

Bernstein, B. (1996). *Pedagogy, symbolic control and identity: Theory, research, critique*. London: Taylor & Francis.

Bezemer, J., & Kress, G. (2016). *Multimodality, learning and communication: A social semiotic frame*. London: Routledge.

Bhabha, H. (1994). *The location of culture*. London: Routledge.

Biesta, G. (2012). The educational significance of the experience of resistance: Schooling and the dialogue between child and world. *Other Education, 1*(1), 92–103.

Blum-Ross, A., & Livingstone, S. (2016). From youth voice to young entrepreneurs: The individualization of digital media and learning. *Journal of Digital and Media Literacy, 4* (1–2). In Special Issue 'From Voice to Influence: Implications for Digital Citizenship and Media Literacy Education' Henry Jenkins & Sangita Shresthova (eds) Available: http://www.jodml.org/2016/06/27/from-youth-voice-to-young-entrepreneurs-the-individualization-of-digital-media-and-learning/. Accessed 24. 02. 17.

Bolas, T. (2009). *Screen education: From film appreciation to media studies*. London: Intellect Books.

Bourdieu, P. (1977). *Outline of a theory of practice*. Cambridge: Cambridge University Press.

Bourdieu, P. (1986). *Distinction: A social critique of the judgment of taste*. London: Routledge.

Bourdieu, P., & Passeron, J. (1990). *Reproduction in education, society and culture*. London: Sage.

Bowman, P. (2011). *Reading ranciere: Critical dissensus*. London: Continuum.

Boyle, J. (2008). *The public domain: Enclosing the commons of the mind*. New Haven: Yale University Press.

Bragg, B. (1985). *Days like these (Single)*. London: Go! Discs.

Bragg, S., Buckingham, D., & Kehily, M. (eds.). (2014). *Youth cultures in the age of global media*. Basingstoke: Palgrave MacMillan.

British Library. (2016). *Children's playground games* [Online]. London: British Library Available: https://www.bl.uk/projects/childrens-playground-games. Accessed 21.09.16.

Brooker, L. (2003). Parental ethnotheories and young children's preparation for school. *International Journal of Early Years Education*, *11*, 117–128.

Bruner, J. (1987). Life as narrative. *Social Research*, *54*, 11–17; 21–31.

Buckingham, D. (2003). *Media education: Literacy, learning and contemporary culture*. Cambridge: Polity.

Buckingham, D. (2007). *Beyond technology: Children's learning in the age of digital culture*. London: Routledge.

Buckingham, D. (2009). *In defence of media studies* [Online]. London: The Guardian Comment is Free. Available: https://www.theguardian.com/commentisfree/2009/aug/22/media-studies. Accessed 23.07.16.

Buckingham, D. (2015a). Why children should NOT be taught to code. *David Buckingham* [Online]. Available: https://davidbuckingham.net/tag/coding/.

Buckingham, D. (2015b). Digital distractions: What's wrong with the debate about Technology. *David Buckingham* (Online). http://davidbuckingham.net/2015/09/25/digital-distractions-whats-wrong-with-the-debate-about-technology-in-education/)

Buckingham, D., & Sefton-Green, J. (1994). *Cultural studies goes to school: Reading and teaching popular media*. London: Taylor & Francis.

Bulfin, S., & Koutsogiannis, D. (2012). New literacies as multiply placed practices: Expanding perspectives on young people's literacies across home and school. *Language and Education*, *26*, 331–346.

Bulfin, S., Johnson, N., Nemorin, S., & Selwyn, N. (2016). Nagging, noobs and new tricks – Students' perceptions of school as a context for digital technology use. *Educational Studies*, *42*, 239–251.

Burawoy, M. (2003). Revisits; An outline of a theory of reflexive ethnogaphy. *American Sociological Review*, 68, 645–679.

Burgess, J., & Green, J. (2009). *YouTube: Online video and participatory culture.* Cambridge: Polity.

Burn, A. (2009). *Making new media: Creative production and digital literacies (new Literacies and digital epistemologies).* New York: Peter Lang.

Burn, A., & Durran, J. (2007). *Media literacy in schools.* London: Paul Chapman.

Burn, A., & Parker, D. (2003). *Analysing media texts.* London: Continuum.

Burn, A., & Richards, C. (Eds.). (2014). *Children's games in the new media age: Childlore, media and the playground.* Farnham: Ashgate.

Burn, A., Banaji, S., & Buckingham, D. (2006). *The rhetorics of creativity: A review of the literature.* London: Arts Council England /Creative Partnerships.

Burnett, C., & Merchant, G. (2014). Points of view: Reconceptualising literacies through an exploration of adult and child interactions in a virtual world. *Journal of Research in Reading, 37,* 36–50.

Burnett, C., Davies, J., Merchant, G., & Rowsell, J. (eds.). (2014). *New literacies around the globe.* London: Routledge.

Butsch, R., & Livingstone, S. (eds.). (2014). *Meanings of audiences: Comparative discourses.* London: Routledge.

Cannon, M. (2016). *Media-making matters: Exploring literacy with young learners as media crafting, critique and artistry.* PhD, Bournemouth University.

Cannon, M., & McDougall, J. (2014). The centre for contemporary cultural studies: 50 years on (CCCS50): A 'pop-up occupation'? *Journal of Media Practice, 15*(2), 147–150.

Carpenter, J. (2006). 'Give it a Try'. *Sources* (28). Bromley: Third Age Trust.

Castells, M., & Cardoso, G. (eds.). (2005). *The network society: From knowledge to policy.* Washington, DC: Johns Hopkins Center for Transatlantic Relations.

Clarke, B., Zimmermann, S., & Svanaes, S. (2013). *One-to-One Tablets in Schools: An evaluation study.* http://www.tabletsforschools.co.uk/wp-content/uploads/2012/12/FKY-Tablets-for-Schools-Stage-2-Full-Report-July-2013.pdf

Comber, B. (2014). Literacy, poverty and schooling: what matters in young people's education?, *Literacy,* 48, 115–123.

Connell, K., & Hilton, M. (2014). *CCCS50: Fifty years on: The centre for contemporary cultural studies.* Birmingham: Midland Arts Centre.

Cope, B., & Kalantzis, M. (eds.). (2000). *Multiliteracies: Literacy learning and the design of social futures.* New York: Routledge.

Cornelissen, G. (2010). The public role of teaching: To keep the door closed. *Educational Philosophy and Theory, 42*(5), 523–539.

Coughlan, S. (2016). 'Social divide stays in online learning'. *The Guardian,* 27.7.16.

Csikszentmihalyi, M. (1996). *Creativity: Flow and the psychology and discovery of invention.* New York: Harper Collins.

Cullum, P., Hallett, R., & Wood, J. (2014). *Creativity, enterprise and co-production: The future is now.* Birmingham: Presentation to HEA Annual Conference https://www.heacademy.ac.uk/system/files/resources/1_7_cullum_hallett_wood.pdf.

Curtis, A. (2016). *Hyper-Normalisation*. London: BBC http://www.bbc.co.uk/programmes/p04b183c.

Curzon, R., & Millard, L. (2013). *Transformation of the student learning experience through student engagement – Examples of students as partners, co-producers and authors*. Newport: Presentation to Society of Research into Higher Education conference.

Dart, J. J., & Davies, R. J. (2003). A dialogical story-based evaluation tool: The most significant change technique. *American Journal of Evaluation*, *24*(2), 137–155.

Davis, A. (2014). To read or not to read: Decoding synthetic phonics. In POLICY P. P. O. E. (ed.), Oxford: Wiley-Blackwell https://www.heacademy.ac.uk/flexible-pedagogies-new-pedagogical-ideas.

Davis, O. (2016). *Lessons from Rancière-Jacotot for a Critical Pedagogy of Neoliberalism's Double Text*. Jacques Ranciere and Critical Pedagogy, Coventry University, 20 May, 2016.

De Abreu, B., Lee, A., McDougall, J., & Melki, J. (eds.). (2017). *International handbook of media literacy*. New York: Routledge.

De Certeau, M. (1984). *The practice of everyday life*. Berkeley: University of California Press.

Dejaynes, T. (2015). "Where I'm From" and belonging: A multimodal, cosmopolitan perspective on arts and inquiry. *E-Learning and Digital Media*, *12*, 183–198.

Deleuze, G., & Guattari, F. (1993). *A thousand plateaus*. Minneapolis: University of Minnesota Press.

Deuchar, R. (2009). *Gangs, marginalised youth and social capital*. Stoke on Trent: Trentham.

Dezuanni, M. (2015). The building blocks of digital media literacy: Socio-material participation and the production of media knowledge. *Journal of Curriculum Studies*, *47*, 416–439.

Dezuanni, M., O'Mara, J., & Beavis, C. (2015). 'Redstone is like electricity': Children's performative representations in and around Minecraft. *E-Learning and Digital Media*, *12*, 147–163.

DFE. (2013a). *Computing programmes of study for key stages 1 and 2*. London: DFE.

DFE. (2013b). The primary national curriculum. *In*: *EDUCATION*, D. F. (eds.), London: HMSO.

Doerr-Stevens, C. (2015). "That's not something I was, I am, or am ever going to be": multimodal self-assertion in digital video production. *E-Learning and Digital Media*, *12*, 164–182.

Dredger, K., Woods, D., Beach, C., & Sagstetter, V. (2010). Engage me: Using new literacies to create. *Journal of Media Literacy Education*, *2*(2), 85–101.

EMEL. (2014). *E-Media Education Lab* [Online]. Brussels: Media animation. Accessed 15.6.15.

Facer, K. (2011). *Learning futures: Education, technology and social change.* London: Routledge.

Feigenbaum, A., Frenzel, F., & McCurdy, P. (2014). *Protest camps.* London: Zed Books.

Fenton, N. (2013). *Publics, politics and power.* Keynote Presentation. Sheffield: *Media Education Summit.*

Fenwick, T., & Edwards, R. (2010). *Actor-network theory in education.* Abingdon: Routledge.

Fielding, M. (2004). Transformative approaches to student voice: Theoretical underpinnings, recalcitrant realities. *British Educational Research Journal, 30,* 295–311.

Formosa, M. (2000). Older adult education in a Maltese University of the third age: A critical perspective. *Education and Ageing, 15*(3), 315–339.

Foucault, M. (1984). *The Foucault reader.* London: Penguin.

Frau-Meigs, D. (2012). Transliteracy as the New Research Horizon for Media and Information Literacy. *Medijske Studije 3*(6), 14–27.

Frau-Meigs, D. (2014). *No coding without decoding.* Keynote Presentation. Prague: *Media Education Summit.*

Frau-Meigs, D., Velez, I., & Flores, J. (eds.). (2016). *MIL Public policies in Europe: A cross country comparison.* London: Routledge Studies in European Communication Research and Education.

Freire, P. (1970). *Pedagogy of the oppressed.* New York: Continuum.

Freire, P. (2004). *Pedagogy of Hope: Reliving Pedagogy of the Oppressed.* London: Continuum.

Fuchs, C. (2012). Some reflections on Manuel Castells' book 'Networks of outrage and hope. Social movements in the internet age'. *tripleC – Open Access Journal for a Global Sustainable Information Society, 10*(2), 775–797.

Fuchs, C. (2016). Henryk Grossmann 2.0: A critique of Paul Mason's book "postcapitalism: A guide to our future". *Triplec, 14*(1), 232–243. http://www.triple-c.at CC-BY-NC-ND: Creative Commons License, 2016.

Gamber-Thompson, L., & Zimmerman, A. (2016). DREAM-ing citizenship: Undocumented youth, coming out and pathways to participation. In H. Jenkins, S. Shreshova, L. Gamber-Thompson, & A. Zimmerman. *By any media necessary: The new youth activism.* New York: New York University Press.

Garde-Hansen, J., Hoskins, A., & Reading, A. (eds.). (2009). *Save as... digital memories.* London: Palgrave.

Gauntlett, D. (2015). *Making media studies.* London: Polity.

Gee, J. P. (2004). *Situated language and learning: A critique of traditional schooling.* New York: Routledge.

Gee, J. P. (2015a). *Literacy and education.* London: Routledge.

Gee, J. P. (2015b). The new literacy studies. In J. Rowsell & K. Pahl (eds.), *The Routledge handbook of literacy studies.* London: Routledge.

Geertz, C. (1973). Thick description: Toward an interpretive theory of culture. In C. Geertz (eds.), *The interpretation of cultures" Selected essays*. New York: Basic Books.

Gerodimos, R. (2008). Mobilising young citizens in the UK: A content analysis of youth and issue websites. *Information, Communication & Society, 11*(7), 964–988.

Gerodimos, R., & Mihailidis, P. (2016). Connecting pedagogies of civic media: The literacies, connected civics, and engagement in daily life. In E. Gordon & P. Mihailidis (eds.), *Civic media: Technology, design, practice* (pp. 371–392). Cambridge, MA: MIT Press.

Gibson, R. (2010). Why have School? An inquiry through dialectical materialism. In A. DeLeon & W. Ross (eds.), *Critical theories, radical pedagogies and social education*. Rotterdam: Sense.

Giddens, A. (1991). *Modernity and self-identity: Self and society in the late modern age*. Cambridge: Polity.

Ginsburg, N. (2012). '"Chavs", class and representation'. *A review of Owen Jones, Chavs: The Demonisation of the Working Class (Verso, 2011)*', *International Socialism* 136. http://isj.org.uk/chavs-class-and-representation/

Giroux, H. (1988). *Teachers as intellectuals: Toward a critical pedagogy of learning*. Connecticut: Praeger.

Giroux, H. (2014). *Zombie Politics and Culture in the Age of Casino Capitalism*. New York: Peter Lang Publishing.

Goffman, E. (1990). *The presentation of self in everyday life*. New *edition*. London: Penguin.

Goodman, S. (2003). *Teaching youth media: A critical guide to literacy, video production & social change*. New York: Teachers' Press.

Green, B. (2002). *English in Australia: A literacy project of our own?*

Gregg, M. (2011). *Work's intimacy*. London: Polity.

Gush, C. (2015). 'Sleaford mods: Raging against the austerity machine', *i-D 2015*. https://i-d.vice.com/en_gb/article/sleaford-mods-raging-against-the-austerity-machine

Gutierrez, K. (2008). Developing a sociocultural literacy in the third space. *Reading Research Quarterly, 43*, 148–164.

Gutiérrez, K. D., Baquedano-López, P., & Tejeda, C. (1999). Rethinking diversity: Hybridity and hybrid language practices in the Third Space. *Mind, Culture, and Activity, 6*(4), 286–303.

Hafner, A. (2012). *Production of third spaces for immigrant English language learners: (Re)Negotiating identity and discourse in the secondary classroom*. http://scholarworks.umass.edu/open_access_dissertations/502

Hall, S. et al (eds.). (1980). *Culture, media, language: Working papers in cultural studies*. 1972–79. Centre for Contemporary Cultural Studies London: Routledge.

Hall, S. (2014). *Foreword to Connell, K and Hilton, M. 2014. CCCS50: Fifty Years On: The Centre for Contemporary Cultural Studies*. Birmingham: Midland Arts Centre.

Hallett, R. (2014). *Creativity, Enterprise and Co-Production; The future is now.* Higher Education Academy Special Interest Group workshop, Aston University, 2 July, 2014.

Halvorsen, E., & Sheridan, K. (2014). The maker movement in education. *Harvard Educational Review, 84,* 495–504.

Hamilton, M. (2012). Unruly Practices: What a sociology of Translations can Offer to Educational Policy Analysis. In Fenwick, T., & Edwards, R. (Eds.), *Researching Education Through Actor-network Theory.* Oxford: Blackwell-Wiley.

Hamilton, M., Heydon, R., Hibbert, K., & Stooke, R. (eds.). (2015). *Negotiating spaces for literacy learning: Multimodality and governmentality.* Bloomsbury: London.

Hanley, L. (2016). *Respectable: The experience of class.* London: Allen Lane.

Harris, A. (2004). *Future girl: Young women in twenty-first century.* London and New York: Routledge.

Haw, K., & Hadfield, M. (2011). *Video in social science research: Functions and forms.* Abingdon: Taylor & Francis.

Hawley, S. (2016). Presentation: The sociomateriality of literacy. *Language, Literacy and Identity Conference.* Sheffield University.

Heath, S. B. (1983). *Ways with words.* Cambridge: Cambridge University Press.

HEA (Higher Education Academy). (2014). Flexible Pedagogies, New Pedagogical Ideas. https://www.heacademy.ac.uk/flexible-pedagogies-new-pedagogical-ideas. Accessed 17 February 2017.

Heppell, S. (2014). 'A Better MOOC? http://www.heppel.net/mooc

Heppell, S. (2014). *Notschool.net: the creation of a remarkable project.* http://rubble.heppell.net/heppell/notschool/heroes.html. Accessed 17 Febuary, 2017.

Heppell, S. (2016). *Learnology.* http://rubble.heppell.net/learnology/index.html

Higher Education Academy. (2014). *Flexible pedagogies, New pedagogical ideas.* York: HEA

Hobbs, R. (2014). Digital media literacy: A plan of action. In A. Silverblatt (eds.), *The Praeger handbook of media literacy* Vol. 2. Santa Barbara, CA: Praeger.

Hobbs, R. (eds.). (2016). *Exploring the roots of digital media literacy through personal narrative.* New York: Temple.

Hopkins, T., & Kendall, A. (2017). *Turning Pages, Changing Lives: Evaluation of the Shannon Trust Turning Pages programme.* Project Report. Shannon Trust, London, UK. http://www.shannontrust.org.uk/our-work/turning-pages. Accessed 17 February 2017.

Ito, M., Baumer, S., Bittanti, M., Boyd, D., Cody, R., Herr-Stephenson, B., Horst, H. A., Lange, P., Mahendran, D., Martinez, K. Z., Pascoe, C. J., Perjel, D., Robinson, L., Sims, C., & Tripp, L. (2009). *Hanging out, messing around, and geeking out: Kids living and learning with new media.* Cambridge, MA: MIT Press.

Ivanic, R., Edwards, R., Satchwell, C., & Smith, J. (2007). Possibilities for pedagogy in further education: Harnessing the abundance of literacy. *British Educational Research Journal*, *33*(5), 703–721.

Jackson, S. (2015). Toward an analytical and methodological understanding of actor-network theory. *Journal of Arts and Humanities*, *4*, 2.

Janis-Norton, N. (2015). *Calmer, easier, happier boys*. London: Hodder and Stoughton.

Jenkins, H., Clinton, K., Purushotma, R., & Robison, A. J. (2006). *Confronting the challenges of participatory culture: Media education for the 21st century Building the field of digital media and learning*. Chicago: MacArthur Foundation.

Jenkins, H., Shreshova, S., Gamber-Thompson, L., & Zimmerman, A. (2016). *By any media necessary: The new youth activism*. New York: New York University Press.

Jenks, C. (1993). *Culture*. London: Routledge.

Jewitt, C. (eds.). (2011). *The Routledge handbook of multimodal analysis*. London: Routledge.

Jewitt, C., Bezemer, J., & O'Halloran, K. (2016). *Introducing multimodality*. London: Routledge.

(Disrupted) *Journal of Media Practice*. (2016). http://journal.disruptivemedia.org.uk/about/

Jolls, T. (2011). *Media literacy: Deconstruction/construction*. e-book: www.medialit.com,

Kendall, A. (2015). "*It's all about trying to meet the needs of your community*": A digital literacies approach to engaging parents through social media. Paper presented at *Media Education Summit*, Boston, MA: 4.11.15.

Kendall, A., & Hughes, J. (2011). *Working with the virtual campus*. Birmingham /London: Learning and Skills Improvement Service.

Kerrigan, M. (2013). Students as digital change agents. In E. Dunne & D. Owen (eds.), *The student engagement handbook* (pp. 437–460). Bingley: Emerald.

Kousis, M. (2013). The spatial dimensions of the Greek protest campaign against the Troika's memoranda and austerity. 2010–13' In M. Ancelovici, P. Dufour, & H. Nez (eds.), *Street politics in the age of austerity: From the indignados to occupy*. Amsterdam: Amsterdam University Press.

Kress, G. (2003). *Literacy in the new media age*. London: Routledge.

Lacou-Labarthe, P. (1989). *Poetry as Experience*. Stanford: Standford University Press.

Laing, T. (2010). Virtual learning: A solution to the all-black male school debate and the challenge of black male K-12 outcomes. *Journal of African American Males in Education*, *1* Issue (3), 211–229.

Lankshear, C., & Knobel, M. (2006). *New literacies: Everyday practices and classroom learning*. Maidenhead, Berks, UK: McGraw Hill Education/Open University Press.

Larson, J., & Marsh, J. (2005). *Making literacy real: Theories and practices for learning and teaching*. London: Sage.
Latour, B. (2005). *Reassembling the social: An introduction to actor-network-theory*. Oxford: Oxford University Press.
Lave, J., & Wenger, E. (2005). Practice, person, social world. In H. Daniels (eds.), *An introduction to Vygotsky:* second *edition*. London: Routledge.
Law, J. (2004). *After method: Mess in social science research*. London: Routledge.
Law, J., & Mol, A. (eds.). (2002). *Complexities: Social studies of knowledge practices*. Durham, NC: Duke University Press.
Leander, K., & Boldt, G. (2012). Rereading "A Pedagogy of Multiliteracies": Bodies, texts, and emergence. *Journal of Literacy Research*, *45*(1), 22–46.
Leander, K., & Frank, A. (2006). The aesthetic production and distribution of image/subjects among online youth. *E-Learning*, *3*, 185–206.
Leander, K. M., Phillips, N. C., Taylor, K. H., Nespor, J., & Lewis, C. (2010). The changing social spaces of learning: Mapping new mobilities. *Review of Research in Education*, *34*, 329–394.
Lee, S. (2016). *Curating...You are the disease, I am the curator* [Online]. London: The Observer (Guardian Newspapers). Available: https://www.theguardian.com/commentisfree/2016/mar/27/i-am-the-curator-stewart-lee-all tomorrows-parties. Accessed 27.03.16.
Levine, C. (2015). *Forms: Whole, rhythm, hierarchy, network*. Princeton: Princeton University Press.
LievrouwI, L. H., & Livingstone, S. (eds.). (2006). *The handbook of new media (updated student edition)*. London: Sage.
Liu, A. (2004). *The Laws of Cool: Knowledge Work and the Culture of Information*. Chicago, IL: University of Chicago Press.
Livingstone, S., & Sefton-Green, J. (2016). *The class: Living and learning in a digital age*. New York: New York University Press.
Lopez, A. (2014). *Greening media education: Bridging media literacy with green cultural citizenship*. New York: Peter Lang.
MacGregor, N. (2012). *A history of the world in 100 objects*. London: Penguin.
Mann, M. (2005). *Incoherent empire*. New York: Verso Books.
Marcinkiewicz, A. (2011). The university of third age as an institution counteracting marginalization of older people. *Journal of Education, Culture and Society*, *2011*(2), 38–44.
Marsh, J. (eds.). (2004). *Popular culture, new media and digital literacy in early childhood*. London: Routledge.
Marsh, J., & Millard, E. (eds.). (2006). *Popular literacies, childhood and schooling*. London: Routledge.
Marshall, T. (2015). *Prisoners of geography*. London: Elliot and Thompson.
Mason, P. (2015). *Post-capitalism: A guide to our future*. London: Allen-Lane.

Masschelein, J., & Simons, M. (2011). The hatred of public schooling: The school as the mark of democracy. In M. Simons & J. Masschelein (Eds.), *Rancière, public education and the taming of democracy*, Chapter. 11. (pp. 150–165). Chichester: Wiley-Blackwell.

McAndrew, T. (2014). *Digital Literacy in the Disciplines*. York: JISC / Higher Education Academy.

McDougall, J. (2012). *Media studies: The basics*. London: Routledge.

McDougall, J. (2015). Open to disruption: Education *either and* media practice. *Journal of Media Practice*, *16*(1), 1–7.

McDougall, J. (2016). How does boy 17 read a game? In G. Merchant & B. Parry (eds.), *Literacy, media and technology: Past, present and future*. London: Bloomsbury.

McDougall, J., & Potter, J. (2015). Curating media learning: Towards a porous expertise. *E-Learning and Digital Media*, *12*, 199–211.

McDougall, J., Livingstone, S., Sefton-Green, J., & Fraser, P. (2013). *Media and information literacy policies in the United Kingdom* 2013. London: London School of Economics.

McDougall, J., Berger, R., Fraser, P., & Zezulkova, M. (2015). Media literacy, education & (Civic) capability: A transferable methodology. *Journal of Media Literacy Education*, *7*(1), 4–17.

Media Education Association. (2016). *Some success (report on consultation on exams for media studies)* [Online]. London: Media Education Association. Available: http://www.themea.org.uk/2016/05/some-success/. Accessed 23.07.16.

Media Policy Project. (2016). *Screen time advice for a new generation of parents*. London: London School of Economics: http://blogs.lse.ac.uk/mediapolicyproject/2016/07/25/screen-time-advice-for-a-new-generation-of-digital-parents/

Merchant, G. (2005). Electric involvement: Identity performance in children's informal digital writing. *Discourse: Studies in the Cultural Politics of Education*, *26*, 301–314.

Merchant, G. (2006). Identity, social networks and online communication. *E-Learning*, *3*, 235–244.

Mieville, C. (2011). *The city and the city*. London: Pan.

Mihailidis, P. (2015). *Media literacy and the emerging citizen: Youth, engagement and participation*. New York: Peter Lang.

Mihailidis, P., Hobbs, R., McDougall, J., & Berger, R. (2015). Building a global community for media education research. *Journal of Media Literacy Education*, *7*(1), 1–3.

Miller, D. (2008). *The comfort of things*. Cambridge: Polity.

Mills, K. A., & Comber, B. (2013). Space, place and power: The spatial turn in literacy research. In K. Hall, T. Cremin, B. Comber, & L. C. Moll (eds.), *The international handbook of research on children's literacy, learning and culture*. Chichester: John Wile and Co.

Mittell, J. (2015). Afterword: D.I.Y. Disciplinarity: (Dis)Assembling LEGO Studies for the Academy. In Wolf, M (Ed.), *Lego Studies: Examining the Building Blocks of a Transmedial Phenemenon*. London: Routledge.

MIT. (2016). *About Scratch* [Online]. Accessed 21.09.16.

Moje, E. B., Ciechanowski, K. M., Kramer, K., Ellis, L., Carrillo, R., & Collazo, T. (2004). Working toward third space in content area literacy: An examination of everyday funds of knowledge and discourse. *Reading Research Quarterly*, *39*(1), 38–70.

Moll, L. C., Amanti, C., Neff, D., & Gonzalez, N. (1992). Funds of knowledge for teaching: Using a qualitative approach to connect homes and classrooms. *Theory into Practice*, *31*, 132–141.

Mullen, S. (2016) 'Getting back in control of screens in the Home'. *Busy Parents Network Directory* 13. Birmingham: Busy Parents Network.

Neary, M. (2014). *Social science centre, Lincoln: A new type of dissident institution*. Newport: Presentation to Society for Research into Higher Education conference.

Neelands, J. (2013). *Dramatic Futures: why the Arts and Humanities should reclaim the curriculum*. The Arts in Education: Policy, Practice, Futures. Digital Arts Research and Education Seminar, British Film Institute, 21 June 2013.

Nemorin, S., & Selwyn, N. (2016). Making the best of it? Exploring the realities of 3D printing in school. *Research Papers in Education*, 1–18.

Nespor, J. (2012). Devices and Educational Change. In Fenwick, T., & Edwards, R. (Eds.), *Researching Education Through Actor-network Theory*. Oxford: Blackwell-Wiley.

Ng'ambi, D., & Bozalek, V. (2015). Special issue on massive open online courses (MOOCs) – 'disrupting' teaching and learning in higher education. *British Journal of Educational Technology*, *46*(3), 451–454.

Norris, S. (2004). *Analyzing multlimodal interaction: A methodological framework*. London: Routledge.

Nygaard, C. et al. (2013). *Student engagement: Identity, motivation and community*. LIHE/Libri. Farringdon: QAA.

Obrist, H. U. (2014). Hans Ulrich Obrist: The art of curation. *The Guardian*.

Ofcom. (2015). Adults' media use and attitudes report 2015. London: OFCOM.

Ong, W. J. (1982). *Orality and literacy: The technologising of the word*. London: Routledge (Reprint 1988).

Opie, I., & Opie, P. (1954). *The lore and language of schoolchildren*. Oxford: Oxford University Press.

Oxford. (2003). T. F. Hoad (eds.). *The Oxford dictionary of etymology* (online edition). Oxford: Oxford University Press http://www.oxfordreference.com/.

Pangrazio, L. (2014). Reconceptualising critical digital literacy. *Discourse: Studies in the Cultural Politics of Education*, *37*(2), 1–12.

Papert, S. (1993). *Mindstorms* (second edition). Hemel Hempstead: Harvester Wheatsheaf.

Parker, R., & Pollock, G. (1995). *Old mistresses* (reissued edition). UK: Pandora.

Parry, B. (2013). *Children, fim and literacy*. London: Palgrave MacMillan.

Parry, B., Burnett, C., & Merchant, G. (eds.) (2016). *Literacy, media and technology: Past, present and future*. Bloomsbury: London.

Peppler, K. (2013). *New opportunities for interest-driven arts learning in a digital age*. New York: The Wallace Foundation.

Perry, G. (2011). *The tomb of the unknown craftsman*. London: The British Museum Press.

Perry, G. (2015). *Playing to the gallery: Helping contemporary art in its struggle to be understood*. London: Penguin.

Porfilio, B. (2010). Critically examining the past and the "Society of the Spectacle": Social studies education as a site of critique, resistance and transformation. In A. DeLeon & W. Ross (eds.), *Critical theories, radical pedagogies and social education*. Rotterdam: Sense.

Potter, J. (2005). "This brings back a lot of memories" – A case study in the analysis of digital video production by young learners. *Education, Communication & Information, 5*, 5–23.

Potter, J. (2010). Embodied memory and curatorship in children's digital video production. *Journal of English Teaching: Practice and Critique, 9*, 22–35.

Potter, J. (2011). New literacies, new practices and learner research: Across the semi permeable membrane between home and school *Lifelong Learning in Europe* XVI, 22–35.

Potter, J. (2012). *Digital media and learner identity: The new curatorship*. New York: Palgrave MacMillan.

Potter, J. (2014). Co-curating children's play cultures. In A. Burn & C. Richards (eds.), *Children's games in the new media age: Childlore, media and the playground*. London: Palgrave.

Potter, J., & Banaji, S. (2012). Social media and self-curatorship: Reflections on identity and pedagogy through blogging on a masters module. *Comunicar, 38*, 83–91.

Potter, J., & Bryer, T. (2014). *Out of the box: A project evaluation report for shoot smart* – Funded by Into Film. London: Into Film.

Processes Influencing Democratic Ownership and Participation (2009–2012). Brussels: European Union. http://www.fahs.surrey.ac.uk/pidop/

Quinlan, O. (2015). *Young digital makers*. London: NESTA.

Rancière, J. (1991). *The ignorant schoolmaster: Five lessons in intellectual emancipation*. California: Stanford University Press.

Rideout, V., & Katz, V. (2016). *Digital equity: Technology and learning in the lives of lower-income families*. http://digitalequityforlearning.org/

Ridley, D. (2016). The emancipated classroom. In *Post-16 Educator*, *83*, 9–11.

Ross, J., Sinclair, C., Knox, J., Bayne, S., & Macleod, H. (2014). Teacher experiences and academic identity: The missing components of MOOC pedagogy. *MERLOT Journal of Online Learning and Teaching*, *10*(1), 57–69.

Rowe, M. (2014). On the genesis of media literacy in the United States, as seen through the lens of a Wisconsin participant. In A. Silverblatt (eds.), *The Praeger handbook of media literacy*, Vol. *2*. Santa Barbara, CA: Praeger.

Rowsell, J., & Pahl, K. (eds.). (2015). *The Routledge handbook of literacy studies.* London: Routledge.

Salford, J. (2012). *Pedagogies for virtual classrooms.* Online: http://pedagogies forvirtualcampus.wikispaces.com/Phase+2+Design+and+Development.

Salmon, G., Gregory, J., Dona, K., & Ross, B. (2015). *British Journal of Educational Technology*, *46*(3),4510454 542–546.

Scarborough, H. (2001). Connecting early language and literacy to later reading (dis)abilities: Evidence, theory and practice. In S. B. Neuman & D. K. Dickinson (eds.), *Handbook of early literacy.* New York: Guildford Press.

Scott, F. L. (2016). Young children's digital literacy practices at home: Social, physical and classed. In I. Pereira & A. Ramos J. Marsh (Eds.), *The digital literacy and multimodal practices of young children: Engaging with emergent research. Proceedings of the first training school of COST action IS1410* (pp. 173–184). Braga, Portugal: University of Minho 6th - 8th June, 2016. Braga: Centro de Investigação em Educação (CIEd). Accessed Nov 2016 http://digilitey.eu.

Sefton Green, J. (2013). *Learning at not school: A review of study, theory and advocacy for education in non-formal settings.* Cambridge, MA: MIT Press.

Sefton-Green, J. (2005). Timelines, timeframes and special effects: Soft and creative media production. *Education, Communication and Information*, *5*, 99–110.

Sefton-Green, J. (2013). *Mapping digital makers.* London: Nominet Trust.

Sefton-Green, J., & Erstad, O. (2012). Identity, community, and learning lives in the digital Age. In O. Erstad & J. Sefton-Green (eds.), *Identity, community, and learning lives in the digital age.* Cambridge: Cambridge University Press.

Sefton-Green, J., & Rowsell, J. (eds). (2014). *Learning and Literacy Over Time: Longitudinal Perspectives.* London: Routledge.

Selwyn, N., Potter, J., & Cranmer, S. (2010). *Primary ICT: Learning from learner perspectives.* London: Continuum.

Selwyn, N. (2013). *Distrusting educational technology: Critical questions for changing times.* London: Routledge.

Selwyn, N. (2014). *Is technology good for education?* London: Wiley.

Sen, A. K. (2008). Capability and Well-Being. In D. M. Hausman (Eds.), *The philosophy of economics* 3rd Edition (pp. 270–293). Cambridge: Cambridge University Press.

Sharma, G., & Sharma, B. (2012). Leapfrogging in the global periphery: Popular literacy practices of nepalese youth online'. In B. Williams & A. Zenger (eds.), *New media literacies and participatory popular culture across borders*. London: Routledge.

Shaw, J. (2015). In McDougall, J. editorial: Open to disruption: Education 'either/and' media practice. *Journal of Media Practice*, *16*(1), 1–7.

Soep, E. (2016). Afterword: Necessary learning. In H. Jenkins, S. Shreshova, L. Gamber-Thompson, & A. Zimmerman. *By any media necessary: The new youth activism* (pp. 290–308). New York: New York University Press.

Solomon, A. (2016) Against the wall. *The Guardian Review*: 17.9.16

Springer, S. (2016). Fuck neoliberalism. *An International Journal for Critical Geographies*, 2016 *15*(2), 285–292.

Street, B. (2003). What's "new" in new literacy studies? Critical approaches to literacy in theory and practice. *Current Issues in Comparative Education*, *5*, 77–91.

Street, B. (2012). New literacy studies. *Language, Ethnography, and Education: Bridging New Literacy Studies and Bourdieu*, 27–49.

Taylor, M., Klein, E. J., & Abrams, L. (2014). Tensions of re-imagining our roles as teacher educators in a third space: Revisiting a co/autoethnography through a faculty lens. *Studying Teacher Education*, *10*(1), 3–19.

Teachmeet: https://teachmeetuk.wordpress.com/

Tempest, K. (2013). *Brand new ancients*. London: Picador.

Tempest, K. (2014). *Everybody down*. London: Big Dada Records.

Terzi, L. (2005). Beyond the dilemma of difference: The capability approach to disability and special educational needs. *Journal of Philosophy of Education*, *39*(3), 443–459.

Thompson, P., Hall, C., Jones, K., & Sefton-Green, J. (2012). The signature pedagogies project: Final report. *Culture, creativity and education*. Nottingham: University of Nottingham.

Ticklet, L. (2012). 'Distance Learning Breaches Prison Walls'. *The Guardian* 20.2.12 https://www.theguardian.com/education/2012/feb/20/distance-learning-for-prisoners

Todd, S. (2015). *The people: The rise and fall of the working class 1910–2010*. London: Hodder and Stoughton.

Trowler, P., & Trowler, V. (2010). *Case studies of student engagement*. York: Higher Education Academy.

Turnbull, S. (1998). Dealing with feeling: Why Girl Number 20 still doesn't answer. In D. Buckingham (Eds.), *Teaching popular culture*. London: UCL Press.

Twining, P. (2013). *Peter T's bliki* [Online]. Available: http://edfutures.net/PeterT's_bliki. Accessed 30.11.2013.

Tyner, K. (1998). *Literacy in a digital world*. Mawhah, NJ.: Lawrence Erlbaum Associates.

UNESCO. (2016). *Literacy* [Online]. Paris: UNESCO. Available: http://www.unesco.org/new/en/education/themes/education-building-blocks/literacy/. Accessed 19.5.16.

Usher, R., & Edwards, R. (1994). *Postmodernism and education*. London: Routledge.

Van Dijck, J. (2013). *The culture of connectivity: A critical history of social media*. Oxford: OUP. pp. 228.

Van Mourik Broekman, P., Hall, G., Byfield, T., Hides, S., & Worthington, S. (2014). *Open education: A study in disruption*. London: Rowman and Littelfield 978-1-78348-209-2 pp112.

Varnelis, K. (2010). 'The meaning of network culture'. *Eurozine*. Online: http://www.eurozine.com/pdf/2010-01-14-varnelis-en.pdf

Watt, P., & Stenson, K. (1998). 'The street: 'It's a bit dodgy around there', safety, danger, ethnicity and young people's use of public space. In T. Skelton & G. Valentine (eds.), *Cool places, geographies of youth cultures*. London: Routledge.

Weller, S., & Kandiko Howson, C. (2014). *Students as co-developers of learning and teaching: Redefining expertise and student voice through student participation in professional development*. SRHE Research Scoping Study. London: Society for Research into Higher Education.

Wenger, E. (1998). *Communities of practice – Learning, meaning & identity*. Cambridge: Cambridge University Press.

White, H. (2015). *STEAM not STEM* [Online]. Available: http://steam-notstem.com/. Accessed 20.11.15.

Whyte, W. (1956). *The organization man*. London: Simon and Schuster.

Willett, R., Richards, C., Marsh, J., Burn, A., & Bishop, J. C. (2013). *Children, media and playground cultures: Ethnographic studies of school playtimes*. London: Palgrave.

Williams, R. (1961). *The long revolution*. London: Chatto and Windus.

Williams, A. (2009). On the tip of creative tongues: Curate" in New York Times, Oct 2nd, 2009. Access date 11.03.2015. *New York Times*.

Williams, R. (2015). *A short counter-revolution: Towards 2000 revisited*. Ed J. McGuiganLondon: Sage.

Williams, B., & Zenger, A. (eds.). (2012). *New media literacies and participatory popular culture across borders*. London: Routledge.

Williams, P., Leighton John, J., & Rowland, I. (2009). The personal curation of digital objects: A lifecycle approach. *Aslib Proceedings: New Information Perspectives*, *61*, 340–363.

Williamson, B. (2015). *Coding/learning: Software and digital data in education*. Stirling: University of Stirling.

Williamson, J. (1981). How does Girl No. 20 understand ideology? *Screen Education*, *40*, 80–87.

Willis, P. (1980). 'Notes on Method'. In S. Hall et al (eds.), 1980 *Culture, media, language: Working papers in cultural studies 1972–79.* Centre for Contemporary Cultural Studies London: Routledge.

Wilson, A. (2000). There's no escape from Third-Space Theory - Borderland Discourse and the In-Between Literacies of Prison. In David Barton, Mary Hamilton, & Roz Ivanic (Eds.), *Situated literacies: Reading and writing in context.* London: Routledge.

Wilson, C., Grizzle, A., Tuazon, R., Akyempong, K., & Cheung, C.-K. (2011). *Media and information literacy curriculum for teachers.* Paris: United Nations Educational, Scientific and Cultural Organisation (UNESCO.)

Wittel, A. (2016). *Digital transitions.* Saarbrucken: Lambert.

Wolf, M. (eds.). (2014). *Lego studies: Building blocks of a transmedial phenomenon.* London: Routledge.

Wright Mills, C. (1956). *The power elite.* New York: Oxford University Press.

Yancey, K. B. (2004). Postmodernism, palimpsest, and portfolios: Theoretical issues in the representation of student work. *College Composition and Communication*, *55*, 738–761.

Yandell, J. (2014). Classrooms as sites of curriculum delivery or meaning-making: Whose knowledge counts? *Forum*, *56*, 147–155.

Zenger, A. (2012). Constructing '"Local Context" in Beirut: Students' Literacy Practices Outside of Class. In B. Williams & A. Zenger (eds.), *New media literacies and participatory popular culture across borders.* London: Routledge.

Zinck, S. (2013). *Risk Assessment in Youth.* CACAP-ACPEA Child & Adolescent Psychiatry Subspecialty Review.

Zizek, S. (2013). 'The postmodern father' Online: http://www.openculture.com/2015/04/slavoj-zizek-calls-political-correctness-a-form-of-modern-totalitarianism.htm

Index

J. Potter, J. McDougall, *Digital Media, Culture and Education*,
DOI 10.1057/978-1-137-55315-7

Printed by Printforce, the Netherlands